6-19-74

POLITICS AND OIL:

MOSCOW IN THE MIDDLE EAST

POLITICS AND OIL:

MOSCOW IN THE MIDDLE EAST

Lincoln Landis

DUNELLEN PUBLISHING COMPANY

New York — London

International Standard Book Number 0-8424-0029-X

Library of Congress Catalogue Number 72-148702

Printed in the United States of America

First Edition

1973

Martin Robertson & Company Ltd — London

1824047

to

Bess B. Landis

with love

Acknowledgments

I am grateful for the opportunity I have had in this research task to combine an interest in Soviet policy with a case study of its application in the vital and troubled region of the Middle East. It has been most rewarding to examine the dynamics of Soviet foreign affairs in political, economic, and ideological terms in this area where historically Moscow's political ties have been weak; where the primary economic wealth is petroleum, also found in rich quantities in the U.S.S.R.; and where foreign ideologies, atheistic Communism in particular, are not welcomed by adherents to the Muslim faith. Access to Russian source materials, which fortunately has become relatively easy in recent years, has provided the opportunity to compare and contrast Soviet policy statements and propaganda with Soviet actions and Marxist-Leninist ideology.

Appreciation is due to numerous acquaintances I had the opportunity to make in other countries — Iran, Lebanon, Britain, France, the Federal Republic of Germany, and Italy— including scholars, government and private industry petroleum officials, and communications media representatives, whose insight contributed materially to a fuller understanding of developments and trends affecting this inquiry. I am particularly grateful for the guidance and critique of Majid Khadduri of the School of Advanced International Studies, Johns Hopkins University; and to Lev Dobriansky, Paul Ello, Hisham Sharabi, and Ulrich Allers, members of the faculty of Georgetown University.

By no means least, I am indebted to David Abshire for encouraging me to undertake this study when I was research fellow at the Center for Strategic and International Studies of Georgetown University, and to the Center for providing support for my research while I was there. Jon Vondracek provided good counsel on matters relating to publication procedures, and Sevinc Carlson assisted generously by earmarking relevant source materials.

I wish also to give special mention to my wife, Donna, for her unstinting support and thoughtful commentary, to my sons, Jeffrey, Dean, and Lincoln, whose interest always remained high, and to our little Timothy, who contributed in his own way.

Finally, I alone remain responsible for the research findings and conclusions, seasoned as they must be with those prejudices one acquires from one's experiences.

Lincoln Landis

Contents

Chapter

Chapter

Illustrations

Foreword

One of the most important clues to the understanding of Soviet foreign and economic policies is appreciation of the differences between Communist strategy and tactics. Many Western statesmen and scholars have failed to grasp the essence of these concepts. Communist tactics are extremely flexible; they are not necessarily bound to the party line because they are a means to an end. The end is decisive; to attain it, long-range strategy is the guide. While strategy may change here and there, it remains basically consonant with the social and political philosophy of Marxism-Leninism. Tactics serve to achieve strategic goals. More often than not tactics give outsiders the impression of traditionalist behavior, while in reality they are the facade which conceals the true intentions of the CPSU. The Soviet leaders are now sophisticated enough to understand some of the psychological requirements in their dealings with the "imperialists" as well as the "non-committed" countries.

This is particularly evident in economic policy and, more specifically, in the issue of oil. A combination of factors must here be considered: the history of Russian relations with the Middle East, which is the richest petroleum region in the world; the national interest of the Soviet Union; and, part and parcel

of the latter, Soviet political doctrine. It is unfortunate that
during the past years Western observers have promoted the
thought that ideology in the U.S.S.R. is eroding to the point of
disappearing altogether. Their reasoning is that during the past
half-century fanaticism has waned, the Soviet people show little
interest in the issues of Marxism-Leninism, and there is increasing dissent, particularly among intellectuals. Such an estimate,
in this writer's opinion, is superficial. Certainly, the fanaticism
of the twenties and thirties no longer exists, but the ingredients
of revolutionary thinking have become ingrained in the post-
revolutionary masses. These are just as much the basis of their
world view as the Judeo-Christian ethic is for Western civiliza-
tion.

In the U.S.S.R. there has developed a political climate, a
secular religion, which filters the thinking of the people. Imbued
with the principles of their socialist society, they see the world
upside down — or so it seems to us. Opponents of this appraisal
accuse realistic analysts of being "cold warriors." They believe
that the Cold War has ended, whereas all indications are that it
is merely being conducted by the Politburo with different tactical weapons.

I feel the need to clarify this issue because it throws light
on one of the great merits of Dr. Landis' present work. In discussing Soviet oil strategy in the Middle East, he never forgets
the basic Soviet rationale. He does not analyze the economic
issues of oil in an intellectual vacuum. As a result, he contributes importantly to the clarification of Soviet strategy and
tactics as reflected in Soviet Middle East policy.

Dr. Landis correctly describes Soviet long-range planning
as an interaction of ideological and national stimuli. Using pre-
dominantly Russian source material, he analyzes the difference
between Soviet words and deeds, politics and economics,
strategy and tactics. He sheds light on the fact that, contrary
to Marx, politics dominates economics, which is particularly
evident in the oil business. He reminds us that in 1965 a Soviet
writer was candid enough to state that "the program of the
Communist Party of the Soviet Union calls for the utilization

in an ever-increasing scale of these riches [oil] in the construction of Communism." No wonder that Western oil interests in
the Middle East, as Landis writes, "underscore the Party's own
real appreciation of petroleum as a political commodity." He
points to the fact that oil is "an important element in Soviet
strategic planning, which is based upon political, military, and
economic considerations."

Landis differentiates between two periods of Moscow's oil
politics: the first comprises the Leninist and Stalinist era; the
second describes its development since 1953 under Khrushchev
and Brezhnev-Kosygin. The nub of the contemporary Soviet oil
dilemma is what the author calls the "petroleum paradox,"
because the Soviet oil industry is at once deficient and competitive. While the U.S.S.R. has abundant oil resources, it has not
been able to cope with poor planning and faulty technological
development. Indeed, it has difficulties meeting the rising demands for oil (and natural gas) from "the Soviet group," notably
the East European countries. On the other hand, the Soviet oil
industry pretends to be competitive in the international market
in that it exports its own oil to Western Europe and Japan.

This "paradox" is the result of a tactical device toward
what Landis calls the "strategic economic dominance over the
Middle East." It is clear that the Soviets have tried, ever since
the British departed from that area, to fill the political vacuum
aggravated by the Arab-Israeli conflict. The progression of this
conflict gave Moscow an excellent opportunity to penetrate,
with the aim of using Middle East oil for the development of a
"world socialist planned economy." Part of this all-embracing
concept is a Soviet-dominated "world energy delivery system,"
which really means an eventual incorporation of the Middle
East oil riches into this "delivery system." Steps toward this
goal would be first what Landis calls the Soviet position as a
producer, importer, broker — ultimately, the U.S.S.R. would
become a "strategic middleman," with Moscow coordinating
a vast energy system encompassing large-scale imports from the
Middle East and exports to the "capitalist West." These are
steps of communist strategy toward eventual global victory. In

order to achieve this goal, Moscow must set up a world socialist planned economy, of which domination of Middle East petroleum is almost certainly regarded as the inevitable first step.

There is in both the American government and many academics a good deal of euphoria, based on the recent ostentatious show of Soviet good intentions, particularly after President Nixon's visit to Moscow. These optimists will shrug off the arguments of more realistic observers as obsolete Cold War positions. They probably will disagree with Dr. Landis' well-reasoned arguments, because they assert ideology is no longer a force. Many politicians and professors will not bother to distinguish between the tactical sophistication of the Soviets and the cautiously underplayed long-range strategic goals that are inspired by national and ideological considerations, with doctrinal influences more often than not preponderant. Western minds have always had trouble seeing through Moscow's efforts at détente. The SALT negotiations, the nuclear proliferation talks, and the Moscow-Bonn treaty are hailed by wishful thinkers as the beginning of a new era.

Former Undersecretary of State George W. Ball has pointed out that "to anybody burdened with a sense of history, such euphoria seems both threadbare and tiresome."* He reminds us of the mockery of the "Spirit of Geneva" in 1955, of Khrushchev's visit to the United States in 1959, of the Cuban missile crisis in 1962. It may be added that these events happened in an allegedly "relaxed" period, while now, under the Brezhnev-Kosygin regime, Communist orthodoxy has experienced a rebirth.

It matters not whether the Politburo undertakes a campaign for relaxation of tensions because of its economic difficulties, because of what the Soviets regard as the Chinese threat, or because of the social and economic troubles of the satellite states. "Détente" has not prevented Moscow from engaging Soviet power deeply in the Arab world and throughout the Middle East — the withdrawal of Soviet forces from Egypt is not an indication that this policy has changed. Moscow would

*Washington *Post,* September 13, 1970.

like the Suez Canal cleared for its maritime expansion toward the Persian Gulf and the Red Sea; it is tempted by the thought of becoming a power in the Indian Ocean and in fact has concluded a treaty with Mauritius that will provide port facilities for Soviet ships. But as no Soviet foreign policy has just one goal but rather several, Kremlin strategy strives for control of Middle East oil, for domination of this area with the view to eventual penetration into South Asia and the Indian Ocean and, ultimately, Soviet predominance in all of Europe, for which the recent negotiations and agreements are indispensable. (The so-called European Security Conference, and the Moscow-Bonn Treaty are major steps toward greater Soviet influence in Western Europe, consolidiation of control over Eastern Europe, and the disintegration of NATO.)

In view of these strategic considerations, Dr. Landis' book is of great importance. He makes it clear, in no uncertain terms, how future Soviet control of Middle East petroleum conforms to the broad objectives of the U.S.S.R. and would have far-reaching consequences for the free world. Thus the work is of particular interest not only to economists but also to students of international affairs and observers of the Soviet scene.

Kurt L. London

Institute for Sino-Soviet Studies
George Washington University
Washington, D.C.

Preface

While the U.S.S.R.'s Middle East military involvement has been clear enough since the 1967 Arab-Israeli war, its long-range aspirations continue to be fostered in lowkey in the realm of regional politics and petroleum. Looking to shorter-term objectives through a cooperative attitude in summitry and SALT, the Soviet Union does not neglect its patient program to rationalize the needs of ideology and economy through well-rounded Middle East policies pursued actively for nearly two decades.

This study comprises an evaluation of Soviet interest in Middle East petroleum, describing it in terms of a long-range, strategic motivation based upon eventual development of a comprehensive pattern of petroleum import and export trade.

In seeking indications of Soviet motivation, the author has employed primary source materials of Soviet origin, some in the original Russian but the majority available in translations published in Moscow. Applying these materials to the interpretation of Soviet strategy, I have sought to remain mindful of the state role of the Soviet press: ". . . books are the sharpest ideological weapon the Party and the people possess. It is necessary always to keep this weapon honed and ready."*

The author has attempted to give appropriate attention to communist theory. The significance of ideology in the Soviet system is, it would seem, slighted by certain Western scholars who tend to discount its influence perhaps because they fail to grasp its unique vitality and resilience after more than half a century. To them, for example, it may seem reassuring to perceive Communism in conventional guise whenever possible, so that "hawks and doves" appear active in "Kremlin debate" and Soviet trade officials seem counterparts of Western businessmen.

This investigation has taken note that Middle East petroleum has been used as a symbolic device to encourage anti-Western sentiment, already activated by currents of nationalism and revolution among Arabs and non-Arabs of the region. Crude oil and natural gas, as exploitable resources and as an industry, have emerged as objects of Soviet and Soviet-bloc policy in both short- and long-term planning. Moscow's policy makers have been guided both by Marxist-Leninist ideology and Russian national self-interest, as they have attempted to erode Western economic predominance in the region, and create an opening for increasing Soviet-bloc participation in the Middle East petroleum industry as advisers, operators, and long-term trading partners.

Looking into an underlying, strategic rationale to Soviet petroleum policies, this study has noted Moscow's "petroleum paradox," the seeming contradiction posed by appraisals that the Soviet petroleum industry is, at once, deficient and competitive. The former case is suggested by the contrast of abundant reserves with reports of continuing discrepancies in planning, development, and operation of the Soviet oil and natural gas

*"Dostoyaniye naroda" ("Property of the People"), *Pravda,* March 13, 1964, P. 1. It is appropriate to note that the Party Central Committee itself takes direct control of a journal such as *Sovyetskaya kultura,* if it appears to stray from the official course. Dev Murarka, "Soviet Leaders Tighten Control over Arts, Culture," London observer of the Washington *Post,* September 7, 1972, p. E-6.

industries, such that its production appears inadequate to meet rising petroleum requirements; it is given credence by a recent series of agreements providing for the import of Middle East petroleum by the majority of the Soviet bloc. At the same time, the Soviet industry appears competitive as a rival marketer of Middle East petroleum-exporting countries, based upon present Soviet exports to Eastern and Western Europe and Japan, coupled with Soviet negotiations for long-term expansion of her deliveries of crude oil or natural gas to Western Europe, Japan, and the United States.

I have attempted to dispel the "petroleum paradox" by turning to the Marxist-Leninist formula for a "world socialist planned economy" and a "world energy delivery system." Such ideology suggests that the U.S.S.R. could "move in" through preliminary roles of producer and major importer of Middle East petroleum and a broker for the region's industry. Ultimately, the U.S.S.R. could, within the world energy delivery system concept, assume a "strategic middleman" role by simultaneously importing major quantities of petroleum from the national sector of Middle East countries on a barter basis, and, after satisfying domestic needs, exporting crude oil and natural gas from its reservoir of Middle East and indigenous production to traditional Middle East customers of the capitalist world.

The concept of strategic middleman would presumably entail increasing integration of petroleum imports from the Middle East and exports to western countries under the precominant influence of the Moscow center. In ideological terms, the U.S.S.R. would be working toward a world energy delivery system within a world socialist planned economy.

Such a development would have far more than theoretical significance. It would harbor the potential for Soviet political action having strategic consequences far beyond what has emerged in the 1970s as a dramatic Russian political and military presence in the Middle East.

Roots of Soviet Interest in the Middle East

Soviet strategy, the Middle East region — a "problem area in world politics,"[1] — and petroleum are diverse subjects to be weighed for their impact upon one another. Each in its own right is of such complexity and importance in international affairs as to deserve concentrated study. Yet, examing petroleum as a factor in Soviet Middle East strategy promises an approach toward understanding the interrelationship of politics and oil and the shaping of foreign policy of the Union of Soviet Socialist Republics.

Origins of East-West controversies over Middle East petroleum are traceable to early British exploration efforts in Persia and the Anglo-Persian Oil Company concessions, dating from 1901. Western exploitation of these fields was vigorously undertaken after Winston Churchill, First Lord of the Admiralty, made the historic decision to convert the Royal Navy from coal to oil. Britain thereupon acquired controlling stock in the company as a result of Churchill's instructions to Sir John Fisher, Chairman of the Royal Commission on Fuel Oil, in 1912: "You have got to find the oil: to show . . . how it can be purchased regularly and cheaply in peace; and with absolute certainty in war."[2]

Thus, Middle East petroleum had assumed major significance for a Western power; a half century later, a broader Middle East, encompassing two-thirds of the world's proven oil reserves and accounting for 40 percent of world production, appeared important not only to Western powers, but to Communist Russia as well. (See Figures 3 and 5.) Finally, the boundaries separating the Middle East from Russia had become stabilized along a line that divided the rich petroleum resources of the south from prolific fields of the Soviet Caucasus and from the yet-undiscovered rich Central Asian and Siberian deposits.

If there is little mystery surrounding Western attraction to Middle East petroleum today, when the United States, Britain, and France are all major investors in its exploitation and Western Europe and Japan its principal consumers, Russia's precise interest in the region's resources is less clear (see Figures 2, 3, and 4). At least, recent developments in Soviet-Middle East relations seem to justify a reappraisal of traditional views: " . . . the Soviet aim has been a negative one: to deny the oil to the West both in time of peace and in time of war rather than to acquire the oil for its own purposes;" " . . . physical difficulties . . . the question of world markets . . . cash requirements . . . would eliminate any direct attempt by the Soviet Union to take over the Middle Eastern oil fields and operate them commercially . . . ." "Russia would still not be able to operate the oil fields against Western opposition . . . ." "Soviet attempts to enter international oil markets . . . clearly imply that the U.S.S.R. does not need the Middle Eastern oil for its own purposes or even for the needs of the communist bloc;" " . . . major oil-producing countries . . . have never, even in the tensest moments of crisis between the Arabs and the West . . . as much as hinted that they would use their oil to force the West to grant Arab demands."[3]

Recent developing relations between the U.S.S.R. and the majority of Middle East countries are in sharp contrast with centuries of hostility, evident in numerous wars and frontier engagements as czars attempted to expand the Russian Empire southward into the Muslim lands of Turkey, Iran, and Central Asia.

In the eighteenth century, military campaigns against Turkey and Persia were designed to extend Russian control over the Black and Caspian Sea regions. Peter the Great took Baku; Catherine II advanced to the Black Sea, challenged Turkish control of the Bosporus and Dardanelles, and gained Russian access to the Mediterranean. Her "Oriental project" envisioned new invasions of the Caucasus and Persia to seize principal trading centers between Turkey and Tibet, to approach India, and to isolate Constantinople from the East. Her favorite, Valerian Zubov, captured Derbent and retook Baku while General Suvorov prepared to attack the Ottoman capital. Only Catherine's death forestalled the Russian fleet's movement to the Straits, halted the land campaign, and led to withdrawal of expeditionary troops from the Caucasus.[4]

The increasing deployment of Soviet naval and merchant vessels in the waters of the Middle East recalls Russia's prominence in the Mediterranean on such earlier occasions as Admiral Orlov's expedition against Turkey in 1770, and subsequent wars against Turkey and Persia to extend her frontiers toward the Mediterranean and the Persian Gulf. With the treaties of Gulistan (1813) and Turkmanchay (1828), Russia formalized her domination of the Caucasus and the Caspian Sea, both regions which would later yield vast petroleum resources for Soviet exploitation. Plans called for further Russian expansion to dominate the "commercially and strategically important cities of Herat and Kabul" in Afghanistan,[5] a state which successfully preserved its sovereignty and, in recent times, developed relations with Soviet Russia, leading to cooperative ventures, such as construction of a pipeline for long-range deliveries of natural gas to the U.S.S.R. in exchange for Soviet aid.[6]

Nineteenth-century czars perceived new opportunities to revive Russian Mediterranean longings of aggrandizement at the Turks' expense. The "Eastern Question," which concerned realignment of Balkan relationships with major European powers as the Ottoman Empire continued to deteriorate, became a dominant theme in Russia's aspirations toward the Straits. Russo-Turkish wars of 1806-08, 1809-12, and 1828-29 led to Unkiar Skelessi, with its secret clause by which the sultan agreed to exclude warships from the Black Sea, thereby establishing a "Russian lake." Thereupon, in 1841, England, Austria, France, and Prussia joined to counter the aims of Nicholas I by placing the Straits under international control. Furthermore, by inflicting a humiliating defeat upon Russia in the Crimean War (1855-56), England, France, and Turkey frustrated czarist designs and forced St. Petersburg, under the Treaty of Paris, to give up the mouth of the Danube and its exclusive position in the Black Sea.

Halted in the southwest, Alexander II resumed expansion to the southeast with drives toward Tashkent, Bukhara, Samarkand, and Khiva in the Muslim lands of Central Asia, a region later to reveal some of the Soviet's richest natural gas deposits. With the conquest of Merv in 1884, Russian annexation of Turkestan (later retaken by the Bolsheviks and called Soviet Kazakhstan) was complete, and "the British lion and the Russian two-headed eagle were glowering angrily at one another across the uncertain frontiers of Afghanistan."[7] Such successful military ventures to the south encouraged Russia to turn her attention again to the Eastern Question. Claiming the title "protector of Slavs," she intervened in the Balkans in 1876 in behalf of a Greater Serbia,[8] seeking to become established nearer Mediterranean shores.

Having helped to establish the Bulgarian Exarchate as a branch of the Greek Orthodox Church in 1870, Russia, as "champion of Balkan Christians,"[9] started a new war against Turkey (1877-78). Hoping that her Balkan intervention would escape complications with other powers,[10] Russia sought to take Bessarabia away from Rumania and to create a servile "Greater Bulgaria," which was extended southward to acquire a port for probable Russian use on the Mediterranean. Turning away from her former Serbian protégé, Russia attempted, through drafting of the Treaty of San Stefano, to recoup losses incurred under terms of the Treaty of Paris. However, Europe's major powers convened the Congress of Berlin (1878) and overturned the San Stefano accord, frustrating Czar Alexander's "Greater Bulgaria" scheme and ending Russia's pan-Slavist dreams of "domination of Constantinople and the Straits";[11] international control of access to the Black Sea was again established.

Thus halted in her Mediterranean drive, Russia was forced to wait until the early twentieth century to push again along the old Caucasian axis toward the Middle East, when she joined with Britain in partitioning Persia under the Anglo-Russian Agreement of 1907. The discovery of Persian oil enhanced the desirability of extending Russian influence southward, and the new treaty facilitated the establishment of "quasi-complete control of Azerbaijan."[12] Czarist aspirations to reach the Mediterranean were revitalized by secret treaties concluded during World War I; one of them, the Anglo-Russian agreement of 1915, provided for postwar "annexation by Russia of Constantinople, the western shore of the Bosphorus, the Sea of Marmara and the Dardanelles, southern Thrace up to the line Enos-Midia, the islands of Imbros and Tenedos, and a strip of the Asiatic littoral."[13]

The Bolshevik Revolution in 1917 resulted in the temporary loss of czarist territorial acquisitions in the south and spelled a setback for Russian aims to penetrate the Middle East. Faced with strife and turmoil at home, Lenin was unable, during the earliest years, to follow up old designs for a Mediterranean beachhead and a physical presence in Persia. Soon, however, the Bolsheviks retook the Caucasus and Central Asia, which had enjoyed only a short-lived opportunity to savor independence. Subsequently, under the aegis of Communism, probes were resumed toward the Mediterranean and the Persian Gulf, and a new element, petroleum, began to figure in Moscow's expanding relations with the Middle East.

Notes

1. Halford L. Hoskins, *The Middle East: Problem Area in World Politics* (New York: The Macmillan Co., 1954).

2. Winston Churchill, *The World Crisis* (New York: Charles Scribner's Sons, 1963), pp. 132—133.

3. Benjamin Shwadran, *The Middle East, Oil and the Great Powers* (New York: Council for Middle Eastern Affairs Press, 1959), pp. 455—456.

4. Michael T. Florinsky, *Russia,* Vols. I-II (New York: The Macmillan Co., 1955), I, pp. 541, 617.

5. Ibid., II, p. 843.

6. *Pyat'desyat' let sovetskoy yneshney torgovli (Fifty Years of Soviet Foreign Trade)* (Moscow: State Publishing House for International Relations, 1967), pp. 172—173.

7. Florinsky, *Russia,* II, p. 985.

8. Benedict H. Sumner, *Russia and the Balkans (1870-1880)* (London: Oxford University Press, 1937), p. 177.

9. Dwight E. Lee, "The Liberation of the Balkan Slavs," *A Handbook of Slavic Studies,* ed. L. Strakhovsky (Cambridge, Massachusetts: Harvard University Press, 1949), pp. 271—272, 277.

10. Mihailo D. Stojanovic, *The Great Powers and the Balkans* (Cambridge, England: The University Press, 1939), p. 152.

11. Charles Jelavich, *Tsarist Russia and Balkan Nationalism* (Berkeley: University of California Press, 1958), p. 15.

12. Florinsky, *Russia,* II, p. 1310.

13. Ibid., p. 1349.

Economics and Petroleum in Soviet Strategy

Since the question of historical continuity in czarist and Soviet Middle East aims can be presumed to affect Soviet interest in the region to the south, it should be noted that the twentieth century has brought a variety of new conditions requiring consideration. Czarist policies had reflected an interest in approaches to the eastern Mediterranean and territory leading toward India and the Persian Gulf; prior to the 1950s, Soviet relations with the area to the south had scarcely reached beyond the proximate border regions of the contiguous states of Turkey and Iran. In the past two decades, however, Moscow has become increasingly involved with a far greater Middle East, characterized by the far-flung bond of the Muslim culture, in which "the Arab countries . . . form the link between Asia and Africa. . . ."[1]

The discovery of petroleum has been only one development shaping the interests of outside powers and creating new dimensions for diplomacy in the Middle East:

> The fact is that the Eastern Question of our day has little in common with the Oriental problem that preoccupied the chancelleries of Europe one hundred years ago. To be sure, the conflict between Russia and the West still persists, but it is no longer the same Russia—nor, for that matter, the same West—which contests the area. The center of the conflict has moved southward from the Balkans and Constantinople, and

7

the stakes are vastly different. The question of the nationalities and minorities in the old Ottoman Empire has been solved — or, to be more accurate, shunted aside. The strategic interests of the powers no longer take the same form, involved as they are in such new issues as Arab nationalism and oil, Communism, and the emergence of Israel as a state . . . .[2]

Soviet Strategy — Some General Considerations

While natural heir to the czars' interest in the Middle East, Bolshevist Russia developed her own approach to the region in keeping with the bold aspirations of world Communism. Thus, evaluating Soviet strategy became a difficult undertaking, in view of the need to sort out the roles of communist ideology and Russian national interests as determining forces in shaping Soviet foreign policy.

A thoughtful analysis of the comparative function of events and doctrine in the formulation of Soviet foreign policy has suggested that these two forces are intermingled. Marxist-Leninist tenets are seen as "an interpretive modifier to which perceived events are subjected," and as "a set of symbolic referents" for defining Soviet national interest, but, it is noted, rarely are policies formulated exclusively from doctrinal considerations.[3] Rather, it should be presumed that Communist decisions are reached under some of the types of pressure operating upon officials of non-Communist governments, which may have been overstated by a western correspondent, who concluded, a few months after the 1967 Arab-Israeli war, that Soviet Middle East decision makers "can't agree among themselves, or they're playing completely by ear from one day to the next."[4]

The deftness with which Communist dogma shifts to meet new opportunities can be seen in changes of the official credo found in Party programmes adopted over a span of four decades. According to the 1961 programme, "The Communist Party of the Soviet Union will hold high the banner of peace and friendship among the nations. . ."[5] while the 1919 programme had a far different ring: ". . . imperialist war must inevitably become

8

transformed into a civil war between the exploited toiling masses, headed by the proletariat, against the bourgeoisie."[6]

In another revision, the more recent programme, claiming to update previous formulations, states that, in foreign relations, the Party must "work for general and complete disarmament under strict international control."[7] Yet, dogma expressed in the earlier version concluded that "the watchwords of pacifism, 'international disarmament,' 'courts of arbitration,' etc., are not merely a reactionary utopia, but a deception of the working classes. . . ."[8]

Such tactical shifts in the furtherance of Soviet strategy are articulated and given justification through the medium of a totally state-controlled press. Thus, Soviet propaganda strives to explain and support Party policies in terms consistent with the current development of Marxist-Leninist ideology. *New Times,* as an example, published in Moscow in a number of languages including English, appropriately documents Lenin's outstanding leadership by reference to his astute perception that Bolshevism's very survival depended upon conclusion of a swift peace, however unfavorable, with the Kaiser after the October Revolution.[9] At the same time, however, the writer contradicts his first purpose by attempting to portray that episode as an example of the principled character of the new Communist state.[10] Another Communist organ, *World Marxist Review,*[11] fulfills the task of continuing to relate Soviet strategy to its doctrinal origins in Marxism:

> Marx and Engels advanced the principle of internationalism as an indispensable condition of man's liberation from exploitation, oppression, and war. The working class in all countries has a common aim - - to abolish capitalism and build Communism. As Lenin pointed out, "capital is an international force. To vanquish it, an international workers' alliance, an international workers' brotherhood, is needed."[12]

Another theoretical journal, *Kommunist,*[13] attempts to rationalize the Soviet Union's elaborate bureaucratic structure apparently required to further the cause of Communism, which, according to Marx, was to have been an inevitable development:

> Communist indoctrination of the workers is the task of not only Party organizations, government organs, councils of workers'

deputies [representatives], trade unions, Communist youth organizations, army political organs, and numerous social organizations, ministries, and departments which are concerned with training and educating the youth carry on this work under leadership of the Party.[14]

Moscow's journal, *International Affairs,*[15] points to the significant role of the Party in creating conditions for the ultimate triumph of Communism: ". . . the general line of the Communist Party . . . all its activities, all its successes, its strategy and tactics . . . are subordinated to the great goal of serving the cause of the working class, the cause of all mankind."[16]

The Party's flexible tactics occasionally result in declarations that appear discordant with Soviet policies, as occurred during the period just preceding the 1956 Hungarian Revolution. Thus, less than a year before Soviet troops re-entered Budapest and ruthlessly put an end to the Imre Nagy government and popular rebellion, Moscow's public pronouncements strongly supported the cause of sovereignty:

Desire for the seizure of colonies is alien to the Soviet state - - our social system is based on the elimination of all colonial and national oppression and enslavement, for fraternal cooperation and friendship between peoples is one of our most important precepts.[17]

The same declarations described "the basic principles of the Soviet state's foreign policy from the first days of its existence," in terms quite remote from the reality of Soviet actions in Eastern Europe in the fall of 1956:

This policy does not and cannot have aims such as the seizure of foreign territories, the subjection of other peoples, be they in Europe or in other continents. It does not and cannot have aims such as the imposition of its will or system upon other peoples, for intervention in the international affairs of other states.[18]

A Communist theoretician acknowledged the dichotomous stance the Party is compelled to assume in furtherance of Soviet strategy, in what Kremlinologists might perceive as a rare moment of candor: "Unfortunately we very often forget that the role which the Party is called upon to play as the vanguard of the revolution is one thing in theory and quite another in practice. . . ."[19]

The Soviet Union's strong support of "peaceful coexistence" with capitalist countries, undertaken in the mid-1950s, constituted a shift in the ideological rationale of Soviet foreign policy. Pursuance of the Communist millenium now appeared, at least for the time being, to be shelved in favor of a kind of humanitarianism here and now:

> One of the urgent tasks of further development in international trade and economic cooperation is the expansion of commodity circulation between the socialist countries and the West. . . .
>
> The nations place great hopes in the UN Geneva Conference on Trade and Development. All countries seeking the strengthening of economic ties, the further lessening of international tension and the welfare of all mankind are interested in its success.[20]

Meanwhile, Soviet articles specializing in economics indicated that the strategy of peaceful coexistence pointed toward a primary goal of revitalizing Soviet economy by infusions of modern capitalist technology and the acquisition of larger amounts of western hard currency.[21] The perils inherent in adopting such policies toward the West quite understandably caused apprehension among ideologues of world Communism, who saw fit to warn Soviet bloc economic planners that peaceful coexistence "must necessarily stop short of the point where it might jeopardize the victory of socialism in the economic competition. . . ."[22] The Party's sensitivity to the danger of "too much peaceful coexistence" was illustrated in the Soviet press in the aftermath of the 1968 Czechoslovak intervention, despite the fact that large-scale economic ties between that country and the West had not yet been permitted to develop. On that occasion, *Pravda* stressed that true Czech patriots stood for even greater economic ties with the U.S.S.R.[23]

Soviet leaders since the mid-1950s have been increasingly faced with Communist Chinese charges of "revisionism" as a result of peaceful overtures to the West; the Moscow Party leadership has found itself, as the predominant voice of world Communism, hard-pressed to rationalize the peaceful coexistence policy with the orthodoxy of Marxism-Leninism. The Central Committee of the Soviet Communist Party was quoted in a letter to the Chinese Party's Central Committee in 1963, explaining that "peaceful coexistence does not imply conciliation between socialist and bourgeois ideologies." The Soviet note then sought to invoke the spirit of world revolution by adding:

> The peaceful coexistence of states with different social systems pre-
> supposes an unremitting ideological, political, and economic struggle
> of the working people inside the countries of the capitalist system,
> including armed struggle when they find that necessary and the steady
> advance of the national liberation movement among the peoples of the
> colonial and dependent countries."[24]

Subsequent developments leading to the Arab-Israeli crisis
and its accompanying pattern of diplomatic contacts between
the U.S.S.R. and the United States evoked further Chinese
charges of Muscovite heresy against the proletarian revolution.[25]
Despite the appearance of such serious dissension within the
world Communist movement, however, the leadership of the
Communist Party of the Soviet Union appears to be committed
to fashioning such tactics as will contribute most effectively to
the realization of Party aims. The conclusion of cooperative
U.S.-Soviet agreements in 1972 could be rationalized in terms
of peaceful coexistence, and, since they followed closely
President Nixon's visit to Peking, the Peoples Republic of
China was not in a strong position to charge "Soviet revisionism."

Economics and Politics in the U.S.S.R.

> "Economic competition is the main battlefield of the two world
> systems.[26]
>
> — St. Goranov, Sofia, Bulgaria, 1967

In Western democratic countries, where products are sold
on a competitive, domestic market, capitalist economics permit
a significant, if gradually decreasing, measure of competition
among agricultural and industrial enterprises. By contrast, the
Soviet Government, under Party direction, plans, supervises,
and operates its sprawling monopoly of production and distribution of the preponderance of goods and services in the
U.S.S.R. This socialist economy of the Soviet Union has also
become a "senior partner" to the national economies of other
members of the Soviet bloc in a structure of individual production systems, coordinated under the predominant influence
of Moscow.

While Communist states have amended Marxian theory in order to reap advantages of capitalism through such accoutrements as profit motive and limited private property, ultimate control of production bears the unmistakable totalitarian brand. These economies permit no free competition; technological research is the province of government scientists; production is planned in deference to broad political guidelines; and the "market" is not a prime reflection of supply and demand, as the terms are understood in Western economies, since prices are set by the government. This supremacy of the Party and its governmental functionaries is evident not only over economic affairs of the U.S.S.R., itself, but also operates decisively in the Council for Mutual Economic Assistance (COMECON) of the Soviet bloc. The political overtones of Marxist-Leninist economics might well be expected, then, to affect the role of petroleum in Soviet foreign economic policy toward the Middle East.

While Russian Communism has been based upon "scientific, economic laws," which are an outgrowth of an "inevitable" Marxian theory, Soviet socialism has become a reality through the Soviet leadership's view that the national economy must be subservient to the maintenance of the Party's monopoly of political power within the state, and the projection of that power abroad.

Such a political rationale underlay early Bolshevist economic policies. In accordance with Marxism, Lenin swiftly implemented nationalization measures against the bourgeois power embodied in the 1917 economic and social fabric of Russia. He had realized the necessity of currying favor with workers and peasants by expropriating the gentry and middle class, and probably knew that the problem of establishing a viable economy would have to be deferred to the future.

Paradoxically, when the Party was faced with desperate economic conditions in the early 1920s, political domination over economic affairs was sacrificed and much of Russian agricultural and factory production had to be returned to the private sector under Lenin's New Economic Policy. After a

13

dramatically successful economic recovery, the Party again came to assert complete dominance over the national economy, and, through the years of Stalin and Khrushchev to the present, has retained tight control. Absolute power had been essential to implement Stalin's forced collectivization of agriculture and massive industrialization, adopted in the late 1920s. Subsequently, the Communist Party has seen fit to attempt numerous liberalization reforms, but has never ceased to look upon its economic system as "totalitarianism harnessed to the task of rapid industrialization and economic growth."[27]

Over the years the Party has steadily institutionalized its control over the national economy, with the avowed aim of creating an abundance of agricultural and industrial production in support of "socialist construction." Senior economic planners turned to the task of building Communism, and, from their vantage point in Moscow, proceeded to plan development of Soviet petroleum resources hundreds of miles to the south.

Political Domination of the Economic System

The Central Committee of the Communist Party of the Soviet Union has been able to exercise control over the Soviet economy through capabilities that accompany totalitarian rule:

(1)   The power to concentrate a preponderance of productive forces in any desired sector of the economy.

(2)   The unifying tendency of central planning by means of which spontaneous local economic trends are contained within bounds determined by the superior state authority.

(3)   The absolute state monopoly over internal and foreign trade.

(4)   The pressure of propaganda and terror, which may be called upon to present an appeal and a threat to achieve mass cooperation in fulfilling production schedules.

Political control over the economy is also supported by the day-to-day activities of an apparatus of Party functionaries, engineers, clerks, auditors, plain-clothesmen, agronomists, administrators, executives, scientists, technicians, agitators, and trade-union functionaries. This bureaucratic aggregate of state officials bears the responsibility of working toward the implementation of Party-conceived plans and programs. They follow the detailed guidance embodied in five- or seven-year plans to produce and distribute goods and services for the country's overall domestic and foreign requirements, as defined in Kremlin chambers. While political control over the economy may not lead to "western efficiency," it has emerged in the Soviet Union as a catalyst providing momentum for the economic system, dedicated to the accumulation of economic power in furtherance of Moscow's domestic and global aspirations.

Despite the adoption of the capitalistic features of incentive pay, enterprise profit schemes, and a limited operation of market principles, Party theoreticians continue to pay homage to Marxism by noting, for example, the ideological purity of the Soviet petroleum industry:

> The socialist oil and gas industry has fundamental advantages over the capitalistic. It is based on social ownership of the means of production. The liquidation of private ownership did away with the exploitation of man by man and created the prerequisites for the planned and proportional development of the oil and gas industry in the system of the national economy in the interests of the workers.[28]

The Liberman reforms of 1966 appear to have brought little relaxation in the Party's firm control, despite Premier Kosygin's statement that "by 1968 profits, sales, and rate of return on investment will replace fulfillment of quotas as the main standards of success for every Soviet firm."[29] While certain changes have appeared as "a repudiation of formerly sacred doctrines, " they seem, according to a Western observer, to resemble little more than a stop-gap antidote for the system's ills. Far from presaging a turn to private initiative as a challenge to established political control, Libermanism, not unlike earlier revisionist reforms, has been seen by that observer to promise dubious results in attempting to meet the challenge of modern industrialization.[30]

During its half century of rule in Russia, the Party has sought to institutionalize its monopoly over economic life as a kind of state upon a state. This formalized, permanent function of the Party, a sharp departure from the orthodox Marxist tenet that its role was only temporary, has become a part of Soviet ideology: "Marxist political economy, which arose as a study of the revolutionary downfall of capitalism, became enriched after the victory of the socialist revolution by a new section — the political economy of socialism, which became the theoretical foundation of the economic policy of the Communist Party and of the Soviet Government."[31]

Social discipline is achieved and Party dominance is intensified by official compulsion over the labor force. Accordingly, the "democratic" Stalin Constitution of 1936, which proclaimed "the right to work," is interpreted as "the obligation to work conscientiously" in furtherance of "socialist democracy . . . to tackle the problems of Communist construction."[32]

The Soviet Union's vast petroleum resources have contributed mightily to the economic power and, hence, to the political stance of the Soviet Union. (See Figure 1.) Most of the rich regions were an inheritance from czarist expansionism — portions of the Ukraine annexed by Catherine the Great; the Baku region of Azerbaijan, subjugated in the early nineteenth century as a springboard for penetration of the Middle East; the Volga-Ural "second Baku" region, taken despite continuing Tatar opposition into the twentieth century; and Turkestan, with its recently found wealth of Mangyshlak, Central Asia, and Siberia, absorbed in the latter part of the nineteenth century.[33]

Shortly after the Bolsheviks seized power in Russia, most of the petroleum-rich area quickly became independent of Moscow as newly proclaimed national republics, thanks to the temporary weakness of Lenin's new regime. The petroleum wealth was, however, again forcibly annexed to Russia by the Bolsheviks when the Red Army invaded Azerbaijan (1920), Volga-Ural (1920), and Turkestan (1922) regions, ending their short-lived independence.[34] (See Figure 1.)

These petroleum resources are appropriately awarded, in keeping with Marxism-Leninism, a lofty role in the struggle for a Communist society:

> For the creation in our land of the material/technical foundation of Communism, petroleum and natural gas - - advanced varieties of fuel and valuable raw material for the chemical industry — have great significance....The Programme of the Communist Party of the Soviet Union calls for the utilization in ever-increasing scale of these riches in the construction of Communism.[35]

Final planning decisions affecting overall industrial and agricultural production are made, not at the pinnacle of the economic structure, but by a higher political voice, the Party, which, after due regard for economic factors, sets priorities for how much, and where, petroleum is to be produced:

> Directives [of the 23rd Congress of the Communist Party of the Soviet Union] prescribe the establishment of new oil-producing centers in Western Siberia and Western Kazakhstan, and a significant increase in the production of petroleum in the old oil-producing regions; provide for the further adaption of progressive methods of developing petroleum deposits and intensification of the production of petroleum to raise production of in the country in 1970 to 345-355 million metric tons.[36]

Reflecting its concern for the economic consequences of incompetence, the Party reinforces its control over the economy by publishing criticism of the professional capacity of important officials of the economic bureaucracy. The front page of *Pravda*[37] thus appeared to sound a warning to the highest official of the petroleum and chemical industries:

> ... the Minister of the Chemical Industry, Comrade Kostandov, and the Minister of the Petroleum-Refining and Petrochemical Industry, Comrade Fedorov, are not exercising sufficient control over major construction.[38]

The political leadership's guidelines for petroleum production are not always accepted with silent compliance. The rationale of political directives to the petroleum industry is occasionally challenged on cogent grounds by a Party economic journalist from the Ukraine. A Communist writer, in one of a series of published economic critiques, cast doubt upon the effectiveness of Soviet central planning as it directs regional petroleum development:

> It is planned that by 1968 oil will begin to be transported to the Republic from Kazakhstan (Mangishlak) through the Caspian Sea and overland and from the Stavropol region. Deliveries of oil brought from afar will increase faster than the growth of refining capacities of Ukrainian plants.
>
> Simple arithmetic shows that this is very costly to the government. The shipment of one ton of oil costs .35 rubles per kilometer. Thus,

not counting the cost of extraction, the delivery of a ton of oil to the Ukraine from Mangishlak costs about 5.7 rubles, and from the Stavropol region, 412 rubles.

Extraction of a ton of Ukrainian oil costs, of course, much less (twice as cheap as Krasnodar and 2.7 times as cheap as Baku, as an example). . . . However, one must consider that the cost of production of Ukrainian oil decreases every year since its rapid growth occurs and will continue to occur as a result of newly discovered deposits in the eastern oblasts of the republic.

. . . Certainly, in order to deliver to the Ukraine millions of tons of oil from Kazakhstan and the Stavropol region, it is also necessary to invest collossal expenditures, a huge amount of critical metal either in construction of a gigantic oil pipeline system or in the expansion of the tanker fleet, tanker trucks, and an increase in the throughput capacity of railroads. So wouldn't it be more prudent from the over-all point of view of the state to turn a part of this money, material resources, metal, and labor of Soviet people over to prospecting and development of new oil resources in the Ukraine?[39]

The Party's assertion of control over production planning and day-to-day operation of the petroleum industry is matched in another economic function — the Party's domination over planning and conduct of Soviet foreign trade.

Political Domination of Foreign Economic Relations

"Curiously, it is rather as an international Capitalist that Soviet foreign economic policy has captured the fancy of the world.[40]
— Joseph S. Berliner

Just as the U.S.S.R. has resorted to capitalistic measures to achieve increased efficiency in industrial and agricultural production, she looked abroad in order to obtain necessary capital to develop her socialist economy, sometimes behaving like an orthordox capitalist. Foreign commerce, like the domestic economic system, is seen to be dutifully performing its state role, as required by the Party.

Foreign trade was nationalized shortly after the Revolution and has since served as an "arm of the state." Every aspect of Soviet foreign trade is and has been under direct state control.[41]

The Soviet economy has already drawn greatly upon Czechoslovakia and East Germany, the most industrialized members of the "socialist camp," in order to make up for its own economic shortcomings. The evidence has seemed quite convincing that "peaceful coexistence" was instituted by

Khrushchev in the hope that sophisticated machinery and possibly hard currency could be obtained from capitalist states in order to augment the Soviet Union's technological development.[42] Soviet efforts to acquire Western technological assistance in the early 1970s, such as U.S. computers and machine tools for the Kama River Truck Plant and West German technology in long-term barter for Soviet natual gas, are illustrations of the success of Soviet foreign economic policy.

Foreign economic relations are furthered by Soviet trade unions, another instrument of political control employed to pressure workers for greater production effort. Soviet trade unions carry out an international role with political overtones in duties assigned by the Party in foreign countries:

> The Soviet trade union, reared by the great Party of Lenin in the spirit of proletarian internationalism, in fraternal fashion shares its rich experience with the young trade centers of the countries of Asia and Africa, and gives them all possible aid and support.[43]

It has already been noted that the Party employs its press to critique industrial ministers as it asserts political direction of the economy. The Soviet press also plays a role in stimulating popular support for foreign trade programs, and, at the same time, gaining public acquiescence for the Party's domination of such republic economies as that of the Ukraine.[44] In trade practices with underdeveloped countries, the U.S.S.R., like other major powers, has apparently not neglected the opportunity of realizing political gain.[45]

When the Party has implemented measures of active foreign trading, there have been frequent Western accusations of "economic warfare"; such intense rivalry in the world market would seem to be merely a logical extension of Marxist-Leninist ideology into the realm of foreign trade. As in Communist dogma, which espouses any means to achieve desired ends, foreign trade, along with other tools of the Soviet regime such as the press, trade unions, cultural exchanges, and perhaps military pressure, performs an appropriate role in furtherance of Russian Communist global objectives. It should be noted that non-Communist states also subordinate trade to political aims through the more subtle means of restrictive commerce legislation. Since the mid-1950s, when the Soviet Union's industrial potential was reaching the point to permit large-scale export of goods and raw materials, Party leaders have frequently invoked Lenin in their use of foreign trade to strengthen the Soviet economy and to spread Communist influence in the world.[46]

Soviet petroleum has been described as a powerful instrument of Soviet foreign economic policy in a report of the United States Senate:

> ... Soviet oil is a commodity entirely under government control and consequently can be employed in the interest of the state in any manner deemed useful by the heads of government. The economic profit motive, while undoubtedly present in all engagements entered into with respect to oil supply of provision of technical services relating to oil exploration, production, refining or transport, invariably has been subordinated to whatever ulterior purposes have been components of Communist state policy. This has given the Soyuzneftexport an inestimable advantage in competing with private enterprise as represented by the major oil companies inasmuch as these are compelled to operate at a profit in order to continue to exist.[47]

It seemed that a resource the Russians were developing in greater abundance in the late 1950s would be an ideal commodity, both to use for establishing better relations with other states, and, as a tool of economic warfare, to make inroads into the traditional Middle East petroleum markets in Western Europe:

> The Russian oil monopoly organization dealing with foreign markets - - Soyuzneftexport - - began to make itself felt abroad once again from 1958 onwards; it had done so already once in the twenties, but had relinquished its positions in Europe early in the thirties when oil demand within the U.S.S.R. had left little if any exportable surplus. Now that vast and prolific oil fields had been found and developed, oil had once more become a suitable export commodity, indeed one of the few where the Soviet Union could match foreign competition as far as quality and performance were concerned. In respect of cost and price of oil Soviet Russia could meet foreign competition at any likely level since it could make available the marginal production of a very large and concentrated enterprise at "what the market would bear"; it could obviously recoup losses incurred on exports by manipulating its domestic sales.[48]

Eager to accommodate the Soviet "oil offensive," which developed after emergence of "second Baku," the Volga-Ural petroleum region, was Enrico Mattei, Italy's "oilman without oil,"[49] who welcomed increased deliveries of Soviet crude to compete with Western oil companies.

The Soviet Union's criticism of western oil interests operating in the Middle East seems to underscore the Party's own appreciation of petroleum as a political commodity, as indicated in the principal journal of Moscow's Institute for World Economics and International Affairs:

> As is well-known, oil is the commodity most linked to politics. In the struggle to acquire control over petroleum resources, the interests of the companies and imperialistic states mesh.[50]

We have seen the close relationship between Communist economics and politics, and how the latter dominates the former in the Soviet economic system, placing the economy, including the Soviet petroleum industry, in the service of the state. It would seem hardly surprising, then, that the country's petroleum wealth would constitute an important element in Soviet strategic planning, based as it is upon political, military, and economic considerations. Furthermore, the oil and natural gas resources of the neighboring Middle East region, the subject of this study, would seem to become a factor to be considered in Soviet production and foreign trade planning.

Soviet Strategy and Middle East Petroleum

This inquiry into Soviet motivation will review Soviet policies toward the Middle East and then appraise political and economic aims that have concerned petroleum within the framework of those policies. "Soviet Middle East strategy" in usage here is seen to comprise specific aims operating within the broad context of aims to advance Russian influence throughout the world. The component term "Middle East," far from suggesting any geographical constraints to long-range Soviet goals, is intended merely to reflect the application of global strategy to specific regional objectives which appear likely to contribute materially to the realization of overall aims. "Middle East petroleum" will be examined to evaluate its possible role as one element in Soviet strategy formulation.

"Petroleum in Soviet Middle East strategy" is considered to be located primarily in the major oil-producing countries of the Middle East and the North African littoral, which,
as Muslim states, "form the link between Asia and Africa."[51]
Petroleum is considered in a broad sense, embracing such
stages of the oil and natural gas industry as exploration, production, refining, transporting, and marketing to the extent
that they appear to affect the broad issue of Soviet motivation. This petroleum is considered to have no single nationality: it is both Arab and non-Arab. As already noted, the
possible influence of the Soviet Union's own petroleum industry upon the formulation of Soviet Middle East policies
should not be overlooked. Furthermore, it should be reconized that petroleum is a significant factor in the oil-transit
countries of the region, through whose territorial domain
pipelines and tankers carry crude and gas to be processed and
marketed elsewhere.

Two chronological periods will provide a framework for
reviewing Soviet Middle East policies, as a prelude to examining the possible impact of petroleum upon those policies.
The first period — from the Bolshevist Revolution through
the reign of Stalin — witnessed such extremes of policy as
the outright use of military force and the apparent temporary retirement from active pursuance of aims in the
region, as will be discussed.

The other period — from the end of the Stalin era in
1953 to the present — seems to reflect a new concerted
policy encompassing the steady development of political,
economic, and military relations with the majority of countries of the Middle East, including the North African littoral.

Notes

1. V. Kudryavtsev, "The Middle East Knot," *International Affairs,* No. 9,
September, 1967, p. 30.
2. Walter Laqueur, *The Soviet Union and the Middle East* (New York:
Frederick A. Praeger, 1959), p. vii.
3. Jan F. Triska and David D. Finley, *Soviet Foreign Policy* (New York:
Macmillan, 1968), p. 129.

4. Anatole Shub, "Soviets Mum in Mideast Shifts," Washington *Post*, November 15, 1967, sec. A. p. 16.

5. "The 1961 Party Programme," *The U.S.S.R. and the Future,* ed. Leonard Schapiro, Appendix A (New York: Frederick A. Praeger, 1963), pp. 280-281.

6. "The 1919 Party Programme," *The U.S.S.R. and the Future,* ed. Leonard Schapiro, Appendix B (New York: Frederick A. Praeger, 1963), p. 315.

7. "The 1961 Party Programme," p. 281.

8. "The 1919 Party Programme," p. 315.

9. "It needed the genius and vision of Lenin, his unsurpassed political realism, to pilot the Soviet ship of state through the stormy seas of those years. Ordeal followed upon ordeal and not only in the military field. As one of its first external acts the Soviet government, by a grim irony of fate, was obliged to conclude a very onerous peace with the Kaiser, whose hordes threatened the existence of the young Soviet republic. Lenin displayed the highest statesmanship on this issue, shunning the left phrasemongers and convincing the Party of the necessity of making a temporary compromise by signing the peace treaty in order to save the gains of the revolution. That was the only right decision." "Architect of Soviet Foreign Policy," *New Times,* April 26, 1967, p. 1.

10. "The Soviet state was born a peace-loving state. That followed from the very nature of the new social system, which had no need either of conquest to appropriate other peoples' riches or of war hysteria to swell "Big Business" profits. But the peace program Lenin proclaimed from the rostrum of the Congress of Soviets encountered only resistance from the capitalist powers. Not only every kind of lie and slander, but armed force was used in an effort to strangle Soviet Russia, the state that called for peace." *Ibid.*

11. *World Marxist Review,* published monthly in Prague, represents the international communist movement.

12. Asen Charakcheyev, "Internationalism — an Effective Force," *World Marxist Review,* March, 1966, p. 8.

13. *Kommunist,* published in Moscow, is the theoretical journal of the Central Committee of the Communist Party of the Soviet Union.

14. V. Stepakov, "Aktivno formirovat' marksistko-leninskoye mirovozzreniye i kommunisticheskuyu moral' sovetskikh lyudey," ("Actively Forming the Marxist-Leninist World Outlook and the Communist Morality of Soviet People"), *Kommunist,* No. 17, November, 1966, p. 28.

15. *International Affairs,* the Communist Party's in-depth journal on international politics, is published monthly in Moscow in English.

16. A. Yermonskiy and O. Nakropin, "General Line of Soviet Foreign Policy," *International Affairs,* September, 1966, p. 84.

17. K. Ivanov, "Soviet Foreign Policy and the Present International Situation," *International Affairs,* November, 1955, p. 18.

18. *Ibid.*

19. Edward Taborsky, "The Communist Parties of the 'Third World' in Soviet Strategy," *Orbis,* Vol. XI, No. 1 (Spring, 1967), p. 145. Quotation is from remarks of José Manuel Fortuny.

20. "An Important Factor in Strengthening Peace," *Pravda,* March 23, 1964, p. 1. Trans. by Joint Publications Research Service, Department of Commerce, Washington, D.C., No. 23, 867 (March 25, 1964), pp. 5-7.

21. "Numerous obstacles to Soviet export of machinery and other finished goods still exist in Western countries. It is hoped that farsighted groups in the West having an interest in the further increased growth of mutual trade with the Soviet Union will remove these obstacles." G. Rubenstein, "Nekotorye voprosy razvitiya vneshney torgovli" ("Several questions Concerning the Development of Foreign Trade"), *Voprosy ekonomiki,* September, 1966, pp. 113—114.

22. Karl-Heinz Domdey, "Economic Contacts between the Socialist and Capitalist Countries of Europe," *World Marxist Review,* September, 1965, p. 13.

23. "Only a pitiful handful of political ignoramuses dream about 'broadening the scope' for flirtation with imperialist monopolies, which seduce simpletons with their big moneybags, 'fat' credits, 'advantageous deals,' and similar lavish promises that lead directly to the yoke of dependence on foreign capital." Raymond H. Anderson, *"Pravda* Cautions Czechs on Trade," New York *Times,* September 3, 1968, p. 7. © 1968/67 by the New York Times Company. Reprinted by permission.

24. F. Michael, *Common Purpose and Double Strategy,* Washington, D.C.: Institute for Sino-Soviet Studies, George Washington University, November, 1966.

25. "The recent Middle East events are unmistakable signs showng that the renegades Brezhnev and Kosygin are nearing the end of their days. Brezhnev and Kosygin, like Khrushchev, are nothing but passing clowns on the stage of history. They will be drowned in the current of the people's revolution." "Brezhnev's Renegade Features Revealed More Clearly," *Peking Review,* July 21, 1967, p. 11.

26. St. Goranov, "The World Socialist System — Materials for Propagandists in Primary Political Education Schools," *Politicheska provseta (Political Education),* No. 3, March, 1967, pp. 61-68. (Translated by Joint Publications Research Service, Department of Commerce, Washington, D.C., No. 40,921, May 8, 1967, p. 5.)

27. R.W. Campbell, *Soviet Economic Power* (Cambridge, Mass.: The Riverside Press, 1960), p. 8.

28. Yu Malyshev, V. Shmapov, V. Tuschenko, O. Koposova, *Ekonomika Neftyannoi i Gazovoi Promyshlennosti (Economics of the Petroleum and Natural Gas Industry),* (Moscow: Nedra Press, 1966), p. 7.

29. Marshall I. Goldman, "Economic Revolution in the Soviet Union," *Foreign Affairs,* XLV (January, 1967), p. 319.

30. "The Russians do not have too much choice; it is like trying to go up the down escalator. As their economy becomes more complicated, it becomes harder and harder to move forward at a rapid rate. Without the Reform, their economy may well be carried backward. With the Reform, they hope it will be able to move forward — at the very least, hold its own." *Ibid.,* p. 331.

31. "Tcoreticheskiy seminar — aktualniye problemy politicheskoy ekonomii sotsializma" ("A Theoretical Seminar — Actual Problems in the Political Economy of Socialism"), *Kommunist,* No. 14, September, 1966, p. 48.

32. "Inalienable social and political rights imply strict observance by all members of society of their duties: to safeguard and increase public property, work conscientiously, maintain law and order and defend the socialist Motherland. Socialist democracy is incompatible with an individualistic attitude and anarchistic disregard for civic duty, with any actions detrimental to the public interest."

"Theses of the Central Committee of the CPSU," *Information Bulletin—Documents of the Communist and Workers' Parties, Articles and Speeches,* No. 13 (July, 1967) (Prague: Peace and Socialism Publishers, 1967), p. 33.

33. Roman Smal-Stocki, *The Captive Nations* (New York: Bookman Associates, 1960), pp. 26-28; Alexander G. Park, *Bolshevism in Turkestan* (New York: Columbia University Press, 1957), p. 6.

34. David J. Dallin, *The New Soviet Empire* (New Haven, Conn.: Yale University Press, 1951), p. 87; Lev E. Dobriansky, *The Vulnerable Russians* (New York: Pageant Press, 1967), inside cover; Firuz Kazemzadeh, *The Struggle for Transcaucasia (1917-1921)* (Birmingham, England: Templar Press, 1951), pp. 283-284: Roman Smal-Stocki, *The Captive Nations,* pp. 36-37.

35. "Neft' i Gaz v stroitel' stvye kommunizma" ("Petroleum and Natural Gas in the Construction of Communism"), *Kommunist,* No. 14, July, 1965, p. 78.

36. D. Vinogradskiy, "Pervoye sobraniye aktiva rabotnikov neftedobyvayushchey promyshlennosti" ("First Meeting of the Organization of the Oil-Production Industry"), *Neftyanoye Khozyaystvo* ("The Petroleum Industry"), June, 1966, p. 72.

37. *Pravda,* published in Moscow, is the Communist Party's principal daily newspaper.

38. "Large-Scale Chemical Production — in High Gear!" *Pravda,* November 16, 1966, p. 1. Trans. by Joint Publications Research Service, U.S. Department of Commerce, Washington, D.C., No. 38, 729 (November 21, 1966), pp. 5-6.

39. T. Honta, "Hekotoriye problemy razvitiya neftyanoy i gazovoy promyshlennosti Ukrainy," *Kommunist Ukrainy,* No. 1, (January, 1967) pp. 79-83, p. 81.

40. Joseph S. Berliner, "Soviet Economic Policy in the Middle East," *Middle Eastern Affairs* (Council for Middle Eastern Affairs, New York) (August-September, 1959), p. 287.

41. Abram Bergson, *Economic Trends in the Soviet Union* (Cambridge, Mass.: Harvard University Press, 1963), pp. 300-301.

42. The Soviet Minister of Trade, writing in an article in the weekly newspaper *Moscow News* for English-speaking countries, acknowledges that the U.S.S.R. highly values foreign trade as a direct link to economic development.

"The Soviet Government regards the extensive development of foreign economic relations, especially trade, as being very important. The Soviet Union is among the world's leaders as regards both volume and pattern of foreign trade. Our achievements in this field are inseparably linked with our economic, scientific and engineering progress, with improving the material and cultural standards of Soviet citizens." Nikolay Patolichev, "Trade with 100 Countries," *Moscow News,* (August 19-26, 1967), p. 8.

43. K. A. Guseinov, "O mezhdunarodnom znachenii bratskikh sviazey sovetskikh profsoyuzov s profsoyuzami stran asii i afriki." (The International Significance of Fraternal Ties between Soviet Trade Unions and Trade Unions of Asian and African Countries"), *Rabochiy klass i rabocheye dvizheniye v stranakh azii i afriki (The Working Class and Workers' Movement in Asian and African Countries),* ed., I.V. Milovanov *et al.* (Moscow: *Nauka* Press, 1965), pp. 37-38.

44. From Izmir to Brussels, from Tokyo to Montreal—everywhere the creative effort of the working people of our Republic is laid like a cornerstone in the building of a great cause: the strengthening of the Soviet Union's position in the world market, further development of foreign trade relations on mutually convenient terms, and the continuing growth of our country's reputation, as the Fatherland of the Great October Revolution." M. Makhynya, "Known on all Continents. Ukraine and the World," *Radyanska ukraina*, February 28, 1967, p. 3. *Digest of Soviet Ukrainian Press*, XI, No. 4 (April, 1967), pp. 27-38.

45. "It is highly questionable that the Soviet Union meets many domestic requirements through much of its trade with the less developed countries. In regard to items such as coffee, cotton, rice, spices, and fish, there is evidence that the U.S.S.R. has resold substantial quantities as a loss on the world market after purchasing them from weak nations in economic difficulties. It is therefore only natural to assume that price-cutting favorable trade terms and the acceptance of commodities from underdeveloped nations that have trouble selling their produce in the international market indicate more of a political than an economic aim." M. Gehlen, "The Politics of Soviet Foreign Trade," *The Western Political Quarterly*, XVIII, No. 1 (March, 1965), pp. 104-115.

46. The CPSU Central Committee's theoretical journal points out: "Now, to a greater degree than ever, the profound thought of V.I. Lenin is revealed, to the effect that our socialist government exerts the primary influence on the international revolution through its economic policy." *"Svet oktyabrya* ("The Light of October"), *Kommunist*, No. 15, October, 1966, p. 11.

47. "Problems Raised by the Soviet Oil Offensive," Study prepared for U.S. Senate Judiciary Committee by Halford L. Hoskins. Committee Print. Washington, D.C.: Government Printing Office, 1962, p. 4.

48. *Ibid.*, p. 138.

49. ". . .Mattei managed to extricate himself to some extent from an awkward situation: whereas the two assumptions on which his policy of the preceding years had been based — an accord of a temporary nature with the oil companies and the possession of crude oil of his own — had not materialized, he obtained supplies from another source which gave him what he needed at a low price and under conditions which reduced his dependence on the oil powers-that-be. He turned to the Russians who stood at the ready to make, for the first time, a major impact on the oil supply of a Western European country." Paul H. Frankel, *Mattei, Oil and Power Politics* (New York: Frederick A. Praeger, 1966), pp. 137-138.

50. R. Andreasyan, " Arabskiy Vostok: Novoye stolknoveniye s neftyanym imperializmon" ("The Arab East: New Clash with Oil Imperialism"), *Mirovaya Ekonomika i Mezhdunarodniye Otnosheniya (World Economics and International Relations")*, No. 3, 1967, p. 112.

51. Kudryavtsev, "Middle East Knot," p. 30.

Oil and Soviet Policies of Opportunism in the Middle East, 1917-53

Soviet Foreign Policy Trends

During the period beginning with the October Revolution in 1917 and extending through World War II, the Soviet leadership of Lenin and Stalin sought primarily to maintain "the integrity of Soviet power within Russia,"[1] and, subsequently to that war, Stalin endeavored to install the Soviet system in the "great new vacuums"[2] which had been created.

The Leninist Era

Vladimir Ilyich Lenin, who directed Soviet foreign policy until 1922, remained loyal to the Bolshevist Revolution, while exhibiting great tactical skill in overcoming serious problems of statecraft:[3] His defensive foreign policy, which, it has been said, "aimed to divide the forces of the enemy and weaken the united front against Bolshevism . . . [and] to win time even at the expense of serious loss of territory or apparent loss of honour,"[4] revealed a strong pragmatism.[5]

Lenin's regime, struggling for survival against the White armies, "faced with staggering problems of economic reconstruction at home, despairing of help from the Allies, and convinced that their survival depended on the spread of revolution to other countries, placed all [its] hopes on Germany."[6] The year 1920 was a "connecting link" between the "abnormal state of intervention and civil war with the absence of all official relations [with the West] which prevailed in 1919, and the general pattern of official relationships which was established during the period 1921-1924." The end of the Civil War "gave to Lenin and his associates for the first time the opportunity to fashion with some degree of deliberateness their policies toward the Western governments."[7]

In the ideological realm, changes were required to justify relations with other states since the expected socialist revolution in Europe had failed to materialize. Lenin reported to the Second Congress of the Comintern in 1920 that Communists in other countries ought to work with bourgeois elements in the struggle against imperialism.[8] "Soviet policy throughout 1920 was an ambivalent and seemingly contradictory one . . . [since] the Bolsheviki needed the help of the Western powers in their effort to restore economic life in Russia,"[9] a factor keenly appreciated by Lenin in shaping foreign policy.[10]

Foreign Commissar Chicherin is said to have been pessimistic about achieving economic gains from France or Britain at the Genoa Conference of 1922, although the occasion would advance Russia's image among other nations.[11] Bolsheviks hoped "by offering crumbs of economic favor to one capitalist group or another" during the year prior to the conference to keep the enemy divided until "the world revolution could take place and draw their fangs."[12]

Mindful of its great need to establish relations with Europe, the Soviet regime could not help but feel an affinity for Germany, with whom there appeared to be a basis for substantial cooperation.[13] The treaty of Rapallo of 1922, then, was a welcome stroke of Soviet diplomacy since it appeared to drive "an entering wedge, on terms favorable to Moscow, into the problem of diplomatic recognition and the resumption of trade relations between Russia and the West."[14] Yet Britain seemed to be the country most sought after by Russia in furtherance of her

diplomatic and commercial position.[15] Establishment of
de jure relations with London in February, 1924, presented
only a short-lived opportunity for Moscow to break out of its
isolation after Lenin's death the same year, since Soviet foreign
policy failed to avert Britain's severence of diplomatic ties in
1927.[16]

The close of the Leninist era witnessed difficult times for
Soviet foreign policy in Asia. During the mid-1920s, the newly
established U.S.S.R. looked toward China with ambivalence:
" . . . both of the two objectives, the defeat of international
imperialism and the defeat of indigenous capitalism, were too
close to the Communist heart for either to be wholly rejected."[17]

The Stalinist Era

The new regime sought to stabilize the diplomatic front in order
to facilitate the drastic restructuring of the domestic economy
by forced collectivization and massive industrialization. Under
Stalin, the U.S.S.R. succeeded in gaining recognition by other
states, developed international commerce, and emerged as a
vocal force in opposition to the unchallenged growth of Nazism.

"Socialism in one country" was the dominant theme justi-
fying the defensive nature of Soviet foreign policy to the period
of the Second World War. Until the mid-1930s, Moscow's policies appeared to support both the pursuit of conventional diplomacy with other states and efforts to subvert those governments
through the Comintern.

In Asia, developments involving China and Japan in the
period leading to world war would largely escape the impact of
Soviet policy. Moscow's efforts to further Bolshevism in China
failed in the face of Chiang Kai-shek's victories, primarily because Chinese conditions had not ripened.[18] Japan appeared as
a distant but growing danger in its movement into Manchuria,
where, in forming a threat to the Far East regions of the U.S.S.R.,
she continued to cause concern to the Soviet leadership.[19]

In Europe, where the threat of Fascism was growing, Russia
began to acquire a "respectable" international image in Maxim
Litvinov's active role with members of the League of Nations.

Admission to the League and formal recognition by the United States in 1934 were followed by treaties of mutual assistance with France and Czechoslovakia in the succeeding year. A strong advocate of "collective security" to counter the Fascist threat, Moscow found it advisable to bring the Comintern into the unique position of supporting capitalist governments. Stalin's venture into the Spanish Civil War was a temporary measure complicated by problems of political stability on the domestic scene. [20]

As Britain and France displayed a lack of resolve to contain Hitler's expansion at the expense of Austria and Czechoslovakia, Stalin perceived that he could, through an agreement with Germany, gain a temporary respite to make preparations for military defense of the homeland.[21]

His non-aggression pact with Hitler in 1939 set the stage for an articulation of Soviet aims in the Middle East, as contained in proposals for a "Four-Power Pact," including the U.S.S.R., Germany, Italy, and Japan. These plans enunciated not only Moscow's expansionist intent toward the Indian Ocean, but also its desire to take possession of new oil resources, to include even the Sakhalin fields of its impending ally, Japan. (See Appendix 2.)

Since their joint victory in World War II, Soviet Russia and the United States have gravitated to opposing poles in a war of words, political maneuvers, diplomatic confrontations, nuclear arms rivalry, and competition in space exploration. The end of the war brought Russia not only the satisfaction of having gained, with the aid of its allies, a magnificent victory, but dramatic gains on the international level of politics. Soviet foreign policy, which had followed a defensive orientation since the first years of the Bolshevist regime, now found that, with the aid of postwar turmoil and the Red Army's occupation forces, Russia was in a position to consolidate its power in neighboring regions.[22]

Foreign Communist parties would again play a role . . . Stalin re-created a formal structure for the international Communist movement, which he had dissolved during his wartime alliance with Britain and the United States, by establishing the Communist Information Bureau in 1947. Apparently intended to "tighten discipline within the new Soviet empire and consolidate Stalin's control there,"[23] the organization was jolted the following year by the defection of Yugoslavia. In relation to the capitalist West, the beginning years of a protracted Cold War coincided with the closing years of Soviet foreign policy during the Stalinist era.

Soviet Middle East Policy Trends: The Case of Iran

While the new Soviet regime was busily engaged in civil war against the Whites and their western interventionist allies, it was not likely that the Bolsheviks were concerned about the relatively remote Middle East — Turkey, Afghanistan, and Persia. However, with the recapture of the Ukraine, the Caucasus, and Central Asia, geographical contact was again established with those southern neighbors.

The general tone of Soviet policy toward Turkey, Afghanistan, and Persia appeared to be the same: ". . . directed and restricted largely to the promotion of nationalistic and anti-imperialistic tendencies, as a check to the influence of Britain."[24] In view of this uniform policy toward these three Muslim states, this study of the petroleum factor in Soviet Middle East strategy focuses upon Soviet relations with oil-rich Persia, or Iran, during the rule of Lenin and Stalin.

The Leninist Era

While the early need to consolidate Bolshevist strength led to conclusion of peace with Germany and withdrawal from Russia's outlying regions,[25] Lenin did not lose interest in "the nations of the East," which lay beyond Russia's old borders.[26] Illustrative of a new approach to Iran was the Bolshevist repudiation of the 1907 czarist treaty with England, which had divided the country and granted a number of concessions, coupled with Soviet assurances of friendship and concern for Iranian sovereignty.[27] Moscow took the position that the old

Russian colonialism was at an end.[28] Lenin's government appealed to Teheran to seek its own independent course and thus to contribute to all humanity.[29]

Soon, however, the Bolsheviks' sympathy for Iranians began to take on a more active form, as indicated by a 1919 appeal "to the workers and peasants of Persia" to struggle against their "oppressors."[30] The following year, the Third Communist International dispelled any illusions that such oppressors were merely British imperialists, when, at its Second World Congress and its First Congress of the Eastern Peoples at Baku, declarations were made to struggle against landowners, bourgeoisie, and native rulers.[31]

The new Soviet state began to assume a more vigorous posture in outlying regions as White armies retreated. In 1920, while bringing the civil war to a victorious conclusion, Lenin's regime brought Communism to power in Russian Azerbaijan, seen as essential to a Communist campaign against Persia. "Moscow was now in a direct line of control of the Communist offensive south of its Asian borders."[32] The new Soviet leadership in the Transcaucasus viewed prospects for extending socialism into the Middle East as bright. "Now Soviet Azerbaijan with its old and experienced revolutionary proletariat and its sufficiently consolidated Communist party will become a revolutionary beacon for Persia, Arabia, and Turkey. . . . "[33]

Within a month of establishing control in Russian Azerbaijan, Red Army units, in a move later attributed to the primary influence of Stalin,[34] entered the Persian port of Enzeli, and, as they took over the whole of Ghilan province,[35] moved to proclaim a Soviet socialist republic with its capital at Resht.[36] Soon, however, military successes came to be tempered by political considerations. According to a Western historian, "Moscow . . . came to the conclusion that . . . the cultivation of good relations with the central government and the gradual infiltration of Iran with Communist propaganda through the Soviet Embassy in Teheran . . . would better suit its purposes [than] highhanded direct action aiming at the sovietization and detachment of several Iranian provinces in connivance with discontented elements of Iran."[37] The threat posed by remaining British influence has been seen as helping to persuade Moscow to "sacrifice its revolutionary foothold in Persia to strengthen the hand of a unified nationalist government in Teheran, which would be capable of controlling provincial and tribal leaders . . . ."[38]

Although Red Army forces had not yet left Ghilan, the political climate between Moscow and Teheran had improved, leading to the establishment of diplomatic relations in May, 1920.[39] Soon thereafter, the Soviet Government concluded security treaties with Persia, along with Afghanistan and Turkey, affirming the principle of outlawing aggressive war.[40]

The agreement with Persia was evidence of the new Bolshevist position of influence in Teheran in that the treaty stipulated Russia's right, if Moscow considered that a third power was threatening its southern border, to dispatch Soviet troops into Persia. Barely two years after withdrawal of the Soviet expeditionary force in Ghilan, Russia was already in a position to declare, in conformity with the new pact, her readiness to defend Persia by sending forces to eject the British from its territory.[41]

The Stalinist Era

After Lenin's departure from the scene and Stalin's consolidation of power, the 1927 Treaty of Non-aggression and Neutrality symbolized continuing good relations between Moscow and Teheran. Yet, as far as Soviet economic relations with Iran were concerned, a Western observer concluded that Russia enjoyed considerable profit at her neighbor's expense.[42]

The rise of Hitler alarmed Stalin and heightened the importance of Europe as the focal point of impending international discord. Understandably, the U.S.S.R. reoriented its attention westward, compelled to forgo an active diplomacy in the south, perhaps recalling the policy of Alexander II who, somewhat more than a century earlier, had shelved his aspirations toward Turkey to meet a Napoleonic threat in Europe.

The Soviet press has summed up Soviet-Iranian relations prior to World War II, noting that "as long as the governing classes of Iran honestly fulfilled their undertakings, friendly relations between the two countries developed to their mutual benefit."[43]

The new decade, which began in an era of Soviet-German friendship following the Molotov-Ribbentrop Non-agression Pact of 1939, brought the Middle East to the forefront of Soviet strategy and diplomacy.

A reminder of long-range Russian aims appeared in secret documents on Nazi-Soviet relations, revealing the draft of a "Four-Power Pact" of November 13, 1940, with secret "Protocol Number One." The documents spelled out "spheres of influence" for Germany in "Europe and Central Africa;" for Italy in "northern and north-eastern Africa;" for Japan in "south-eastern Asia;" and then stated: "The Soviet Union declares that its territorial aspirations center south of the national territory of the Soviet Union in the direction of the Indian Ocean."[44] Two weeks later, a clarification of the Russian "sphere of influence" was conveyed by Molotov to the German ambassador in Moscow. In that note the Soviet Commissar for Foreign Affairs expressed willingness to approve the pact draft, provided that "the area south of Batum and Baku in the general direction of the Persian Gulf is recognized as the center of the aspirations of the Soviet Union,"[45] and stated Soviet interest in annexing Japan's Sakhalin oil resources.[46] (See Appendix 1.)

The Nazi invasion of Russia a few months later did not distract Stalin from pursuing ambitions toward Iran, which Molotov had so recently made clear. After agreement with Britain, which was dispatching military forces to southern Iran, the U.S.S.R. sent Red Army units into the five northern provinces in August, 1941, after invoking the Soviet-Iranian treaty in effect for two decades, on grounds that hostile elements "might attempt to transform Iran into a base for attacks on the U.S.S.R."[47]

After the occupation began, it became apparent that Allied personnel were forbidden by Russia to enter her northern zone of responsibility in Iran, and, according to a Western historian, systematic domination through techniques of "Sovietization," soon to be applied in postwar Eastern Europe, was underway in Iran.[48] Regardless of whether the U.S.S.R. was intending to create a satellite state, she soon indicated her intention of supporting Iran's interests by agreeing, under terms of a tripartite treaty with Britain and Iran in January, 1942, "to jointly and severally respect the territorial integrity, sovereignty, and political independence of Iran,"[49] and to remove military forces of the U.S.S.R. and Britain "not later than six months after all hostilities between the Allied Powers and Germany and her associates [were] suspended."[50] The following year, Stalin joined Churchill and Roosevelt in Teheran and affirmed by joint declaration that the three powers were "at one with the Government of Iran in their desire for the maintenance of the independence, sovereignty and territorial integrity of Iran.[51]

The Soviet Union undertook diplomatic efforts in 1944 to seek oil concessions in Iranian Azerbaijan, but the government in Teheran decided to turn down the overtures from Moscow. After a few months, it appeared that the U.S.S.R. might be attempting to "turn back the clock" to the period of its short-lived intervention in Ghilan in 1920-21. By August, 1945, amid a renewed campaign of agitation for autonomy for the Iranian province of Azerbaijan, a popular revolt broke out against the Teheran government. A new government was quickly established, and, while a similar revolt took place in neighboring Kurdistan province, the latter was based upon ethnic, rather than political, currents.[52] Iranian appeals to the United States for assistance were in vain, since Washington was unable to gain Moscow's agreement to withdraw, along with British-U.S. forces, by January 1, 1946, three months ahead of the date set in 1942.[53] 1824047

In December, Moscow radio reinforced Soviet aims by announcing formation of a "National Government of Iranian Azerbaijan" in Tabriz. The Iranian National Army was dispatched to Azerbaijan in order to quell the "secession," but its 1,500 soldiers were confronted by some 30,000 well-equipped Red Army troops.[54] Again, the United States intervened with the U.S.S.R. in behalf of Iran's sovereignty. Stalin, hosting a conference of foreign ministers in Moscow, gave the following explanation to justify the Red Army's role: "Iran constituted a threat to the Russian oil fields of Baku; the U.S.S.R. had the legal right to remain in Iran until at least six months after the termination of World War II; and the Soviet-Iranian treaty of 1921 permitted Soviet troops to remain on Iranian territory when the U.S.S.R. was threatened from the south."[55]

Faced with Soviet refusal to terminate occupation of Azerbaijan, the Iranian government sought help from the fledgling United Nations, but her call to gain removal of Soviet forces appeared to bring only an echo from the days of Ghilan.[56]

The U.S.S.R., forced into defending an untenable diplomatic position, resorted to stalling tactics. When the Security Council decided in April to defer any action on the case, Moscow declared, in conjunction with announcing a "new Soviet-Iranian oil agreement," that the Red Army would withdraw the following month. After evacuation of all forces the Iranian Government moved swiftly to deal with separatist elements and again took charge of its northern provinces.

Announcement of the Truman Doctrine, April 13, 1947, an event of lasting importance in the development of an American foreign policy after World War II, made a timely impact upon Soviet-Iranian relations, although it had been intended primarily to halt Soviet aggressive meddling only in Greece and Turkey. This courageous pledge to oppose Communist imperialism gave the Iranian Parliament determination to rally against the "Soviet-Iranian oil agreement," which had been drawn up while the Red Army was still in occupation of Azerbaijan. The rejection by the Majlis (parliament) of the agreement in October, 1947, was also induced by resentment over Soviet "defrauding" of Iranian interests in the joint operation of the Caspian Sea Fisheries Concession during the previous two decades.[57]

The demise of the carefully conceived oil agreement evoked Communist threats to sever diplomatic relations because of hostile activity by the Iranian government against the U.S.S.R.[58]

Recent Soviet press accounts chide the United States, whose response to Moscow's threat against Greece and Turkey in 1947 is seen as foreign meddling. One such article calls to task the Truman Administration for alleging that subversion was being exported by the U.S.S.R. into the Middle East.[59]

After the year 1946, which has been cited as "the highest point of Soviet expansion,"[60] a more passive period in Soviet diplomacy toward the Middle East seemed to prevail during the balance of the Stalin era.

The issue of Middle East petroleum, it has been noted, became an occasional factor in Soviet-Iranian relations during the period ending in 1953. A more detailed examination will place the role of petroleum in this early phase of Soviet policy toward Iran in clearer perspective.

Middle East Petroleum Industry — An Object of Soviet Policy? The Case of Iran

When, at the turn of the century, the Persian Government granted a sixty-year oil concession to the Australian D'Arcy, the conflict between a British desire to secure the lifeline of India and Russian ambitions in the direction of the Persian Gulf became sharper. Both countries established a *modus vivendi*, agreeing in 1907 to divide Persia into a "Russian sphere" in the north, a "British sphere" in the south, and a central buffer zone.[61]

Two years later the Anglo-Persian Oil Company was formed, and in 1914 the British gained controlling interest, which Churchill felt was as significant as Disraeli's purchase of Suez Canal shares.[62]

The Leninist Era

During the initial years of the Soviet regime, marked by serious dislocation in industrial and agricultural production and the need to develop diplomatic ties and foreign trade, there was no indication of direct Soviet interest in Iranian petroleum.

The Stalinist Era

While Britain proceeded to dominate Iranian oil development into the 1930's, there was no significant Soviet effort in the direction of Middle East oil until the joint occupation of Iran during World War II. Since the U.S.S.R. possessed only a negligible concession in Semnan, it was not surprising that when, in 1943 and 1944, British Shell and the American companies Standard Vacuum and Sinclair undertook surveying activity in the area of Baluchistan in southeastern Iran, Communist objections were quickly heard in the Majlis. Thus, the deputy of the Tudeh (Communist) Party, Radmenesh, demanded that other foreign countries be permitted to participate in petroleum surveys, and called for Iranian development of her own oil resources without the help of foreign concessions.[63]

In the light of subsequent Soviet opposition to Western oil interests in the Middle East as "trappings of imperialism and neocolonialism," it is well to look into the nature of Moscow's interest in Iran, as reflected in the Teheran visit of Deputy Foreign Commissar Kavtaradze in September, 1944. The Soviet envoy demanded an oil concession to include all five provinces under Red Army occupation. Moscow appeared to be seeking to obtain oil supplies for prosecution of the war, and, at the same time, to contain the growing American presence by pressuring Iran to refuse all foreign concessions.[64]

The second of these possible aims appeared to be realized when Teheran announced the rejection of all foreign proposals for oil concessions — American, British, or Soviet. Yet the heated Muscovite reaction to this new Iranian policy suggested possible Soviet anger at failing to get a foothold in the country's oil development. The Communist press assailed the Iranian

Government as "disloyal and unfriendly," and Commissar Kavtaradze took the unprecedented step of calling a press conference in Teheran to attack the Iranian Government. The assembly of editors, organized by the Tudeh Party,[65] heard Kavtaradze outline the advantages of a Soviet-Iranian oil agreement: "greater employment in Iran . . . training of Iranians for skilled jobs . . . development of Iran's natural resources and wealth . . . larger market for agricultural produce in the areas under concession . . . the Soviet government would guard the health and welfare of the workers and their families."[66] In a sudden tactical shift, local Communists, who formerly had opposed "foreign oil concessions," now strongly vocalized their support of the Soviet proposals.[67]

Although diplomatic means had failed, there was little doubt that the issue of obtaining oil rights would again emerge. The left-leaning Iranian press stepped up criticism of "imperialist Britain," while the Kremlin appeared ready to adopt a more forceful attitude toward Iran.

In 1945, after trying unsuccessfully to establish an Azerbaijanian National Government of Iran, Stalin used the presence of military force to support his diplomacy; when Iran sought removal of Red troops according to a 1942 agreement,[68] petroleum emerged as an underlying Soviet objective — the U.S.S.R. wanted to be majority stockholder in an oil concession in Iran.[69]

When the United Nations became concerned about the Red Army's indefinite stay in Iran, Stalin made an agreement in April, 1946, for troop withdrawal, but included a "rider clause" granting the U.S.S.R. oil concessions, along with a mild call for "improvements" within Iranian Azerbaijan:

(1) The Red Army was to be evacuated within one month and a half after March 24, 1946,

(2) A joint stock Irano-Soviet oil company was to be established and ratified by the Fifteenth Majlis within seven months after March 24,

(3) With regard to Azerbaijan, since it is an internal Iranian affair, peaceful arrangements will be made between the Government and the people of Azerbaijan for the carrying out of improvements in

accordance with existing laws and in benovolent spirit toward
the people of Azerbaijan.[70]

The concession would make the U.S.S.R. majority stock-holder for the first twenty-five years of the company and equal partner for a similar period. After the U.S.S.R. withdrew the Red Army in May, the Majlis did not move to ratify the oil proposal; strong Soviet tactics in pursuance of oil rights in Iran had apparently not brought instant results. Furthermore, it seemed, at least to some observers, that Soviet policy over the years, during which time the U.S.S.R. was felt to harbor ambitions for direct participation in Iran's oil industry, had come to nought.[71]

The U.S.S.R. had not, however, given up hope that the recent agreement would ultimately be ratified by the Iranian parliament. Her bid for a concession in Middle East petroleum production continued as a subject of debate in the Majlis through 1946 and into 1947. During arguments over ratification of the proposed treaty, one delegate charged that the Soviet proposal was the "worst agreement in the past hundred years of Iranian history."[72] Iran's steadfast resistance to the Soviet offer was probably encouraged by announcement in 1947 of the Truman Doctrine, since its implied application to Iran's current policy dilemma was expressed by United States Ambassador George Allen.[73]

The Iranian Government moved carefully but surely to resolve again the problem of rebellion in the northern provinces, and, at the same time, to arrive at a decision on the oil concession with Moscow on the legislative level. In October, 1947, the Majlis took final action on the U.S.S.R. proposal, declaring the Soviet-Iranian negotiations null and void.[74] While the Majlis stipulated that Iran might later agree to sell to Russia such additional oil as might be discovered in the subsequent five years, the U.S.S.R. reacted sharply, threatening to break diplomatic relations with Iran.[75]

While the Soviet Union had been unsuccessful in her attempt to gain an Iranian concession, there was an indication that she would in the future regard the growing strategic importance of Middle East petroleum as an issue of contention in the impending Cold War, as suggested during the following month by a prominent Soviet political scientist:

> The significance of the question of northern Iranian oil extends beyond the framework of local commercial relations between the U.S.S.R. and Iran. This question has in our time become one of the vital questions of international politics, and the struggle ensuing with respect to it is a part of the world struggle between the forces of democracy and the forces of reaction.[76]

Summary

During the period from 1917 to 1953, as we have seen, Soviet policies toward oil-producing Iran did not follow a consistent pattern, as a result in large part of the rising threat of Hitlerite Germany and also the intervention of such outside influence as that of the United Nations and the United States.

If one is to judge apparent Communist interest in the Middle East and Asia from the nature of Soviet literature produced during this period, one is confronted by an anomaly: Until the mid-1930's, when nationalist movements had met with little success in those regions, large numbers of books and periodicals on the Middle East and Asia were published by the U.S.S.R.; yet, from the first years of World War II until Moscow's diplomatic offensives of the mid-1950's, a period in which Middle East revolutionary movements were growing, pertinent Soviet publications were rare.[77]

We have seen that Iran, while experienced in frequent border warfare with czarist troops, and, consequently, "the better able to calculate the dangers inherent in the Soviet embrace,"[78] also became schooled in the negative features of British imperialism. Despite early pressures from the new Soviet state in the form of Comintern appeals to Muslims "in the East" to overthrow their rulers, and the military take-over of the province of Ghilan, Moscow had to abandon such programs in order to face its pressing economic and diplomatic problems. Thus, even during the Leninist era, it had become possible for Iran to choose better relations with the Bolsheviks as a defensive measure against British domination, and Soviet-Iranian treaties and commerce quickly served to symbolize the new relationship.

During the Stalinist era, Soviet-Iranian relations did not continue to develop after the non-aggression treaty of 1927, until the period of World War II Allied occupation. While some Western observers have suggested that the U.S.S.R. never attempted to become involved in Iran's oil industry,[79] Moscow made determined efforts, as we have noted, to combine military and political means toward achieving concession rights 1944-46.

In an observation some fifteen years ago that "the center of world politics today is the most promising oil region of the globe, the Middle East," a German authority on the Soviet oil industry noted that the U.S.S.R. "has long tried to obtain oil concessions in Iran, but negotiations have never terminated in a contractual agreement," and referred to a purported admission by the Soviet premier to Ambassador Bedell Smith:

> Stalin . . . emphasized how important it was for the Soviet Union to get a larger share in the exploitation of the world oil deposits and maintained that first Britain and then the United States had laid obstacles in her way when she endeavored to obtain oil concessions.[80]

We have seen that Russia under Lenin and Stalin conceived of a "Middle East" comprised primarily of Turkey, Afghanistan, and Iran, and that her foreign policy followed a rather uniform pattern toward them. Of these states, only Iran possessed oil riches and therefore came to be involved in whatever petroleum interest the Soviet Union developed with regard to the region to the south.

During the period encompassed by Stalin's successors, however, a much different "Middle East" would emerge, including other oil-producing states, and, in addition to non-Arab Iran, the region would include many Arab states, some possessing petroleum riches. It will be seen that the appearance of this new ethnic factor promised to influence political relations between states both within and outside of the region, and to become enmeshed in questions concerning Middle East petroleum.

Notes

1. George F. Kennan, *Soviet Foreign Policy, 1917-1941* (Princeton, N.J.: D. Van Nostrand Co., 1960), p. 114.

2. Jan F. Triska and David D. Finley, *Soviet Foreign Policy* (New York: Macmillan, 1968), p. 11.

3. Historian Louis Fischer described Lenin as a leader who, though "held within relatively narrow limits by the principles and morals in whose name he and his party made the revolution, ... nevertheless found sufficient room for manoeuvring and for avoiding those rocks on which less gifted statesmen would have broken their ships — and their heads." Louis Fischer, *The Soviets in World Affairs* (2 vols.; London: Jonathan Cape, 1930), I, p. 461.

4. *Ibid.,* p. 462.

5. "When the German offensive threatened in 1918, [Lenin] advised appealing for assistance to the 'Franco-British imperialist brigands'; when Allied intervention commenced he weighed the possibility of German aid against the French and British. He tried to use the antagonism between Japan and the United States, and between England and France. His policy was to win the support of business elements within capitalist countries by offering them concessions and trade ... " *Ibid.,* 461-462.

6. George F. Kennan, *Russia and the West under Lenin and Stalin* (Boston: Little, Brown and Co., 1960), p. 155.

7. *Ibid.,* p. 166.

8. Xenia J. Eudin and Robert C. North, *Soviet Russia and the East, 1920-1927* (Stanford, Calif.: Standford University Press, 1957), pp. 63-65.

9. Kennan, *Russia under Lenin and Stalin,* p. 166.

10. Fischer, *Soviets in World Affairs,* I, p. 463.

11. Louis Fischer writes that, according to Chicherin, "[The Bolsheviks] felt that [the Genoa Conference] rested on a misunderstanding, on the supposition, in foreign quarters, that the NEP represented the Thermidore of the Communist Revolution. . . . They attended in order to assert Russia's natural position on the international stage, and, perhaps, to establish normal relations with individual countries." *Ibid.,* p. 333.

12. Kennan, *Russia Under Lenin and Stalin,* p. 166.

13. "The Bolsheviks' opposition to Versailles established not merely this sentimental link [with the Germans], whose significance must not be underestimated, but also an economic and political bond between Russia and Germany." Fischer, *Soviets in World Affairs,* I, p. 330.

14. Kennan, *Russia under Lenin and Stalin,* p. 222.

15. "The pact with the Germans had been important as a means of frustrating any attempt by the capitalist powers to form a united front in their commercial and diplomatic dealings with Russia. It had improved Moscow's bargaining power vis-a-vis the West. But Britain remained the key target." *Ibid.,* p. 226.

16. *Ibid.,* p. 278.

17. *Ibid.,* p. 266.

18. Historian Fischer, noting Stalin's rationale for lack of success in China, concluded: "Time is a decisive factor in revolutionary analyses. . . . Revolution is not an article of export or import. It develops when it has struck deep roots in national soil." Fischer, *Soviets in World Affairs,* II, p. 679.

19. Kennan, *Russia under Lenin and Stalin,* pp. 262-263.

20. *Ibid.,* p. 312.

21. *Ibid.,* p. 328.

22. "To Stalin, the new 'socialist allies' of the Soviet Union in Europe and Asia were all only satellites, to orbit obediently and remain dependent upon the Soviet Union. Their sole purpose was to serve the U.S.S.R., which by then had a highly developed socialist system, in order to strengthen it further. Pursuant to the 'socialism in one country' policy, this was a logical and proper view. To milk the satellite economies, to subordinate their politics, and to rearrange their social systems to fit the new role — all these were imperative to fulfill the Soviet principle." Triska and Finley, *Soviet Foreign Policy,* p. 12.

23. Triska and Finley, *Soviet Foreign Policy,* p. 13.

24. Kennan, *Soviet Foreign Policy, 1917-1941,* pp. 66-67.

25. "Architect of Soviet Foreign Policy," *New Times,* April 26, 1967, p. 1.

26. Noting that "one of the pillars of Lenin's foreign policy was friendship for the nations of Asia," historian Louis Fischer went on to quote the Soviet leader: "The aim of the Soviet Government, he wrote, must be to 'group around itself all the awakening peoples of the East and fight together with them against international imperialism.' " Fischer, *Soviets in World Affairs,* I, p. 463.

27. Writing in a major political journal for foreign audiences, a Soviet writer recalls: "Shortly after the victory of the Great October Socialist Revolution the Soviet Government declared on December 7, 1917, in its historic appeal "To The Working Moslems of Russia and the East" that the Anglo-Russian Treaty of 1907 "on the partition of Persia is torn up and destroyed" and that "as soon as hostilities cease the troops will be withdrawn from Persia, and the Persians will be ensured the right freely to shape their own destiny." Kh. Grigoryev, "An Action Contrary to the Interests of Iran and International Security," *International Affairs,* December, 1955, pp. 59-60.

28. "Ever since it came into being, the Soviet state has recognized the right of the oppressed peoples, including the Iranian people, to independent national development . . . and based its relations with Iran on equality." *Ibid.,* p. 59.

29. ". . . the Soviet Government made a declaration to the Iranian Government, in which it again renounced all rights and privileges acquire in Iran by the czarist government. On behalf of the Russian people it expressed confidence that men of world renown would "by a powerful effort shake off their age-long slumber, overthrow the tyranny of the infamous plunderers, and join the fraternal ranks of the free cultured peoples for further creative endeavor for the benefit of all mankind." *Ibid.,* p. 60.

30. Foreign Commissar Chicherin proclaimed: "The time for your liberation is near, the hour of death will soon strike for English capitalism against which a broad revolutionary movement is spreading evermore threateningly among the toiling masses of Britain itself. The working people of Russia stretch out to you, the suppressed masses of Persia, their fraternal hand." Sepehr Zabih, *The Communist Movement in Iran* (Berkeley: University of California Press, 1966), p. 10.

31. ". . . as early as 1920 there appeared the first signs of an aspect of Communist policy not present in the expansionism of Czarist Russia. The Second Comintern World Congress called on the assembled Muslims to unleash a holy war against Britain and to overthrow the sultans, emirs, and khans — in other words, the traditional forms of government in the East. The Congress created a Council

for Action and Propaganda as an instrument in the common struggle of the Bolsheviks and the Eastern peoples. . . ." Günther Nollau and Hans Jürgen Wiehe, *Russia's South Flank* (New York: Frederick A. Praeger, 1963), p. 5.

32. Zabih, *Communist Movement in Iran,* p. 10.

33. M. Sultan Galiev, "K obyavleniyu azerbaidzhanskoy sovetskoy respubliki" ("Declaration of the Azerbaijan Soviet Republic"), *Zhizn Natsional 'nostey,* No. 13 (May 9, 1920), p. 1, quoted in Eudin and North, *Soviet Russia and the East,* p. 96.

34. "In 1920, an unsuccessful attempt was made by Stalin, in his capacity as Commissar for Nationalities, to bring a portion of Northern Iran under direct Soviet control." Kennan, *Soviet Foreign Policy,* n. 1, p. 67.

35. George Lenczowski, *Russia and the West in Iran, 1918-1948* (New York: Greenwood Press, 1968), p. 52.

36. Eudin and North, *Soviet Russia and the East,* p. 96.

37. Lenczowski, *Russia and the West,* p. 60.

38. E.R. Goodman, *The Soviet Design for a World State* (New York: Columbia University Press, 1960), p. 60.

39. A recent Soviet version recounts the period leading to the resumption of diplomatic ties, but avoids making any reference to the Red Army occupation of Ghilan:

"The Western Powers then sought, as they do now, to embroil Iran with the land of Soviets. The then rulers of Iran, for their part, were not loath to meet the British colonialists half-way. . . . But various sections of the Iranian population sympathetic to Soviet Russia insisted on normalizing relations with her." Grigoryev, "Action Contrary to Interests of Iran," p. 60.

40. G.I. Tunkin, "New Principles of International Law," *New Times,* No. 35, August 30, 1967, p. 4.

41. K. Radek, *Vneshnyaya Politika Sovetskoy Rossii,* 1923, p. 74, as quoted in Ivar Spector, *The Soviet Union and the Muslim World, 1917-1956* (Seattle: University of Washington Press, 1956), p. 56.

42. ". . . the Soviet Union consistently strove to maintain Iran in a state of economic subjection by dumping on her markets Russian manufactured goods to the detriment of both foreign competitors and the native industry: . . . profiting by the fact that she was the only import market for the northern provinces, Russia did not hesitate to take advantage by compelling Iran to conclude trade agreements often prejudiced to the latter's interests. . . . " Lenczowski, *Russia and the West,* pp. 95-96.

43. "Early Soviet Contacts with Arab and African Countries," *Mizan,* Vol. VIII (March/April, 1966), p. 61.

44. "Nazi-Soviet Relations, 1939-41," *Documents from the Archives of the German Foreign Office,* U.S. Department of State Publication 3023, 1948, p. 257 as quoted in Lenczowski, *Russia and the West,* p. 193.

45. *Ibid.,* pp. 193-194.

46. *Ibid.*

47. E. Carman, *Soviet Imperialism: Russia's Drive Toward World Domination* (Washington, D.C.: Public Affairs Press, 1950), p. 122.

48. Lenczowski, *Russia and the West,* p. 195.

49. Carman, *Soviet Imperialism,* p. 123.

50. *Ibid.*

51. *Ibid.*

52. "Autonomous Azerbaijan [of 1945] was governed by a Communist terror regime that devoured hundreds of victims; Kurdistan's rulers included no genuine Communists, only members of old and respected families. No secret police stalked about in Mahabad, and only one Kurd, a certain Mahmodi, was put to death, and only after he had been caught three times in possession of information destined for the Teheran government. Hundreds fled to Teheran from Tabriz, but only a few Kurds left their country. Tabriz imposed the death penalty for listening to a foreign radio broadcast, but this was not illegal in Mahabad." Nollau and Wiehe, *Russia's South Flank,* p. 55.

53. Lenczowski, *Russia and the West,* p. 216.

54. Carman, *Soviet Imperialism,* p. 125.

55. *Ibid.,* p. 126.

56. Spector, *Soviet Union and Muslim World,* p. 114.

57. H.L. Hoskins, *Middle East Oil in U.S. Foreign Policy* (Washington, D.C.: Library of Congress, 1950), p. 61.

58. Lenczowski, *Russia and the West,* p. 312.

59. *International Affairs,* the leading Soviet political journal for foreign consumption, states: "In the spring of 1947, under the pretext of countering a non-existent threat, the U.S.A. foisted the Truman Doctrine on Greece and Turkey, which were to allow the U.S.A. to use their territories as a springboard for a new war, and a startling point for further inroads into the eastern part of the Mediterranean. U.S. apologists of the Truman Doctrine did not even take the trouble to conceal its anti-Soviet character." A. Kafman, "U.S. Big Stick in the Mediterranean," *International Affairs,* August, 1967, p. 72.

60. Hisham B. Sharabi, *Governments and Politics of the Middle East in the Twentieth Century* (Princeton, N.J.: Van Nostrand Co., Inc., 1962), p. 96.

61. Benjamin Shwadran, *The Middle East, Oil, and the Great Powers* (New York: Council for Middle Eastern Affairs, 1959), p. 7.

62. Hoskins, *Middle East Oil,* p. 68.

63. Lenczowski, *Russia and the West,* p. 216.

64. *Ibid.,* pp. 217-218.

65. A. Ardekani, "Towards a National Democratic Front in Iran," *World Marxist Review,* VIII, No. 9 (September, 1965), pp. 29-34.

66. Lenczowski, *Russia and the West,* p. 219.

67. *Ibid.,* p. 219.

68. Carman, *Soviet Imperialism,* p. 123.

69. Spector, *Soviet Union and Muslim World,* p. 115.

70. Lenczowski, *Russia and the West,* pp. 229-300.

71. Spector, *Soviet Union and Muslim World,* p. 116.

72. Lenczowski, *Russia and the West, 1918-1948,* pp. 309-310.

73. In September, 1947, the American envoy to Teheran declared: "Iran was perfectly free to accept or reject the Soviet offer, and that if she chose to reject it, she could count on the support of the United States against threats and pressure." *Ibid.,* pp. 310-311.

74. A Western scholar has drawn a striking parallel between these events and a previous episode in Soviet-Iranian relations, which in 1921 had led to the defeat of

Iranian revolutionary groups after Moscow pulled out the Red Army from Azerbaijan. Spector, *Soviet Union and Muslim World,* pp. 115-116.

75. *Ibid.,* p. 312.

76. E.L. Shteinberg, *Sovetsko-iranskiye otnoshenii i proiski v anglo-amerikanskom imperializme v irane 1947 (Soviet-Iranian Relations and the Intrigues of Anglo-American Imperialism in Iran in 1947),* (Moscow: *Pravda* Press, 1947), p. 23.

77. A Western political scientist has noted: "Between 1917 and 1955 Soviet interest in the East manifested itself in inverse ratio to the real importance of the Asian revolution." Walter Laqueur, *The Soviet Union and the Middle East* (New York: Frederick A. Praeger, 1959), pp. 2-3.

78. H. L. Hoskins, "Soviet Economic Penetration in the Middle East," *Orbis,* III, No. 4 (Winter, 1960), p. 466.

79. "Russia successfully prevented Western penetration into northern Iran, which it considered part of its own defense perimeter, but it never attempted to exploit the oil of that region for itself. In fact, because of that, the northern Iranian oil fields remain unexploited to this very day." Shwadran, *Middle East Oil,* p. 455.

"The Russian oil industry has appeared nowhere except Spitzbergen as an explorer seeking concessions. . . . " J.E. Hartshorn, *Oil Companies and Governments* (London: Faber, Ltd., 1967), p. 241.

80. Heinrich Hassmann, *Oil in the Soviet Union,* trans. Alfred M. Leeston (Princeton, N.J.: Princeton University Press, 1953).

Petroleum in the U.S.S.R.'s Concerted Middle East Drive Initiated in 1954

Soviet Foreign Policy Trends

A growing nuclear stalemate between the United States and the Soviet Union in the post-Stalinist period encouraged the latter's adoption of "policies of economic competition and winning favor in the underdeveloped world."[1] During the rule of Khrushchev and Brezhnev-Kosygin there seemed to be a continuation of these new trends which showed that "the strength of Communism as a set of ideas and ideals was declining while Soviet military power was increasing."[2]

The Khrushchev Era

The gradual re-emergence of France and Germany, which had been facilitated by the U.S. Marshall Plan policy, began to confront the Russia of Stalin's successors with a potential threat to the preservation of her new "socialist bloc."[3] Soviet strategy was to seek an alliance with "neutral states," as indicated by Khrushchev's enunciation of a Third World camp, consisting of "colonial and semicolonial" areas of Asia, Africa, and Latin America, on the occasion of the Twentieth Party Congress in 1956. Khrushchev's view that war between the

48

forces of imperialism and socialism was no longer inevitable became the basis of a new foreign policy orientation toward the capitalist West, which called for socialist vigilance to prevent war, while economic competition between the two systems would result in victory for socialism. "Wars of national liberation" in colonial areas where local conditions had ripened would be supported.[4]

Meanwhile, the absence of Yugoslavia from the socialist bloc contributed to unstable currents in Eastern Europe, along with a challenge to Moscow's monolithic hold on world Communism by a "purely orthodox" China, which threatened to rearrange the postwar interstate relationships on the unacceptable basis of equality with the U.S.S.R.[5] The main external threat to success of the socialist camp was the United States, perceived by Moscow's leadership, it has been said, to be following a middle course between the extremes of "lukewarm coexistence" and "aggressive liberation," while serving as "protector" of France and Germany.[6]

Under Khrushchev, Russia achieved "unparalleled" gains in space exploration and military development, which led to threats of the use of military force as "a regular feature of Soviet diplomatic exchanges."[7] At the same time, in harmony with "peaceful coexistence" in Soviet foreign policy, Moscow's press emphasized the "peace" theme:

> The Soviet people, like the people of the People's Democracies, are standing unanimously for *peace* and international cooperation and vigorously supporting their government's *peace*-loving foreign policies.
>
> In the present situation active struggle for *peace* becomes of prime importance. To be active in the struggle for *peace* means to follow the intrigues of its enemies and promptly expose them. At the same time it presupposes the utilization of every opportunity offered by the current international situation to strengthen *peace*ful cooperation between peoples.
>
> Undoubtedly, the noble cause of the preservation and stabilization of *peace* enjoys the support of the peoples of all countries. Resolutely championing *peace*, the Soviet Union has won the love and sympathy of the working people of the whole world.[8]

(emphasis added)

The term "peaceful coexistence," according to Western scholars, has come to misrepresent its original meaning in

Leninism as "an expedient tactic for survival in adversity," and to serve a different purpose, "shifting some attention from the military to more flexible political and economic means for pursuing foreign policy goals."[9] Khrushchev's revision of Soviet strategy, symbolized by his denunciation of Stalin, could not help but lead to ideological complications with far-reaching consequences for future Soviet policy. One analysis aptly characterizes Khrushchev's contribution to Marxist-Leninist dogma as replacing Stalin's "socialism in one country" by "socialism in one region," which emphasized "the interests of the party-state system as a whole above those of the Soviet Union and hence of any other individual state, although endeavoring to define specific system interests as compatibly with Soviet national interests as possible."[10]

The Brezhnev-Kosygin Period

To date, the Khrushchev legacy of foreign policy doctrine remains largely intact, although events of recent years have appeared to place new strains upon Soviet policy decisions with respect to relations with states both outside and inside the socialist bloc. United States intervention in the Dominican Republic and, more importantly, in Vietnam was followed by a Soviet decision to provide military and economic assistance to Ho Chi Minh on an increasing scale. Within the bloc, differences with China continued to degenerate into new hostility on ideological and political fronts, while Eastern Europe became the scene of massive military intervention by the U.S.S.R. with token Warsaw Pact support against its member, Czechoslovakia. The so-called Brezhnev Doctrine of 1968 asserted the new concept that the U.S.S.R. has a right to use military force when the gains of socialism in a country are seen to be in jeopardy. Thus, Soviet policy making appears to be increasingly hampered by problems involving cooperation on a government-to-government as well as on a party-to-party level among the socialist states. [11]

Recent Soviet writings reflect a continued development of "peace-loving principles" in terms of a new concept quite alien to world revolution to destroy capitalism — that of measures to enhance "international security". Thus, the Soviet press attempted to adapt the historical record of communism in Russia in order to rationalize the Moscow summit accords with the United States on the heels of President Nixon's 1972 visit to Peking:

> " . . . peaceable foreign policy has won the Soviet Union high authority in international affairs, and has had an important impact on the strengthening within international relations of the tendency toward peace and security."[12]

Soviet Middle East Policy Trends

Just as Soviet foreign policy under Lenin and Stalin had its own regional application for a relatively compact "Middle East," Moscow's subsequent strategy came to be applied to a broader "Middle East," which was undergoing development and change amid conflicts and wars.

The Khrushchev Era

The last years of Stalin's rule had been marked by a retiring attitude toward the Middle East, in the wake of Iran's rejection of a Soviet oil concession proposal. In the interim, anti-Western sentiment in Iran had surfaced strongly during the short rule of Mohammed Mossadegh, when Western oil properties were nationalized.[13] After the dynamic premier's ouster, the United States, now the growing personification of "the West," proceeded toward the creation of a Middle East military alliance apparently intended to contain the Soviet Union. Surging nationalism and increasing antipathy to the Western presence, as reflected in Nasser's revolution in Egypt, seemed to prepare both Arab and non-Arab states of the Middle East for Soviet diplomatic successes, which were not long in coming.

An initial step in bettering Soviet-Iranian relations was taken in December, 1954, when certain outstanding border disagreements were cleared up. The U.S.S.R.'s new foreign policy trend toward conciliation with such non-Communist states was accompanied by appropriate shifts in its propaganda. Ignoring past Red Army efforts to gain a foothold in the oil-bearing northern provinces, the Soviet Union's principal English-language journal devoted to foreign policy declared:

> The Soviet Union, basing its relations with other countries, small countries included, on the principles of mutual respect for sovereignty and territorial integrity, equality and peaceful coexistence, has always endeavored to settle all issues with Iran in the spirit of good-neighbor relations and mutual understanding.[14]

A similar tone was evident in Soviet pronouncements concerning Eastern Europe, less than two years before Moscow's bloody suppression of the Hungarian Revolution:

> The trade and cooperation in the economic, technical, and cultural spheres, now existing between the Soviet Union and the People's Democracies, are based on the principles of sovereign equality and mutual respect for interests and contribute to the steady expansion of the economy of these countries.[15]

Possibly a determining factor for Soviet strategists who may have been undecided about a new Middle East policy was U.S. efforts for military agreements, which led to the Turkish-Iraqi pact in 1955. Viewed by one Western observer as "the turning point in Soviet Middle East policy," this agreement appeared to alert the U.S.S.R. that the time had arrived to become systematically involved in this vital region.[16] The Soviet press sought to discredit this treaty and to stimulate opposition by referring to the touchy oil question in the states' relations:

> Despite the terror rampant in the country, the Iraqi public are protesting against the Turko-Iraqi treaty which runs counter to the country's national interests and enhances the threat to peace in the Middle East. . . .
>
> The treaty does not, of course, eliminate the differences between Iraq and Turkey, of whom the latter, as press reports show, has not renounced her old plans for annexing Iraq's rich Mosul oil fields. At the same time in the view of Ankara ruling circles, the treaty must back up Turkish claims to Arab leadership. Ankara, it should be noted, is not against renewing certain claims of the Ottoman Empire.[17]

Between 1954 and 1956, the U.S.S.R. signed trade agreements with Egypt, Lebanon, Syria, and Yemen, providing for the shipment of some Soviet petroleum products to Russia's new partners in the area of the oil-rich Middle East. The agreements stipulated that they would guarantee "equal and mutual advantage."[18] The Soviet press, beamed to western audiences, pointed out that, by way of contrast, United States "assistance" to underdeveloped states retarded their development and served as an outlet for weapons sales, while U.S.S.R. relations with Eastern Europe were devoted to the furtherance of peace.[19] Another writer spoke of the Soviet Union's wide reputation for service to peace,[20] while a third Soviet writer saw peace as a primary goal of Moscow's foreign policy,[21] specifically to be sought by discouraging alliances and weapons rivalry.[22] "Capitalist profits" were seen as motives behind "economic militarization of the capitalist countries."[23]

The Soviet press explained that American assistance was "shackling" underdeveloped countries, unlike Soviet aid programs.[24] In discussing the Czechoslovak-Egyptian agreement of 1956, which included arms deliveries from the socialist bloc, a writer explained that Czech motivation in assisting the Third World was similar to that of the U.S.S.R., based on "principles of mutual respect, sovereignty, non-interference in internal affairs, equality, mutual benefit, and businesslike economic co-operation."[25]

By contrast, United States "aid" and "co-operation" were seen to be a "screen behind which the imperialist countries . . . are pursuing their own selfish aims — exploitation of Middle Eastern oil and other resources."[26] On the occasion of the Iranian Shah's visit to Moscow in 1956, when the U.S.S.R. offered technical assistance "with no strings attached," Chairman of the Presidium of the Supreme Soviet Voroshilov emphasized Soviet friendly intentions toward Iran:

> Iran has often found in the past and finds now and in the future
> the Soviet Union as a dependable friend in everything concerning

> the strengthening of its national independence and sovereignty, and
> the strengthening of peace and security. . . . The Soviet Union does
> not seek in Iran or in any other country for that matter any special
> rights or advantages for itself, and has no territorial or other claims
> with respect to Iran. Our country does not threaten now, nor will
> it constitute a threat to friendly Iran.[27]

The U.S.S.R.'s new diplomacy toward Iran met with rapid success. In 1956, Iran granted the U.S.S.R. "most favored nation" rights, and, while adhering to her policy not to accept agreements involving Soviet loans, signed an additional trade pact. Her trade with the Soviet bloc increased to the point that, by 1958, Iran was sending one-quarter of her exports to that area.[28] The same year brought Soviet-Iranian accord on regular rail service linking Moscow and Tabriz and the joint use of certain rivers. Negotiations continued into 1959 on proposals for the construction of dams, bridges, and railroads, but no firm agreements materialized.[29]

Meanwhile, cooperation between the two countries faltered because of Iran's acceptance of the Anglo-American "northern tier" defense alliance embodied in the Baghdad Pact.[30] A tense interlude prevailed until 1962, when the Shah assured Khrushchev that he would not permit the establishment of "foreign rocket bases" in Iran. The U.S.S.R. sent a mission to Teheran in December in order to build friendly relations, and the following year signed trade agreements, providing the first Soviet loan to Iran, which totalled forty million dollars and included commitments to build dams.[31]

Relations between the two countries have continued to improve. In recent years Soviet propaganda has been designed to overcome the harsh impressions of the five-year Red Army occupation of Iran's northern provinces during World War II and its aftermath:

> . . . Soviet troops treated the Iranians in friendly fashion and respected
> their laws and customs. They left an excellent memory of themselves
> with the Iranian people.[32]

Within Iran, the Tudeh Party had been advised in 1955, after Soviet-Iranian government relations were on the upswing, to continue its work "to defeat reaction" by linking with other parties in a national front.[33]

The Brezhnev-Kosygin Period

Soviet relations with the Middle East continued to develop as the Soviet Union and Eastern Europe provided economic and military assistance. While formal government-to-government relations between the U.S.S.R. and Iran grew closer, *World Marxist Review* was slow to relent in criticism of the Teheran government on a doctrinal level for "betraying" its people and "losing its independence" to the United States.[34] That journal continued with charges alleging terror and deprivations on the part of the Shah's regime:

> In this country which is one vast prison the prevailing atmosphere is that of fear, suspicion, and mistrust. Political organizations of both the working class and the national bourgeoisie have been smashed and their leaders jailed. Not a single legal newspaper or journal of the opposition appears; deputies instead of being elected are appointed by the Shah.[35]

The broad approach taken by Soviet policies in the Middle East is indicated in the U.S.S.R.'s willingness to build influence in diminutive·Yemen, known for its strategic location rather than for oil. Here, as *New Times* would seem to indicate, Moscow seeks to develop Marxist ideology amid patently un-Marxian conditions: "the Soviet Union is helping the Yemen to build enterprises which are bringing into being a Yemeni proletariat, destined to play a big part in the country's future."[36] In a similar effort to find orthodox truths in unlikely circumstances, Soviet authors have described how the workers of oil-exporting Saudi Arabia are going forward in the struggle to obtain independence, as a part of the larger effort in the Arab cause.[37]

Of particular significance in the present period is the dramatic emergence since the 1967 Arab-Israeli war of the U.S.S.R. as the "superpower of the Arab cause," with a permanent battle fleet in the Mediterranean with berthing rights in Arab ports, a developing naval presence in the Indian

Ocean, and a major military assistance, training, and advisory role in Arab states. Meantime, the Persian Gulf and Indian Ocean have acquired new strategic importance for the super-powers.[38]

Middle East Petroleum — A Symbolic Device to Encourage Anti-Westernism?

It is not surprising that the richest natural wealth of the Middle East region would become a factor, in at least an indirect fashion, in the Soviet's expanded policies of aid and trade. Although the actual recipients of such aid did not, until recently, include major oil or gas producers of the region, the "oil-transit countries" of Egypt and Syria, which have received large Soviet bloc assistance, have been developing their petroleum industries with growing success.

There are indications by Soviet writers, during the period from the middle 1950s to the present, that Middle East petroleum played a role in Soviet policies as a vehicle for development of anti-Western sentiment among Arabs and non-Arabs, and among states with great or little oil wealth.

The Khrushchev Era

A few months after the Turkish-Iraqi Pact was approved, an agreement in Baghdad brought together those two countries with Iran and Pakistan in a defense alliance backed by Britain and the United States, a move certain to bring Soviet disapproval. Moscow's press pointed to the role supposedly played by Western oil companies in arranging for Iran to join the pact,[39] and described these interests as keeping that country in servitude so that she could not help joining "an aggressive military bloc."[40] *International Affairs* took the oil companies to task for a series of politically inspired crimes in such countries as Iran, Syria, Lebanon, Jordan, and Yemen, in a "battle for oil":

> The oil monopolies of the US and Britain have in their struggle for
> oil fields and pipelines turned the countries of the Middle East into

an arena of intrigues, provocations, political murders, and coups d'état. The bloody events in Iran, Yemen, Syria, the Lebanon, and Trans-Jordan smell strongly of oil. The British oil monopolies had an interest in the murder of the Syrian dictator Husni Za'im, who was closely connected with Wall Street, and that of Hajir, the former Iranian Prime Minister. The murder of people well known for their pro-British sympathies, such as Abdullah, King of Trans-Jordan, the Syrian General Hinnawi, organizer of the second coup d'état in Syria, the former Prime Minister of the Lebanon, Riad Solh, and the Iranian Prime Minister, General Ali Razmara, were necessary to the oil monopolies of the United States. All these bloody events are a reflection of the Anglo-American battle for oil in the Middle East.[41]

The same organ supported resistance by Syria and Lebanon against existing transit arrangements for oil movement from Iraq and Saudi Arabia through company-owned pipelines.[42] While the anti-Western Mossadegh regime in Iran from 1951 to 1953 was recognized to be part of "the national liberation movement,"[43] the pro-Western successor rule of the Shah was subjected to Tudeh opposition which called for overthrow of the government, granting of broad freedoms, and economic progress entailing "liquidation of the oil monopolies."[44]

The Brezhnev-Kosygin Period

Proposals for an Islamic Pact, which would seek to bring a measure of political unity to both Arab and non-Arab Middle East countries, brought denunciation in the Soviet press. When Saudi Arabia, Iran, and Jordan seemed interested in such a grouping, the Kremlin may have reckoned its possible effect upon millions of Soviet Muslims and been wary of the unifying force of religion in the Middle East. The Soviet press continued its attack upon the Western oil companies as a vehicle for allegations against the Islamic Pact, charging them with a host of heinous political crimes:

These seven [oil companies] have dictated and are dictating the policies of the imperialist countries in the Middle East in other oil-rich regions. On their orders the unobliging kings and presidents of the Near East and Middle East are overthrown, interventions are organized, pacts and blocs are formed, and doctrines of imperialist robbery are pronounced. The evil shadow of the seven was evident behind the three-power intervention in Egypt, behind the American

57

intervention in Lebanon, behind the murder of Iran's progressive prime minister Mossadegh who had dared to express concern for the national interests of his country, and behind the innumerable other crimes of the imperialists in this region.[45]

The year 1966 brought challenges to the major Western companies by petroleum enterprises owned partially or wholly by West European governments. This period saw the advent of negotiations and agreements between Arab and non-Arab oil-producing states with Entreprise de Recherches et d'Activités Pétrolières (ERAP) of France, Ente Nazionale Idrocarburi (ENI) of Italy, and Hispanoil of Spain. During the same time negotiations were undertaken between the producing countries and several states of Eastern Europe, culminating in contracts for barter of Middle East oil in exchange for Soviet bloc machinery and equipment. A Soviet book dealing with economic development of Iran advised that country to be cautious about signing agreements with such new Western entrants into Middle East petroleum development as ERAP, but did not consider the Communist barter trade, which, as will be seen, provided for petroleum operations and equipment from the Soviet bloc, to reflect any similarly inhibiting influence upon the flexibility of Iranian economic planning:

> While assuring a considerable increase in Persia's oil revenues, the agreements draw Persia even more deeply into the meshes of dependence on foreign capital, and thereby create the conditions for strengthening the influence of foreign capital on the further course of the country's economic development.[46]

As the Western companies of the consortium in Iran and Iraq Petroleum Company carried out annual negotiations with the respective host countries in late 1966, the Soviet press reiterated an Iranian newspaper charge that Western states considered Iran as an appendage — to supply raw materials and to absorb exports. The Soviet writer, who applied the same analysis to oil companies operating in Iraq, did not clarify that exports to the Middle East oil-exporting states in exchange for the latter's petroleum are, for the most part, in the form of producer's and consumer's goods from Communist countries, and hard currency from the capitalist West:

> ... there are signs of a constant endeavor to slow down the economic
> development and frustrate the fulfillment of economic plans in the
> oil producing countries. The Teheran newspaper *Kayhan* explains the
> consortium's unwillingness to satisfy Iran's demand by the fact that
> the West needs an economically underdeveloped Iran as a supplier of
> raw materials and as a marketing outlet for industrial goods. The
> monopolies have been pursuing a similar policy in respect of Iraq.[47]

The Iranian press furnished economic data to support that
country's side in the continuing negotiations, which were
quoted by Moscow. The Soviet correspondent seemed to play
upon Arab-Iranian differences apparently to show that diverse
Western interests operating throughout the Middle East are
responsive to some obscure supreme management and indulge
in no real competition with one another. Reference was made
to the seeming anomaly in the fact that Kuwait's oil income
exceeds that of Iran, while the latter has greater proven oil
reserves:

> Director [of the consortium] John A. Warder declares that any rapid
> increase in oil production in Iran is impossible unless new markets are
> found. This caused bewilderment in the Iranian press which is of the
> opinion that proven oil reserves in the country exceed 5,000,000,000
> tons, which is 20 times more than in Kuwait. Nevertheless Kuwait's
> income from oil last year was 114,000,000 dollars greater than Iran's.[48]

The implication that the Western-owned Iranian consortium
could arrange a more equitable balance in production of the
two countries did not take note of the fact that only two of
the seven consortium members,[49] British Petroleum and Gulf,
also participated in Kuwait Oil Company.[50] The Soviet press
spoke of Western petroleum interests when it noted that "Iran
will not be endlessly patient about the losses to its national
interests resulting from the activities of foreign oil vampires,"[51]
despite the fact that the U.S.S.R. had concluded a long-range
barter contract for Iranian gas and negotiated for oil rights in
northern Iran.

Soviet interest in the on-going negotiations between
Western companies and Iran and Iraq appeared in the charge
by a Soviet writer that Western countries employed hard currency as a device to influence foreign policy of oil-exporting
states.[52] In dealing with the issue of Western oil operations
in Iran, writers for the U.S.S.R.'s leading governmental

newspaper appeared to provide conflicting information about the companies' motivation:

> [Certain representatives of the oil monopolies] urge an even more intensive exploitation of the Arabian and Iranian deposits, so that their wealth "may not fall into the hands of the Communists. . . . "[53]
>
> "We cannot remain indifferent to the fact that our oil reserves in an enormous area remain unexploited solely because the consortium wishes it." So declared Deputy Bala in the Iranian Parliament, speaking of the "frozen" territories.[54]

While presenting allegations to the effect that Western companies in Iran and Iraq were trying to "drive a wedge" between Middle East oil-exporting states and attempting to "explode OPEC" (Organization of Petroleum-Exporting Countires), a Soviet foreign affairs observer appeared to reflect precisely such a national objective as he, even in his argument, appeared to portray regional differences, in terms of Vietnam policy, between Saudi Arabia on the one hand, and fellow-Arab Iraq and traditional rival Iran on the other:

> [Iran and Iraq] have been faced with a stiff diplomatic battle over every new barrel of oil. At the same time, Saudi Arabia, which plays a considerable part in imperialist plans in the Middle East, has had its oil output increased by 22 percent. Another thing to take into account is that according to the *Guardian,* the U.S. expeditionary corps in Viet Nam is being supplied with oil from Saudi Arabia.
>
> The negotiations at Teheran and Baghdad once again revealed the efforts of the monopolies to drive a wedge between the oil-producing countries and to explode OPEC.[55]

Just as Western negotiations with Iran and Iraq were being completed at the end of 1966, an oil crisis developed in Syria concerning payments to that country by Western-owned Iraq Petroleum Company (IPC) for oil pipeline rights. The movement of oil to eastern Mediterranean ports of Syria and Lebanon was interdicted within Syria, causing pressure on IPC to grant increased rates. Now, the Soviet press reflected what appeared to be a trend in Soviet policy in support of Arab oil, as distinct from Middle Eastern states' oil, against "the imperialists."[56] As IPC refrained from agreeing to Syria's initial demands, *International Affairs* suddenly seemed aware of elaborate details in a charge that IPC was linked to a widely acknowledged conspiratorial effort against the Syrian regime involving "western imperialists and their Middle East agents":

> It is well known that for many years, the IPC [Iraq Petroleum Company] has been spending a great deal of money to corrupt officials, and pay its agents in the country. The IPC's stubborn refusal to satisfy Syria's legitimate demand is closely tied in with the subversive activity which the Western imperialists and their Middle East agents have been carrying on against Syria. Some details of the plot against Syria were revealed a short while ago. CENTO's intelligence agencies, together with men in reactionary Arab regimes, said the Cairo Rosa el Youssef, had worked out a plan to overthrow the existing regime in Syria. To implement this plan a great number of experts who took part in the invasion of Cuba arrived in the Middle East. There was to be co-ordinated action against Syria by the Israeli army, the U.S. Sixth Fleet, which was to be off the coast of Syria, and a fifth column inside the country.[57]

It seems appropriate to note, however, that no diplomatic protests were registered by the anti-Western B'ath regime of Syria concerning such types of activity, nor were appeals made to the United Nations.

When Syria and IPC reached an accord in early 1967, resulting in resumption of westward oil movement from Iraq, *Pravda* hailed "victory . . . for Arab and non-Arab petroleum-exporting countries:

> The evident retreat of the oil company means victory not only for the Syrian people, but for all the other Arab and non-Arab petroleum-exporting countries, which wage the continuous and arduous struggle against the oil monopolies for their legal rights. Playing a vital role in this victory was the support given Syria by Arab countries — U.A.R., Iraq, Lebanon, Algeria and others. This is a vivid example of the vast importance of unity of actions in the struggle of the developing countries for their economic independence.[58]

In what appears to be an inference of negotiations for petroleum barter arrangements between Iraq and members of the Soviet bloc, another writer suggested that Iraq might be able to market its oil without using the marketing structure serving IPC: ". . . searches for new markets for Iraqi oil are already undertaken and not without success."[59]

Encouragement of Arab resistance to "oil imperialists" could also be heard from Egypt, not yet an oil-exporting country, over Radio Cairo's "Petroleum of the Arabs" program beamed to neighboring Muslim states.[60] In Soviet writings, reference has occasionally been made to the Organization of Petroleum Exporting Countries (OPEC), whose members until recently included Iran, Iraq, Kuwait, Saudi Arabia, Libya,

Indonesia, Venezuela, Abu Dhabi, and Qatar. OPEC gains have been seen as blows against "oil imperialism" in the Middle East:

> In 1966 the oil monopolies were forced to made a series of concessions to members of OPEC. The consortium for exploiting Iranian oil, after lengthy negotiations with the Iranian Government in December, 1966, was obligated to increase from year to year the production of oil in the country, to return 1/4 of the region of the concession not presently being exploited, and to allocate to the national oil company for 1967-71 period 20 million tons of oil at the lowest price for subsequent sale by Iran itself. The ARAMCO company in September of the same year agreed not to deduct discounts from the reference prices for calculation of the income of Saudi Arabia and to pay her compensation for use of these discounts since 1961. The same is true of negotiation of the Kuwait Oil Company with the principality of Kuwait. In August, 1966, Iran was successful in concluding with the French governmental company ERAP an agreement, unprecedented in the history of relations of Near Eastern countries with foreign capital. For just the right to explore for oil (and not for a concession!) and for sale of a certain amount the company was prepared to allocate Iran 91.5 percent of the profits.[61]

The same author called for unified action in order to support Syria and Iraq against the Iraq Petroleum Company during the oil stoppage caused by seizure of the IPC pipeline at the end of 1966: "The struggle of Syria and Iraq with the oil monopolies is difficult and complex. In the final analysis, only unified actions of the oil-exporting countries can inflict a serious blow against the cartel, and deprive the monopoly of freedom of maneuver and of the opportunity to employ a boycott."[62] The U.S.S.R., engaged in providing technical assistance and equipment to such states as Syria, could contrast her disinterested relationship toward Middle East countries with the West's "imperialistic position."[63]

The dramatic events in the Middle East during the spring of 1967 were interpreted by a Soviet press that at times seemed too hurried to reflect a consistent trend in the development of Soviet policy. While published materials could not always agree as to "the ultimate aggressor," or "the aggressor's objectives" in the Arab-Israeli war of June, the Western oil companies were not neglected in the determinations of guilty parties. *World Marxist Review* praised Arab efforts in recent negotiations to increase their own share of petroleum profits, adding "in an attempt to prevent this, the oil monopolies are using Israel to

fight against the Arab peoples."[64]   Border incidents involving
Israel and Jordan during the previous November had been interpreted as attacks ordered by the U.S. Mediterranean Fleet.[65]
A few weeks later, the same writer, using the theme of Israel
as "imperialism's chief shock force in the Middle East," began
to focus attack upon the oil company symbol in a new role of
playing off Arab against Arab "for imperalist ends": "There is
an unmistakable connection between foreign oil interests and
the policy of certain Western powers. 'Gunboat politics' are of
no use now, and the tactic has been to inflate enmity between
Arab countries, build up tension, and split the Arab world
through secret diplomatic and other moves."[66]

With the outbreak of Arab-Israeli hostilities, personification of the oil companies as "forces of imperialism" became
commonplace in the Soviet press. Articles seemed to shift
abruptly from making slurs against "reactionary Arab regimes"
to supporting "all Arab countries in their just struggle against
the Israelis, the imperialists, and the oil companies." *New
Times* presented a "summary of production and profits" of
the Western companies entitled, "The Imperialist Stake in the
Middle East Oil,"[67] with a companion article, "Aggression
Against the Arab World," which bluntly charged the Western
powers with responsibility for the war and its consequences:

> The recent spate of inflammatory articles in the reactionary British
> and American press were obviously meant to incite Israel first against
> Syria and then against the United Arab Republic. There were also
> many promises of Western "moral" and every other kind of support.
> It can therefore be validly said that Anglo-American imperialism is
> directly responsible for the bloodshed in the Middle East.[68]

During the weeks of the 1967 Arab-Israeli crisis, the Party
press urged Arab solidarity in boycotting United States and
British oil markets. As the boycott got underway "because of
Western assistance to Israeli aggression," Moscow's *Izvestiya*[69]
began to accuse the companies themselves of having been the
actual aggressors: ". . . one way or another, the cartel got wind
of a portent debunking the myth of its invulnerability. It
seemed that the cartel would have to retreat if it was to be opposed by the real solidarity of at least several of the Arab

countries. And this is one of the main reasons behind the thirst for revenge which made the cartel eager to attack the Middle Eastern countries."[70]

The Soviet press continued to encourage the Arab countries to maintain their boycott as ". . . a concrete and effective expression of Arab solidarity and a form of opposing the Israeli aggression and those who inspired it . . . "[71] Since such a policy was not fully enforceable, and alternative markets did not exist, the Soviet Union may have been more interested in exploiting anti-Western feeling than in furthering the Arab oil producers' welfare:

> The anti-imperialist sentiments in the Arab countries are expressed in many forms, including the rapture [sic] of diplomatic relations and boycott of U.S. and British goods, and an organized withdrawal of capital deposited in City and Wall Street Banks. A powerful weapon in the hands of the Arab countries is the oil boycott. This is the first time in the history of the Middle East that the Western world has been made to feel who is the real owner of Arab oil. Let us add that the Western Powers depend heavily on Arab oil.[72]

After the Arab countries meeting at Khartoum decided to give up the costly oil embargo, the Soviet press, in an abandonment of its former position, switched to support of the new Arab position: "It was . . . a matter of sober calculation. Refusal to pump oil for the United States, Britain, and Federal Germany caused no actual shortage of oil and oil products in Western Europe. . . . "[73] Furthermore, the press began increasingly to extend the anti-imperialist theme to include non-Arab states of the Middle East, and, consequently avoided chiding Iran for undermining the 1967 Arab oil boycott by increase of its own shipments to the "imperialists."

Soviet writers interpreted Israel's decisive military victory over Jordan, Egypt, and Syria in 1967 as "a failure for imperialism." For example, "imperialism's three general strategic objectives," of which "not one has been achieved," appeared in the Soviet press a month after the war:

> . . . to smash the progressive regimes in the United Arab Republic and Syria; . . . to scare the Arabs into accepting the existence of an Israel that would fulfill the role of imperialist bailiff in the Middle East; . . . and to tighten imperialist control over the Arab world, guarantee the Western monopolies unhindered exploitation of Arab oil for a long

time to come, put an end once and for all to tendencies to break the grip of the international oil cartel on Arab oil. . . .[74]

World Marxist Review noted somewhat similar objectives, but on this occasion neglected to charge the oil companies with connivance in the June war: ". . . the imperialists and their agents in Tel Aviv did not achieve their main political goals in this aggression, viz., to weaken the progressive regimes, to reverse the revolutionary trend in the Arab world, to split the united Arab movement."[75]

A few months after the Arab-Israel War, *International Affairs* presented a revised analysis of the "motives of imperialism," scarcely mentioning the oil interests, upon whom attacks had been carried out with such regularity during the Arab boycott. A new "strategic appraisal," while continuing to charge "the imperialists" with seeking to liquidate the "progressive regimes," perceived a grandiose scheme. According to the purported plan, Israel sought Sinai in order to force nationalization of the Suez Canal, and wanted to take all of Jordan to help the United States "encircle independent Asia from the south" by establishing a corridor from the Indian Ocean based across Arabia, Jordan, Israel, Cyprus, and Greece. The United States, as part of its "total strategic plan" to prepare to assault the Soviet Union from the south, encouraged Israel to attack:

> . . . the U.S. encourages and promotes Israel's ventures, the more so as they are directed against the national liberation movement of the Arab peoples and can be developed into a "local war" as part of the total strategy, a war that it will suit the U.S. to wage through other people, without deploying an American expeditionary force. It can therefore be said that the Middle East crisis precipitated by Israel's aggression has become an integral part of U.S. strategy.[76]

Subsequently, *Kommunist* charged that the companies were guilty of conspiracy in the hostilities: "An analysis of the events in the Near and Middle East, following the beginning of the Israeli aggression against the Arab countries, shows that the Western monopolies which earn huge profits from petroleum production in this area of the globe played an important role in the preparation and implementation of these events."[77] Continuing U.S. diplomatic support of Israel during the years after 1967 enabled Soviet propaganda to persist in linking

Middle East oil with "Western imperialism,"[78] through nationalization of Iraq Petroleum Company in 1972.

Middle East Petroleum and Petroleum Industry — Objectives of Soviet Policy?

Just as in an earlier period the Soviet Union had displayed an interest in participation in Middle East oil production, as we saw in the case of Iran near the end of World War II, she again pursued oil development rights in the region, and succeeded in gaining oil exploration rights. In addition, the U.S.S.R. and the Soviet bloc, whose petroleum requirements have always been met by internal production, with surplus for export, have undertaken long-term arrangements to import Middle East crude oil or natural gas.

The Khrushchev Era

As relations with Iran were changing for the better, the U.S.S.R. attempted to establish trade links with Iran, which included provisions relating to petroleum. When the Shah was visiting Moscow in 1956 and again two years later, as the United States was tempting Iran with a military defensive pact, the U.S.S.R. offered to provide its southern neighbor with equipment and technical assistance for its petroleum industry. The following year, the Russians reportedly proposed an arrangement for exploration rights in Iran, under which Iran would receive a record 85 percent of profits.

> Significant of one of the possibilities of future action was the report by Reuters in 1959 that the Soviet Union had offered to develop the oil in the northern provinces by the Caspian on a 15-85 percent split in profits, conditioned on Iran ousting foreign military bases from its soil. The Ambassador was reported to have offered, in an interview with Shah, to duplicate Soviet activities in Afghanistan by building dams, roads, railroads, and power stations.[79]

Although such efforts came to nought at that time, the U.S.S.R. soon became the major purchaser of Iran's overall exports.[80]

A Soviet writer, who undertook to prepare a "historical account" of economic relations with Iran, made no mention of the Stalin-Kavtaradze efforts of 1944-47, when the U.S.S.R. failed to impose its own conditions for oil concessions.[81] Possibly new tactics for similar aims were embodied in Soviet "assistance packages" with specific provisions for drilling test wells. Since the earlier efforts to penetrate Iran's oil industry had been rebuffed, a preliminary position within Middle East petroleum production now sought in states whose mineral prospects did not appear bright:

> In the fall of 1957 the Soviet Union made economic agreements involving substantial Soviet loan offers both to Egypt and Syria. ... The Syrians will get a geological map, exploration for petroleum ores and water resources, irrigation projects, improved oil storage facilities, a fertilizer plant, and an agriculture research laboratory. In addition, the Soviet Union will drill eighteen test oil wells, will build four hundred miles of railroad, five dams and hydroelectric stations, and a number of bridges. Egypt will get marine workshops, a drydock, building materials facilities, petroleum and mining projects, and other industrial projects.[82]

The Brezhnev-Kosygin Period

Soviet publications began to emphasize the petroleum theme of each country exploiting its own resources. A *New Times* journalist, speaking of the Syrians' gratitude for Soviet assistance, quotes one citizen's remarks: "Soviet geologists discovered rich oil deposits in our country. Now we have enough oil for ourselves and for export. The government has decided not to grant concessions to foreigners."[83] Soviet assistance programs for the Middle East have provided for increasing amounts of technical assistance and equipment in the development of petroleum industries in such other states as Algeria and Egypt along with loans for construction of crude oil refineries.[84] The road to economic and cultural development of Middle East countries is seen to lie in relations with the Soviet bloc rather than with "the imperialists."[85]

Algeria, the first country in the class of petroleum exporters to receive Soviet technical assistance, is looked upon in

Pravda as a model for development of petroleum-producing states, which have chosen to take over the crude oil and natural gas properties from foreign companies:

> The example of the way independent Algeria is handling the problem of exploitation of its natural resources shows that newly independent states, once having won back their rights from foreign monopolies, can use these resources in the cause of their own development. Of course the development problem has many facets. Of no small importance, for example, is the absence of technically trained national cadres. The Soviet gift to Algeria of an instructional center, including an institute and technicum for oil and gas, is evidence that with the help of friendly and selfless aid young states can overcome many serious difficulties.[86]

The question of whether the petroleum industry of the U.S.S.R., second in the world after that of the United States, is able to continue to meet bloc demands naturally arose when, beginning in 1966, such East European members of COMECON as Poland, Czechoslovakia, Rumania, and Bulgaria contracted to import crude oil from such Middle East states as Iran, Iraq, and Saudi Arabia on a long-term barter basis.[87] The same year, the U.S.S.R. became an important customer of the Middle East petroleum industry as well. Thus, according to an agreement with Iran, the Soviet Union has been helping to construct a large steel complex at Isfahan to be paid for by long-term deliveries of Iranian natural gas via a pipeline built jointly by the U.S.S.R. and Iran, which was opened in 1970. This line, traversing very difficult terrain over its long course from the Persian Gulf area,[88] connects with the U.S.S.R. Transcaucasus, the Baku oil and natural gas region. (See Figure 1.) An additional note to Moscow's plans to import the fuel into its own producing regions has appeared in an authoritative report that the Iranian gas will be shipped not only to the Transcaucasus, but to the possibly gas-surfeited Central Asia as well: "In accordance with . . . the Soviet-Iranian agreement signed in January, 1966 . . . Iran will pay for a significant proportion of the installations of a metallurgical plant by supplying natural gas that is needed in the Central Asian republics of the Soviet Union."[89]

The original Soviet-Iranian agreement has been substantially augmented by increasing gas deliveries in exchange for

Soviet assistance in the form of equipment to double the steel plant's output, construction of zinc and lead-smelting plants, railway electrification, and military aid.[90] Planned repayment over twelve years indicates that the Soviet Union is beginning to play an important part in the future economic life of Iran in areas not only involving the petroleum industry but in general industrial development as well. Climaxing her efforts to become established in the Iranian oil industry, the U.S.S.R. concluded an agreement with Iran in 1966 for joint exploration and development operations in the promising Iranian Caspian area. In 1970, the countries signed a treaty expected to double two-way trade.[91] Further efforts are being made to participate in Iran's oil industry to include joint exploitation of Persian Gulf fields released by the consortium. There have been indications that the U.S.S.R. would, as in the case of natural gas, become an importer of Iranian crude oil.[92] One possibility is for Arab and Iranian Gulf oil via the Soviet-Iranian gas pipe line axis.[93] In 1968, the U.S.S.R. was successful in concluding important negotiations with the Iraq National Oil Company (INOC) for the exchange of Soviet technicians, equipment, and consultant services for Iraqi crude oil.[94] By 1972, a year which witnessed signing of a 15-year treaty of friendship between the two countries, a $300 million Soviet investment in Iraqi oil production,[95] and nationalization of Iraq Petroleum Company, the U.S.S.R. was entrenched in Iraq's oil industry.[96]

In addition, it should be noted that "economic cooperation between Iraq and the C.E.M.A. (COMECON) countries has been consolidated year after year . . . the Iraqi-Hungarian joint communique' [concluded recently] . . . says, in part, that Hungary will increase its aid to Iraq in extracting and refining oil . . . the Iraqi Government will repay Hungary in crude oil and other Iraqi products . . . "[97] The Soviet bloc is now importing oil from Iran, Iraq, Egypt, Algeria, Libya, and Syria.

Summary

A more consistent Soviet policy toward the Middle East was undertaken at the end of the Stalinist era. This policy fits smoothly into the general line of Soviet foreign policy since the mid-1950s. A broad campaign of economic assistance and increased trade made available, particularly to the "revolutionary countries" of Egypt, Syria, Iraq, and Algeria, industrial equipment and technicians, arms, and construction loans. The appeal of such aid to states, which recently gained their independence and hope increasingly to develop greater economic stability, cannot be underestimated. Soviet efforts to participate in the Middle East petroleum industry were rewarded at first in countries which were not major oil-producers or major oil-exporters; lately, however, successes have been achieved through agreements which provided for direct U.S.S.R. and Soviet bloc participation in development, production and import, involving particularly the petroleum industries of Iraq and Iran.

The growing Soviet merchant fleet is reportedly increasing in presence at Middle East sources of petroleum supply. In part, this new activity can be illustrated by increasing oil shipments between Egypt and the Aden refinery. Since the closure of the Suez Canal, Soviet tankers have also begun to haul Western-produced Arab oil from the Persian Gulf to fulfill Soviet customer requirements east of Suez, where the U.S.S.R. has been exporting its crude to such countries as Ceylon, India, North Vietnam, and Japan.[98]

It has also been seen that Middle East petroleum appeared prominently in Soviet press treatment of the causes of economic backwardness and conflict between states of the area — Middle East petroleum as it is "controlled by the foreign monopolies . . . the imperialists." In conditions already ripened by nationalism and revolutionary currents in the Middle East, Soviet efforts to emphasize "the imperialists' role" would seem to have been timely and effective. The present state of "good U.S.S.R. relations" with many Middle East states, and a deteriorated relationship between the United States and many countries of the region, suggests that Soviet propaganda, while not the primary factor, has seemingly contributed to growing anti-Western sentiment caused by Arab perceptions of U.S. partisanship toward Israel in the protracted Arab-Israeli conflict.

Notes

1. Jan F. Triska and David D. Finley, *Soviet Foreign Policy* (New York: Macmillan, 1968), p. 25.

2. David J. Dallin, *Soviet Foreign Policy after Stalin* (Philadelphia: J.B. Lippincott Co., 1961), p. 525.

3. *Ibid.,* pp. 525-527.

4. Triska and Finley, *Soviet Foreign Policy,* pp. 23-25.

5. Dallin, *Soviet Foreign Policy,* p. 524.

6. *Ibid.,* p. 529.

7. *Ibid.,* p. 524.

8. K. Ivanov, "Soviet Foreign Policy and the Present International Situation," *International Affairs,* November, 1955, pp. 30-31.

9. Triska and Finley, *Soviet Foreign Policy,* p. 24.

10. *Ibid.,* pp. 17-18.

11. *Ibid.,* pp. 18-21.

12. R. Svetlov, "USSR-USA Possibilities and Reality," *International Affairs,* February, 1972, p. 15.

13. Walter Laqueur, *Communism and Nationalism in the Middle East* (London: Routledge and Kegan Paul, 1956), p. 260.

14. "Successful Negotiations," *International Affairs,* January, 1955, p. 94.

15. G. Andreyev, "United States Imperialist Expansion in Guise of 'AID' to Underdeveloped Countries," *International Affairs,* No. 2, February, 1955, p. 44.

16. Laqueur, *Communism and Nationalism,* p. 261.

17. "The Turko-Iraqi Treaty," *International Affairs,* April, 1955, pp. 111-112.

18. "Soviet Union Expands Its Foreign Trade," *International Affairs,* April, 1956, p. 135.

19. Andreyev, "U.S. Imperialist Expansion," p. 44.

20. "Resolutely championing peace, the Soviet Union has won the love and sympathy of the working people of the whole world." Ivanov, "Soviet Foreign Policy," p. 31.

21. "The Western press often alleges that Soviet foreign policy is designed to sow discord between the capitalist powers. Actually the Soviet Union, far from pursuing any such aims, wants friendship and co-operation with all countries. It stands for friendship between all countries on a peaceful and honorable basis." "Friendship between the Great Powers," *International Affairs,* May, 1956, p. 5.

22. "The Soviet people are firmly opposed to the arms race and to restricted military blocs spearheaded against other powers. They feel certain that the arms race and military blocs are fraught with manifold dangers and constitute the greatest obstacle to normal relations between countries." *Ibid.,* pp. 5-6.

23. Ivanov, "Soviet Foreign Policy," p. 22.

24. Andreyev, "U.S. Imperialist Expansion," pp. 44-45.

25. "Czechoslovak-Egyptian Economic Relations Grow Stronger," *International Affairs*, May, 1956, p. 135.

26. "Session of Baghdad Pact Council," *International Affairs*, May, 1956, p. 133.

27. M.N. Ivanova, *Oktyabrskaya revolyutsiya i iran (The October Revolution and Iran)* (Moscow: State Publishing House for Political Literature, 1958), p. 61.

28. H.L. Hoskins, "Soviet Economic Penetration in the Middle East," *Orbis*, Vol. III, No. 4 (Winter, 1960), p. 466.

29. W.B. Ballis, "Soviet-Iranian Relations during the Decade 1953-1964," *Bulletin of the Institute for the Study of the U.S.S.R.*, XII, No. 11 (November, 1965), p. 21.

30. In retrospect, it has been said concerning U.S. Middle East policy, . . . "The Eisenhower Doctrine, modeled on the Truman Doctrine of 1947 which served so usefully in assistance to Greece and Turkey, was more the outline of a policy than a policy itself, and hardly proved as successful as its predecessor, although it seemed a sound and constructive policy at the time," (Harry N. Howard, "The Regional Pacts and the Eisenhower Doctrine," *The Annals of the American Academy of Political and Social Science*, May, 1972, p. 94.

31. *Ibid.*, p. 22.

32. L. Alekseyev, *Sovetskiy soiuz i iran (The Soviet Union and Iran)* (Moscow: Institute of International Relations Publishing House, 1963), p. 16.

33. "Although the Tudeh Party, as the theoretically grounded and revolutionary party of Iran, enjoying the support of the masses, is much stronger than the different groups of the national bourgeoisie, still it will not be able to defeat reaction with its own forces alone." A. Ardekani, "Toward a National Democratic Front in Iran," *World Marxist Review*, Vol. VIII, No. 9 (September, 1955), p. 31.

34. ". . . a wave of reprisals swept the country. Many members of the nationalist religious organization "Champions of Islam" were arrested. Over the past fifteen years this organization has assassinated a number of prime ministers and ministers (Hagir, Razmara, Zangane). . . . the numerous attempts on top officials of the regime is a reflection of the popular resentment with government policy. . . a policy of betrayal as a result of which Iran is losing its independence and becoming more and more a colony of U.S. imperialists. . . ." A. Husseini, "Another Wave of Terror in Iran," *World Marxist Review*, Vol. VIII, No. 6 (June, 1965), p. 64.

35. *Ibid.*, p. 65.

36. D. Volskiy, "Into the Twentieth Century," *New Times*, May 17, 1967, p. 17.

37. "Although the working class of Saudi Arabia at present consists of no more than one percent of the population, it has, through its selfless struggle for the interests of the workers, won the respect of the broad masses of people. . . . The workers' and general democratic movement in Saudi Arabia has assumed a national scale and is becoming a part of the common struggle of the Arab peoples for their rights and true national independence." I.V. Milovanov *et al.*, *Rabochiy klass i rabochiye dvizheniya v stranakh azii i afriki (The Working Class and Workers' Movements in the Countries of Asia and Africa)* (Moscow: *Nauka*, 1965), pp. 229-230.

38. Alvin J. Cottrell and R.M. Burrell, "No Power Can Hope to Dominate the Indian Ocean," *The New Middle East,* September, 1971, p. 37.

39. "By insisting on her inclusion in the Baghdad bloc [the foreign monopolies] sought both to tighten their grip on the Iranian oil industry and to gain greater access to the other branches of the Iranian national economy. These schemes have undoubtedly become quite realizable now that the imperialists have succeeded in inducing Iran to court disaster by joining the Baghdad bloc." Kh. Grigoryev, "An Action Contrary to the Interests of Iran and International Security," *International Affairs,* December, 1955, p. 57.

40. "Infringement on Iranian National Interests," *International Affairs,* October, 1955, p. 136.

41. S. Belinkov, "Battle for Oil," *International Affairs,* January, 1955, p. 121.

42. "Differences over rentals exist not only between Syria and the Lebanon, on the one hand, and the IPC, on the other, but also between those countries and the U.S. Tapline Company, which owns a big pipeline linking Saudi Arabian oil fields with the Lebanese port of Saida. . . .

It will be seen from this that countries situated in an area which until recently was a colonial preserve no longer allow oil companies to impose unequal agreements upon them as was hitherto the case." "Syria, Lebanon, and Oil Companies," *International Affairs,* June, 1956, p. 120.

43. "The Iranian Oil Problem," *International Affairs,* July, 1955, p. 147.

44. ". . . the People's Party of Iran proposes drafting a united front programme that will meet the interests of the country. . . overthrow of the antidemocratic regime of the Shah: establishment of a national and democratic government; political freedom for the various parties and democratic and patriotic organizations; freedom of speech, press, and demonstrations; withdrawal of Iran from CENTO and a neutral foreign policy; renationalization of the oil industry and liquidation of the oil monopolies; expulsion of military and U.S. advisers from the country; protection of the national economy against foreign monopoly capital, development of the economy and in the first place of a heavy industry." Ardekani, "Toward a National Front," pp. 33-34.

45. M. Vilba, " 'Islam Pact' Seen as Tool for Promoting Western Oil Interests," *Pravda ukrainy,* May 17, 1966, p. 3, trans. by Joint Publications Research Service, Department of Commerce, Washington, D.C., No. 36,009, June 15, 1966, p. 8.

46. I.I. Palynkatis, *Ekonomicheskoye razvitiye irana (The Economic Development of Iran),* (Moscow: State Publishing House, 1966), p. 196, as quoted in "The Present Soviet View of Persia," *MIZAN,* Vol. VIII, No. 5 (September/October, 1966), p. 216.

47. D. Kasatkin, "Middle East: Assault on the Oil Monopolies," *International Affairs,* January, 1967, p. 94.

48. V. Nakaryakov, "Iranian Oil Production Dispute," *Izvestiya,* November 11, 1966, p. 4, trans. by Joint Publication Research Service, U.S. Department of Commerce, Washington, D.C., No. 39,174 (December 19, 1966).

49. R. Andreasyan, "New Aspects of Middle East Countries' Oil Policy," *International Affairs,* September, 1968, No. 1, p. 28.

50. "Taking It Out on the Oil Companies," *Economist,* June 24, 1967, p. 1368.

51. Nakaryakov, "Iranian Production Dispute," p. 6.

52. "In recent years, the haggling of the oil monopolies over the volume of oil output has assumed political significance. On the one hand, using the developing countries' keen interest in obtaining foreign exchange as a means of pressure on them, the West has tried to adjust the foreign policy lines of some of them." Kasatkin, "Middle East: Assault on Oil Monopolies," p. 94.

53. Rachkov, "Neft'-bez mifov;" ("Oil—Without Myths"), p. 2.

54. Nakaryakov, "Iranian Production Dispute," p. 4.

55. Kasatkin, "Middle East: Assault on Oil Monopolies," p. 94.

56. In an article entitled "Arab Oil for the Arabs," *Pravda* reported: "The chairman of the Trade Union Federation of Homs, Gazi Nasif Malki, who is also Chairman of the All-Arab Federation of Petroleum Workers, told me about the important development of labor and the high level of consciousness of the petroleum workers of Syria, about the militant solidarity expressed to them by their class brothers of the other Arab countries."

"I am sure that we will win the battle we have started against the oil company IPK [IPC]" he said, "for we are fighting for our legal rights, and we continuously feel the support of the masses of the Arab countries, and the workers of the whole world." L. Medvedko, "Arabskuyu neft' — arabam!" ("Arab Oil for the Arabs!"), p. 5.

57. P. Gevorkyan, "Syria: Political Aspects of the Oil Conflict," *International Affairs,* February, 1967, pp. 86-87. (Note the reference to "reactionary Arab regimes," a popular phrase in Soviet propaganda prior to the 1967 Arab-Israeli crisis, when new opportunities dictated a theme of "anti-imperialism by all Arabs.")

58. Medvedko, "Arab Oil," p. 5.

59. R. Andreasyan, "The Arab East: New Clash with Oil Imperialism," *World Economics and International Relations,* No. 3, p. 113.

60. ". . . Arab oil-producing countries should value the power of the oil in their hands and its effectiveness as a weapon in the battles the Arab states are now fighting against the states of EEC and other states. . . ." "Arab Oil Can Be Used as Weapon Against EEC," *Daily Report.* Foreign Broadcast Information Service, No. 185 (September 23, 1966), Sec. B. p. 3.

61. Andreasyan, "Clash with Oil Imperialism," p. 112.

62. *Ibid.,* p. 113.

63. "Whenever I talked to Syrian public personalities or government officials they invariably brought up two subjects: construction of the Euphrates dam with Soviet aid, and the defeat of the Iraq petroleum monopoly in the conflict over payment for piping Iraq oil across Syria territory." D. Volskiy, "Troubled Spring," *New Times,* May 31, 1967, p. 16.

64. Jan Prazsky, "Imperialist Intrigues in the Middle East," *World Marxist Review,* Vol. X, No. 7 (July, 1967), p. 2.

65. "The Cairo *Al Gumhuria* comments: 'Israel is not alone. For some powers her aggressive actions are part of their own anti-Arab policy. . . . The Israeli attack on Jordan [November 13, 1966] was undertaken on orders from the U.S. Sixth Fleet.'" M. Kremnev, "Arab East: Provocation Continues," *New Times,* November 30, 1966, p. 17.

66. M. Kremnev, "Tension Centre in the Arab East," *New Times,* December 21, 1966, p. 6.

67. B. Rachkov, "The Imperialist Stake in the Middle East Oil," *New Times,* June 14, 1967, pp. 2-3.

68. "Aggression against the Arab World," *New Times,* June 14, 1967, pp. 2-3.

69. *Izvestiya,* published daily in Moscow, is the official newspaper of the Soviet Government; it rarely deviates from the presentation of indoctrination material appearing in the Party's *Pravda,* giving rise to the critical jibe *"v pravde net izvestii i v izvestii net pravdy"* (in *Pravda* [meaning "truth"] there is no news, and in *Izvestiya* [meaning "news"] there is no truth).

70. B. Rachkov, *"Za kulisami-neft' "* ("Oil — Behind the Scenes"), *Izvestiya,* July 11, 1967, p. 5.

71. Y. Dmitriyev, "Arab Oil Resources," *International Affairs,* August, 1967, p. 102.

72. L. Sedin, "The Arab Peoples' Just Cause," *International Affairs,* August, 1967, p. 28.

73. Igor Belyayev and Evgeniy Primakov, "The Situation in the Arab World," *New Times,* September 27, 1967, p. 10.

74. G. Mirskiy, "Israeli Aggression and Arab Unity," *New Times,* July 12, 1967, p. 4.

75. Prazsky, "Imperialist Intrigues," p. 2.

76. V. Kudryavtsev, "The Middle East Knot," *International Affairs,* No. 9, September, 1967, pp. 29-30.

77. B. Rachkov, "The Petroleum Monopolies and the Israeli Aggression," *Kommunist,* No. 12 (August, 1967), pp. 109-117. Trans. by Joint Publications Research Service, Department of Commerce, Washington, D.C., No. 42,903 (October 10, 1967), p. 90.

78. One Western observer of Kremlin policy has noted: "In urging nationalization of the oil industries, the Russians are suggesting that the Arabs use it as a weapon against the West for its support of Israel." Victor Zorza, "Soviet Oil Moves Threaten West," Washington *Post,* June 7, 1972, p. A-19.

79. Harvey O'Connor, *World Crisis in Oil* (New York: Monthly Review Press, 1962).

80. W.B. Ballis, "Soviet-Iranian Relations during the Decade 1953-1964," *Bulletin,* Institute for the Study of the U.S.S.R., Vol. XII, No. 11 (November, 1965), p. 22.

81. Alekseyev, *Soviet Union and Iran,* pp. 32-42.

82. Robert Loring Allen, *Middle Eastern Economic Relations with the Soviet Union, Eastern Europe, and Mainland China* (Charlottesville, Va.: University of Virginia Press, 1958), pp. 46-47.

83. N. Shimmel, "Damascus Journalist Tells of His Visit to Syria," *New Times,* No. 8 (February 23, 1966), p. 32.

84. Rachkov, "Oil — Without Myths," p. 2.

85. "The path to lasting economic and cultural progress is not through the 'good deeds' of imperialism that are being spread by boastful propaganda and a servile press, but through feats of labor by the peoples of the developing countries, on the basis of mutually advantageous cooperation with the Soviet Union and the other socialist countries." *Ibid.,* p. 5.

86. N. Prozhogin, "Oil and Gas in Sahara Produced Independently by Algeria," *Pravda,* November 14, 1966, p. 4. Trans. by Joint Publications

Research Service, Department of Commerce, Washington, D.C., No. 39,174 (December 19, 1966), p. 4.

87. Andreasyan, "Clash with Oil Imperialism," p. 113.

88. "Start near for Iran-to-Soviet Line," *Oil and Gas Journal,* April 17, 1967, p. 112.

89. Rachkov, "Oil — Without Myths," p. 2.

90. Kyril Tidmarsh, "Russia's Worries with Her Economic Block," London *Times,* April 10, 1968, p. 10; "Russia Increases Aid to Iran," Washington *Star,* June 23, 1968, Sec. A., p. 14.

91. C. Saikowski, "Resource Gap Nags Soviets," *Christian Science Monitor,* October 27, 1970, p. 1.

92. Joe Alex Morris, Jr., "Russia Seeks Entry to Iran's Gulf Oil Fields — Kosygin Eyes Region Dominated by West," *International Herald Tribune,* April 5, 1968, p. 2; Drew Middleton, "Iran — a Strategic Pawn," New York *Times,* April 7, 1968, p. 2.

93. *Petroleum Intelligence Weekly,* April 6, 1970, p. 1; May 11, 1970, p. 4.

94. Baghdad radio broadcast, November 27, 1967, as reported in *MIZAN,* Supplement A, "The Middle East in the Soviet Press," No. 1 (1968), p. 1; John K. Cooley, "Iraq to Develop Vast Oil Field," *Christian Science Monitor,* April 15, 1968, p. 12; Robert E. Hunter, "The Soviet Dilemma in the Middle East, Part II: Oil and the Persian Gulf," *Adelphi Papers* No. 60 (October 1969), The Institute for Strategic Studies, London, p. 11.

95. Marilyn Berger, "Oil, Foreign Policy, and the Energy Crisis," Washington *Post,* April 16, 1972, p. B-5.

96. "U.S.S.R., Iraq Sign Cooperation, Trade Agreements," TASS (Moscow) International Service, September 5, 1972, printed in *Foreign Broadcast Information Service, Soviet Union,* September 6, 1972, Vol. III, No. 174, p. B-1.

97. "C.E.M.A.-Iraq Cooperation Aids in Social, Economic Gains," Radio Moscow in Arabic to Arab world, September 4, 1972, printed in *Foreign Broadcast Information Service,* September 6, 1972, Vol. III, No. 174, p. B-2.

98. Edward Hughes, "The Russians Drill Deep in the Middle East," *Fortune,* July, 1968, p. 104. Courtesy of *Fortune* Magazine.

Soviet Motives and Moscow's "Petroleum Paradox"

The foregoing review of Soviet relations with the Middle East has suggested that the region's petroleum has emerged in a contributory role toward certain ends of Soviet policy. The question arises as to the nature of Soviet strategic motivation involving Middle East petroleum. In a sense, the problem at hand consists of proceeding from the known to the unknown, from the past and present to the future, and from short-range to long-term considerations. As will be noted, this discussion of strategic rationale will lead into a seeming paradox in the Soviet Union's own position as petroleum producer and marketer vis-à-vis the Middle East.

From the Past to the Future

If we are seeking the role of Middle East petroleum in Soviet strategy, we must take into account background and historical factors such as Soviet ideology, Russian national interests, and past Soviet Middle East policies which have related to petroleum in a broad or narrow sense. Lessons from the past may be applied to future conditions, by projecting their pattern of relationships between the major powers and countries of the Middle East upon a presumed future environment. This task entails dealing with both that which may be proven and questions intrinsically conjectural; thus, while evaluations may be derived through objective procedures, they cannot afford to be dogmatic because of presumptive elements upon which projections must be based.

Although ideology and national interests have not been primary objects of study in this research into the political aspects of Middle East petroleum, they tend to shape the general direction of Soviet strategy and must therefore be viewed in their broad application.

The ideological basis of the Soviet system is "Marxist-Leninist," a body of doctrine originally based upon teachings of Marx, interpretations by Engels, and further application of that theory to Russian conditions by Lenin and his successors. The general line of Soviet foreign policy and the U.S.S.R.'s Middle East policies have been justified through relevant interpretations of Marxism-Leninism. Doctrines such as "peaceful coexistence" and "support of wars of national liberation" have been consistent with Soviet emphasis, since the end of the Stalinist era, upon the expansion of trade between the Soviet bloc and other states including the Middle East, on a barter basis for economic and military assistance.

Just as Soviet ideology has been subjected to interpretation or revision according to changing domestic and foreign relationships, it may be expected to evolve further through interaction with new requirements arising from pressures of Russian national interest. The relative importance of ideology and national considerations in the making of strategy is likely to remain controversial, if it can truly be said that "doctrine enters as an interpretive modifier to which perceived events are subjected . . . [and] is a set of symbolic referents by which a specific national interest in any one case can be subjectively formulated."[1]

The Soviet Union's national interest itself can be expected to evolve in a bolder direction as the U.S.S.R. grows stronger economically and militarily; the commander in chief of the

Soviet Navy has explained developments in the Soviet naval art of war which seem to indicate the increasingly global character of Russian national interest: "With the growth of the economic might of the Soviet Union, its interests on the seas and oceans continue to expand greatly, and consequently new demands are levied upon the Navy for their defense against the conquests of the imperialists."[2] Soviet ideology and the country's national interests retain their links with the past — just as there are elements of pure Marxism in Marxist-Leninist theory, there are likely to be strains of Russian Mediterranean and Persian Gulf aspirations embodied in Soviet overtures of friendship and assistance for countries of the Middle East.

Moscow's Middle East policies indicate that, under the influence of idoleogy and national interests, the region's petroleum has played a certain role in Soviet strategy. While recognizing that Soviet intentions are a matter of some speculation, this study will attempt to draw reasonable conclusions from observable trends in order to suggest a rationale for Soviet interest in Middle East petroleum.

Toward Strategic Economic Dominance over the Middle East?

While motives rooted in ideology or national interest may be considered to be essentially political, Soviet interest in Middle East petroleum appears to have been affected by economic considerations as well. In previous chapters, we observed petroleum emerging as a symbolic Soviet device for encouraging anti-Western sentiment, particularly during the Khrushchev and Brezhnev-Kosygin periods; and noted both Middle East petroleum and the petroleum industry evolving into objects of Soviet foreign economic policy, in the Khrushchev era and to the present.

What kind of underlying rationale supports policies which, on the one hand, work toward aggravating of differences between Western capitalist states heavily engaged in development, production, processing, and marketing of Middle East crude oil and natural gas and host countries, and which, on the other hand, seek to establish Soviet technicians and advisers in that region's petroleum production, including states with few proven resources and major oil exporters as well? It would seem plausible that Soviet intentions in the Middle East have been, at least in part, to erode Western economic predominance in the region, and support the gradual establishment of Soviet influence, leading toward a long-range goal of Moscow's strategic economic dominance over the Middle East.

The reduction of Western influence in the Middle East, which is hinged upon its major capital investment in the petroleum industry, seems clearly to have been an aim of Soviet press campaigns waged consistently against "foreign oil monopolies." Denigration of the West's position would seem to constitute a logical preparatory phase for a Soviet expansionist sequel to Russian drives toward the Mediterranean and Persian Gulf.

The appearance of Middle East petroleum and its industry as objects of Soviet foreign economic policy might seem, at first glance, to represent the U.S.S.R.'s effort to establish her position in the region by replacing the Western economic presence with her own. In fact, economic means of penetration would appear more feasible than political methods, in view of certain conditions prevailing in the Middle East. For example, the Soviet Union could not, for the foreseeable future, support through a military occupation a campaign of Sovietization of the region; presently, Moscow has only a quasimilitary presence represented by a new Soviet Mediterranean fleet with access to Arab ports, and Russian Army and Air Force advisers and technicians spread among countries which have included Egypt, Syria, Algeria, Iraq, and Iran. In addition, the Middle East affords no centrally controlled, ideologically based political framework of parties responsive to Moscow, such as would be important to support a program of direct, political penetration. Furthermore, there is an indigenous, unifying strength inherent in both the Muslim religion and Arabism, which tends to resist subjugation to such alien ideologies as Communism. Ironically, so it would seem, the region's divisiveness through deeply seated rivalries and hostilities would also seem, in the long term, to imperil any foreign-imposed political hegemony.

If conditions for Soviet political penetration of the Middle East seem poor, prospects for making economic inroads appear better. Since it is both underdeveloped and abundantly blessed with natural resources, the Middle East remains amenable to economic programs which promise industrial development and social progress, while leaving the existing political structure of individual states undisturbed. Precisely such an approach has been embodied in assistance agreements concluded since the mid-1950s between the Soviet bloc and many countries of the Middle East.

However, the appearance of Middle East petroleum and the petroleum industry as objects of Soviet foreign economic policy does not, in itself, lead to an unassailable conclusion that the U.S.S.R. is attempting to replace Western economic influence with its own. Indeed, it must be presumed that the U.S.S.R. is well aware that Middle East petroleum-exporting countries rely primarily upon Western capital investments as a major source of badly needed hard currency. Furthermore, as Moscow has shown in her foreign economic policy toward the capitalist West and the Middle East through her own quest for hard currency and her barter deals, respectively, she would appear ill-prepared to assume the West's role in the Middle East petroleum industry, even if it were otherwise possible. It would seem reasonable, then, that Soviet policy directed toward eroding Western influence has not anticipated its elimination, but has sought instead, through trade and aid, to bolster the U.S.S.R.'s own relative image among Middle East states as a prelude to participating in the rapidly expanding national sector of their petroleum industries. In this manner, the Soviet Union would anticipate "joining" Western countries in exploitation of Middle East resources, quite in harmony with the producing states' aspirations for industrial development.

Yet the recently expanding U.S.S.R. and Soviet bloc long-range commercial ties with national ministries and petroleum companies of Middle East countries comprise a source of some controversy since they center upon an apparent contradiction concerning the Soviet Union's own potential position as oil and natural gas producer and marketer vis-à-vis Middle East petroleum-exporting states.

Paradoxical Future of Soviet Petroleum — Deficient or Competitive?

Touching upon the question of Soviet strategic motivation is the controversy regarding the capacity of the Soviet oil and natural gas industry. Not only are there conflicting views concerning Russian aims in Middle East petroleum — there is disagreement about prospects for Soviet oil and natural gas production and development itself. What are these prospects, and how do they concern Middle East petroleum?

On the one hand, one might conclude, from a Western economic frame of reference, that the U.S.S.R. would have little need for Middle East crude oil or natural gas; the Soviet Union has ranked as the world's second largest petroleum producer (following only the United States) even before recent large discoveries in Siberia, announced in the mid-1960s and in 1970. The Western petroleum press has noted optimistic reports, such as that of Soviet geologist S.V. Goryunov, concerning the magnitude of "third Baku" resources: ". . . It looks as though Tyumen Province, which occupies over half of the western Siberian lowland area, will by itself turn out to be the world's largest oil and gas region both in size and production," and high Soviet officials reportedly declared, "Discovery of oil and gas in Siberia is one of the greatest events of our time."[3] Six years later, I.I. Nesterov, director of the West Siberian Geological Survey Oil Research Institute, confirmed such optimism.[4]

On the other hand, however, there are indications that tend to offset the optimism generated by assessments of the U.S.S.R.'s petroleum wealth. In the main, they concern the petroleum industry itself.

Case for a Deficient Industry

Deficiencies of the Soviet petroleum industry arise not from the quantity of Soviet crude oil and natural gas reserves, both proven (see Figure 5) and estimated,[5] but from operation of the economic system in the petroleum sector. This condition stems, in part, from non-economic practices in the short-range or day-by-day planning, production, processing, and distribution functions which cause shortages requiring imports from the Middle East. Compounding the ill effects of these practices is the apparently accelerating demand of the U.S.S.R. and other bloc countries due to requirements for further industrialization. This functional deficiency is also apparent in long-range planning — that is, in development of future production, requiring the import of foreign capital investment and advanced technology. This type of deficiency is also aggravated, by rising petroleum requirements within the Soviet bloc.

• Uncertainties Facing Soviet Petroleum Production and Development. In 1967, *Kommunist ukrainy* quoted T. Honda, in Kiev:

> Year after year the plan for the deep prospective drilling in Ukraine is not being fulfilled. The main reasons for this? High frequency of accidents, prolonged stoppage, inferior quality of material and technical provisions, and shortage of qualified workers and engineering and technical cadres.[6]

Such self-criticism appearing in the Soviet press extends to both older, "well-established" elements of the petroleum development, Soviet economic planners may have concluded that early reports of favorable prospects for petroleum development may not have fully reckoned with challenges related to their Siberian location. (See Figure 1.) The initial optimism suggesting the acceleration of Communism seems to have given way to sober reflection upon the formidable tasks confronting large-scale petroleum development. Soviet economists, appraising some of the practical problem threatening development of the vast resources, have cautioned:

> The grandiose program of development of the oil and gas industry, indicated in the Program of the Central Committee of the Communist Party, can be fulfilled only under the condition of the successful

> solution of great and complex tasks for the accumulation of industrial supplies of oil and gas, the drilling of oil and gas deposits and their extraction, an increase in the coefficient of layer output, the curtailment of periods of exploiting the deposits, and so forth.
>
> The solution of these and many other tasks is impossible without a rapid pace in technological progress, the fundamental condition for the attainment of the greatest result from the minimum investment.[7]

A Western journal has suggested that precisely the lack of such "technological progress" has resulted in "the Russians' shortage of high-quality equipment . . . a constant cost handicap which does little to mitigate the fear that some of Russia's largest Siberian reserves may never be economically viable."[8]

Looking forward to the challenge of developing her petroleum resources in Siberia, the U.S.S.R. turned to other Soviet bloc members for assistance. An agreement with Czechoslovakia, concluded in Moscow in September, 1966, provides for that country to furnish "pipe, pumps, and other equipment" for a second major Soviet-East European crude oil pipeline, which will traverse some 4,000 miles from northern Siberia to Czechoslovakia. Apparently, the industries of other East European countries, in growing need of raw material and energy resources, are also subjected to Soviet pressures, which, through COMECON, seem to be able to prevent "excessive trade [for such resources] outside of the socialist countries": "These resources are in the Soviet Union. To develop them and make them accessible to Eastern Europe, Moscow needs credits in form of equipment for which there are no provisions in the Soviet plan."[9] Thus, in a kind of "inverted metropole-colony" relationship, the predominant power in COMECON performs the role of raw material supplier to bloc members, and, in turn, is dependent upon them to help equip Soviet industry. One sign of the U.S.S.R.'s program to develop its petroleum-refining capacity appeared in the provisions of the Five-Year Plan (1966-70) under which "more than 80 up-to-date chemical and petroleum refining plants" were to be imported from Czechoslovakia.[10]

Due to Moscow's slow pace in development, perhaps in part from Czechoslovak truculence in fulfilling its 1966 agreement, both Eastern Europe and the U.S.S.R. are calling upon

Middle East sources to help provide crude oil needed to match rising demands.[11] Experience gained by Soviet economic planners during the *tselina* campaign of the 1950s, when thousands of farm workers were persuaded to settle the virgin lands of western Kazakhstan, might have suggested the kinds of difficulties lying ahead for prospective oil workers in the hostile Siberian environment of the new Tyumen petroleum region. Moscow's *Literaturnaya Gazeta* has inferred that the problem of getting required labor for development of such crude oil and natural gas reserves is critical, with annual manpower turnover reaching seventy percent due to such factors as primitive shelter and the danger of wolves.[12] The same problems appeared to be still unresolved in the region five years later.[13]

The centrally planned, periodic production targets appear to be a source of dismay to Soviet economists concerned about petroleum production, since failures in certain branches of industry cause shortages in inputs to other branches, resulting in compounded failures to meet established goals.[14]

The discrepancy which may exist between official "plan fulfillment" and actual satisfaction of basic necessities does not normally come to the attention of foreigners. However, if one studies the regional press, one finds that, even in the fuel-rich Ukraine; serious distribution problems persist, despite the fact that "the plan" is credited with "overfulfillment." One aptly titled article reflected shortages that would be unacceptable by Western standards:

> The plan for fuel deliveries according to the appropriations of oblasts and market requirement has been overfulfilled during the last eight months. . . .
>
> However, in Vinnytska, Donetska, Krymska, Khersonska, Mykolaywska and other oblasts of the Republic (Ukraine) the plan of fuel supplies is not being carried out. Fuel has not been delivered in sufficient quantities to schools, hospitals, children's and cultural-educational institutions. The goals of setting up networks of yards and warehouses are not being fulfilled as required, as a result of which some localities have no fuel supplies to this day. . . . [15]

Another published self-criticism, while in itself showing a certain remedial tendency, casts doubt upon the viability of the

Soviet petroleum production system and its developmental planning — the persistence of procedures that can allow a major petroleum refinery to make its contribution to "the construction of Communism" by repeatedly refining the same oil over again in order to get added credit for plan fulfillment.[16]

Poor planning and management continue to plague coordination of production among various branches of industry, despite a series of "reforms," inaugurated through the years to increase efficiency. Khrushchev's "regionalization" of planning and operation of the economy through *sovnarkhozy* (economic councils) had sought greater efficiency through added participation by lower levels in the planning structure. The Liberman reforms of 1966, as has been seen, have been intended to infuse certain capitalistic principles to rationalize a system troubled by lack of coordination between principal branches of industry, and hampered by an apparent lack of initiative that results from bureaucratic lethargy:

> *Pravda,* on September 23 (1966), has already reported how, owing to the efforts of two institutes — a metallurgical machine-building institution and an institution of high frequency current — in cooperation with the Moskabel' Plant, a highly productive machine for manufacture of cable enclosed in a protective, welded, aluminum coating was created. This method makes it possible to save large quantities of lead and lower production costs. After the Pravda commentary, the essential difficulties in mastering the machine were overcome. Hundreds of kilometers of cable meeting technical specifications have already been produced. But now there is a new obstacle. The main customer for this commodity, the Ministry of Communications, with which the technical conditions for the cable in the aluminum coating were co-ordinated, is not placing any orders for it. There are no reasons for this except a prejudiced attitude towards new things.[17]

Even the most experienced petroleum industry in the U.S.S.R., the Baku region dating from the early years of the century, was charged a few years ago with allowing oil and gas pipe to be grossly misused:

> The Ministry of Communal Economy of Azerbaijan ... undertook the manufacture of metal posts from oil and gas pipes for street lighting in cities and rayon centers in its machine repair plant.
>
> The investigation also revealed the negligent attitude prevailing in the republic in regard to compressor pump and drilling pipe. A large volume of this material was allocated to organizations having nothing

to do with the drilling of oil. Matters even reached the point at which large quantities of usable pipe were classified as scrap iron, cut up, and sent to be smelted. . . .

Unfortunately, what has been found in Azerbaijan is not the exception to the rule. Evidence of the waste of steel pipe has been noted in many other oil producing and refining areas.[18]

The picture of plan fulfillment and economic success frequently presented in the national press is in contrast with Kiev's *Robitnycha hazeta* portrayal of waste in Ukrainian natural gas and crude oil production:

The densely saturated condensed gas was spreading low above the ground. The wind was blowing it toward the village of Lutyshche, which was being evacuated.

Events were marching fast. The explosions grew stronger. The hole was spewing sand and pieces of rock along with the gas. Falling into a nearby lake like artillery missiles, the rocks threw up fountains of water.

On the night of April 12 the gas and sand had cut through the steel of the elevator and the drilling rig fell down into the hole. Near the top of the derrick surrounded by gas a spark was made by a rock, and a high torch of flame shot up into the sky. In 15 minutes the 53-meter-high steel derrick fell. The red glow from the explosion of the terrible volcano lit up the countryside.

The fire burned for nearly three months. The burning drill hole formed a huge crater. It was only recently that the element was stilled by means of a diagonal drilling. The loss is calculated at about 1 million rubles; more than 2 million cubic meters of natural gas went up in flames in the volcano. . . .

There was no electrical core sampling at the drilling. It would have immediately warned the drillers about the increasing gas content in clay solution. Incidentally, about three years ago at the drilling No. 6 in Kehychivks (Kharkovs'ka Oblast) an open gas gusher was rushing for 6 months. The mistake was repeated.

We must mention another volcano which spewed in the Ukraine. In 1964, following Kehychivka, the Crimean geological prospectors got an open gas gusher, only weaker, on the Arabat arrow (Kherson'ka Oblast). Both made the drilling a waste and led to the loss of hundreds of millions of cubic meters of gas. The state suffered huge losses. As usual, these volcanoes were the result of gross violation of the technology of drilling. . . .

The drilling enterprises have a general high rate of accidents. In 1965 in the Republic [Ukraine] in deep drillings for petroleum and gas there were 290 accidents, and in 5 months of this year, 105. The total losses from these accidents amount to 5.7 million rubles. Here we are referring not only to open gushers, but also to pipe breaks, submersion of drilling instruments under rock avalanches, etc. . . ."[19]

Thus, Soviet sources indicate that, despite the U.S.S.R.'s abundant oil and natural gas resources, deficiencies with the Soviet economy and its petroleum industry tend to create a gap between energy availability and short-term requirements, as represented by existing needs and commitments.

● Soviet Bloc's Growing Demand for Petroleum. *The Christian Science Monitor* quoted Polish economist Stanislaw Albinowski, writing in Warsaw's weekly *Polityka* in 1967, as estimating "that by . . . 1980 . . . the Soviet bloc — including the Soviet Union itself — will need 730 million tons for domestic purposes. That is about 100 million tons more than anticipated total Soviet production."[20]

The vast new discoveries of the Siberian third Baku are beginning to assume more modest proportions, as the problem of rising petroleum demand is being encountered. Not only are estimates of an impending overall shortage in Soviet bloc crude oil production heard from a Communist country, they are circulating in the West as well: ". . . a demand that is conservatively estimated at nearly 15 million b/d by 1980 for all Eastern Europe including Russia. Production* in the U.S.S.R. at that time has been forecast at only 12.6 million b/d."[21] Impending Soviet bloc petroleum shortages are reportedly causing concern among economic planners of other member of COMECON: "Can Russia . . . continue to offer petroleum as a staple export to the West, and still pump enough oil into the Friendship Pipeline to enable Eastern Europe to carry through its own revolutionary changes? . . . the question is certainly being asked in Warsaw, Prague, and Budapest."[22]

The barter agreements East European states have been concluding for the import of Middle East oil appear to be a necessary measure to insure adequacy of petroleum stocks beyond the capacity of Friendship and Brotherhood Pipelines and "third Baku." Predictions of the Polish economist cited earlier imply that COMECON requirements can be satisfied only through continuing to increase crude oil shipments from

*Multiply "barrels per day" by 50 to convert to approximate annual production in metric tons.

the Middle East: ". . . by 1980 Eastern Europe must import at least 90 million tons of oil annually from non-Communist countries."[23] Thus such indications point anew to the monumental economic potential embodied in Middle East petroleum resources, which can hardly escape the scrutiny of Party politico-economic planner. (See Figure 5.) "Kuwait alone has larger proven reserves than the United States and the Soviet Union together. Saudi Arabian reserves are of the same order, and the combined reserves of Iran and Iraq are nearly as large. The Neutral Zone between Kuwait and Saudi Arabia, the Sultanate of Muscat and Oman, Abu Dhabi, reserves which, though smaller, are of international significance."[24]

In the long run, it may be anticipated that new sources of energy will be opened up through such possibilities as development of means for recovering oil from shale and in the exploitation of nuclear power. Despite these future developments, however, the U.S.S.R.'s leading journal on international economic problems has estimated that the world demand for crude oil and natural gas will continue to rise steadily at least through the year 2000.[25] Furthermore, estimates have been prepared of petroleum resources and production on a world-wide basis to the year 2000; the Soviet projections envision a rise in Middle East oil production, not counting Algeria and wealthy Libyan deposits, by six times since 1965, compared with a Soviet bloc production increase for the same period of only four times. The Soviet writer again stressed the crucial importance of Middle East petroleum on a world scale by concluding that the region's crude oil production, again excluding Libya and Algeria, will reach 2.2 billion tons, more than double his estimate for Soviet oil production in the year 2000.

Estimated Growth in Production and Reconnoitered Supplies of Oil in Capitalist Countries
(in million tons)

	1960	1965	1970	1980	2000
Production of oil	931	1,234	1,600	2,550	3,500-3,700
Reconnoitered supply at year end (oil and gas sources)	37,500	44,000	50,000	64,000	90,000

According to our calculations, by the year 2000, 4,600-4,950 million tons of oil will be produced from the world's oil deposits, of which those countries already within the socialist system will produce 1,100-1,250 million tons. The Soviet Union by that time will produce, it appears, not less than 1,000-1,150 million tons. . . .

The share of countries of Near and Middle East in oil production of countries now belonging to the capitalist system, in all likelihood, will increase by the year 2,000 to 57 to 62 percent (in 1965 33 percent). The countries of Africa in the period 1980-2000 will provide 7.5 to 9 percent of oil production of the capitalist world (in 1965 8.5 percent). The share of Latin America by the year 2000 will decrease to 15-16 percent (in 1965 19.4 percent), while US to 9-10 percent (in 1965 31 percent).

The proportion of countries presently in the socialist system will by the year 2000 reach about 24-27 percent of the total world oil production as opposed to 18 percent in 1965.[26]

The Soviet Union's prospects for "third Baku" in western Siberia now appear more modest, when compared with such a forecast of world petroleum resources and crude oil production by a responsible Soviet economist.

The case for a deficient Soviet petroleum industry must necessarily remain on a conjectural basis, since there are no reliable means available in the West to gauge the adequacy of the Soviet Union's petroleum production to meet future requirements. These needs must satisfy domestic consumption; export to Western capitalist states in exchange for advanced technology and hard currency; export to other members of the Soviet bloc; and deliveries to underdeveloped countries, as determined by Party economic planners. Due to the contingent nature of production goal fulfillment within the Soviet Union's central planning system, it would seem that the potential of the U.S.S.R.'s developing petroleum industry to meet projected requirements must even remain conjectural to Soviet economic planners.

Against reports that have described continuing problems in such areas as petroleum planning, development, production, distribution, and refining, coupled with indications of rising petroleum requirements in the Soviet bloc, it is easy to see why the Middle East's vast, viable resources may be increasingly viewed in Moscow as a potential reserve supply to accommodate the goals outlined in Soviet long-range planning.

The abundance of Soviet oil and natural gas resources, tempered by economic deficiencies and confronted by rising petroleum demand, relate to the Soviet Union's competitive position vis-à-vis Middle East petroleum.

Case for a Competitive Industry

An apparently contradictory view of the capacity of the U.S.S.R.'s petroleum industry stems from indications that the Soviet Union's present status as marketing rival of Middle East crude oil and natural gas exporting states is likely to continue into the future indefinitely.

● **The Soviet Union's Position as Natural Competitor of Middle East Petroleum-Exporting Countries.** Western appraisals of Soviet motivation toward Middle East oil and natural gas vary widely, from the view that the Soviet Union's increasing involvement in the region's petroleum industry is a screen for political aggression, to that which sees only ordinary capitalist competition.[27] Likely to affect Moscow's interest in the Middle East is the matter of whether the U.S.S.R. is itself a competitor of the petroleum-exporting countries of that region. There are indications that she is.

By virtue of the aggregate petroleum resources of the Caucasus, Volga-Ural Central Asian, and Siberian regions together, the U.S.S.R. is today, as already noted, the world's second largest producer of crude oil and natural gas. Furthermore, whereas U.S. reserves are dwindling, the Soviet Union has vast, unexploited oil and gas fields, which, in theory, could make Moscow the world's largest producer.[28] The appearance of Soviet petroleum in foreign trade with both Communist and capitalist states is, in itself, indicative of Moscow's natural economic rivalry with Middle East petroleum exporting countires. Increasing Soviet initiatives for exporting additional petroleum to Western European markets and Japan, which are served primarily by Middle East production, suggest an intention to continue in a competitive role vis-a-vis the oil and natural gas industry of the region to the south.

In the late 1950s the U.S.S.R. first embarked upon a major oil export program, making inroads into West European markets by offering cut rates on crude oil and maintaining prices at levels that have been even cheaper than her own captive market in Eastern Europe was obliged to pay.[29]   The Soviet objective has appeared to be the acquisition of hard currency and Western industrial equipment,[30] while, it would seem, attaining the political advantages implicit in becoming a major supplier of West European and Japanese petroleum demand.

Steel pipe obtained by the Soviet "oil offensive" went toward construction of *Druzhba,* the Friendship Pipeline, to carry crude oil from the U.S.S.R. to COMECON partners Poland, East Germany, Czechoslovakia, and Hungary in the early 1960s. In view of expanding Soviet crude oil shipments to the Middle East's customers of Western Europe, the U.S.S.R. could, perhaps, envision extension of the *Druzhba* from Eastern Europe to capitalist clients. Such a development was inferred by an American critic of the Western oil industry, when he noted that the Friendship Pipeline "would bring Soviet crude to the edge of Western Europe."[31]

Another observer has suggested that Russia's oil export plans may begin increasingly to shift, as is occurring in natural gas agreements,[32] from bloc countries to West European markets, as a result of Moscow's search for capital investment to develop her forbidding Siberian energy region.[33] With respect to the substance of such an objective in broad Soviet strategy, it seems appropriate to consider the doctrine of "peaceful coexistence," which, on the one hand, stresses the importance of socialist trade with capitalist states, and, on the other hand, warns of the dangers inherent in such contacts with the capitalist world:

> It should be noted that some of the contacts established by Western countries with the socialist world system only seem to be prompted by genuine economic motives, while actually being designed to serve unsavory political ends. Considerations of economic advantage are thus interwoven with schemes aimed at undermining peaceful coexistence. The decisive factors always are the concrete content, the conditions, the tangible significance and the foreseeable consequences of the relations in question. Whatever the motives and ultimate aims

of one or another set of capitalists and bourgeois politicians in establishing economic contacts between the world systems, only those can hope to succeed who sincerely seek peaceful co-operation.[34]

It is significant that Communist ideologists feel compelled to point out the "risks" of trading with capitalists:

Co-operation between the world systems ("socialist" and "capitalist") must necessarily stop short of the point where it might jeopardize the victory of socialism in the economic competition, the realization of the principles of peaceful coexistence, the advance of the newly free countries in the struggle of the working people in the industrialized capitalist countries. It cannot be carried to a point where the sovereignty of the socialist states and their freedom of action in one or another sphere are jeopardized; where production or its principal branches would be tied to capitalist partners for a prolonged period of time resulting in loss of independence. Nor should co-operation impinge adversely on areas of the economy of decisive importance from the standpoint of the security and viability of the socialist countries. Lastly, it cannot be allowed to lead to developments on the world capitalist market which would run counter to the principles of socialist foreign policy.[35]

A Soviet objective of developing such trade with "hostile capitalism" to gain Western technology and hard currency for developing Siberian petroleum resources is, in fact, quite consistent with current Marxist-Leninist ideology: ". . . promotion of progress in science and technology is the internationalist duty of the socialist countries, a precondition of the political and economic victory of socialism over capitalism on a worldwide scale."[36]

The Soviet Union's foreign economic policy of building up crude oil exports to the Middle East's petroleum market countries of Western Europe became a source of particular interest with respect to Soviet Middle East policy during the Arab-Israeli crisis of 1967. A number of reports in responsible Western periodicals noted that, in the aftermath of the six-day war, the Soviet Union, while strongly supporting the Arab boycott on oil deliveries to countries in Western Europe, stepped up her own marketing efforts among the Middle East's own clients in that region.[37] Moscow has also recently appeared as competitor of Arab natural gas exports; she has reached beyond her Brotherhood Pipeline ties with COMECON (also CMEA) customers of Eastern Europe to hard-currency markets in Western Europe, allegedly arousing resentment from a rival marketer on the North African littoral.[38]

Meanwhile, the U.S.S.R. has also been looking eastward with the aim of exporting, on a permanent basis, both crude oil and natural gas to another Middle East petroleum client — Japan. Negotiations with Japan have persistently sought arrangements for the latter to build a crude oil pipeline across the vast distance from Tyumen in western Siberia to the Pacific port of Nakhodka.[39] In addition, the U.S.S.R. wants Japan to buy Soviet gas after building a gas pipeline across Sakhalin Island and under the Sakhalin Straits,[40] and also to buy liquified natural gas via ship from northern Sakhalin. Yet, as we have seen, the Soviet bloc has already undertaken to import Middle East crude oil from countries such as Iran, Egypt, Algeria, Libya, Iraq, and Syria. The Soviet Union has contracted for long-term Iranian gas, Iraqi crude oil, and, through similar negotiations, may expand oil importation from the region by future arrangements for Iranian and perhaps Arab oil from the Persian Gulf via the axis of the Soviet-Iranian natural gas pipeline or Soviet tankers.

Thus, the U.S.S.R., apparently perceiving its position as competitor of the petroleum-exporting states of the Middle East, has been taking steps to undermine that region's hold on its traditional petroleum markets in Western Europe and Japan, in order to increase exports of crude oil and natural gas through its delivery facilities in exchange for needed hard currency and Western technology. Such a trade pattern, indeed, would appear to complement the optimistic declarations concerning vast crude oil and natural gas discoveries of the Siberian "third Baku" since the middle 1960s and in 1970.

There is a case, then, to challenge the earlier arguments for a deficient Soviet petroleum industry, as Soviet plans appear to anticipate continuation of its present competition with the Middle East and North Africa, and, through new, long-term export arrangements, to acquire a significantly increased competitive stature in future energy commerce as a rival of the Middle East.

The Soviet "Petroleum Paradox" Defined

In attempting to appraise the nature of Soviet interest in Middle East petroleum, which has given rise to policies apparently aimed at eroding Western influence and creating conditions favorable for entry of the U.S.S.R. as a participant in the region's industry, this study has placed attention upon a Soviet "petroleum paradox." This seeming contradiction, reflected by a discrepancy between current assessments, respectively, of a deficient, or a competitive, Soviet oil and natural gas industry, appears to be relevant to the Soviet Union's interest in the world's strongest petroleum industry, that of the neighboring Middle East.

We can conclude that, since the Soviet Union's industry appears to be inadequate to meet foreseeable requirements of the Soviet bloc, as defined by existing commitments, an increasing and unfettered access to Middle East crude oil and natural gas takes on strategic, or long-range, importance for the U.S.S.R. Since Soviet economic planners have prepared the basis for vastly increased export programs involving clients of COMECON, Western Europe, and Japan, the Middle East oil and natural gas exporting countries will continue indefinitely in a rival marketing role for the same listed customers. Obviously, the U.S.S.R. cannot be both deficient and competitive; she must be one or the other.

The relevance of Middle East petroleum, then, seems to be established in accordance with the contradictory alternatives of Moscow's petroleum paradox. However significant this conclusion may be in its broad justification for Soviet interest in Middle East petroleum, it would seem to provide an unhappily vague evaluation as long as the petroleum paradox persists without clarification.

Moscow's petroleum paradox is a function, it would seem, of three elements: an abundance of energy resources, increasing demand represented by growing domestic needs and foreign markets, and a deficient economic system unable to cope with the problems of short-range and long-range petroleum requirements. The paradox, then, is structured upon a scarcity, or inadequacy, not of reserves, nor of markets, but of economic viability and petroleum productivity.

Notes

1. Walter Laqueur, *The Soviet Union and the Middle East* (New York: Frederick A. Praeger, 1959), p. vii.

2. S.G. Gorshkov, "Razvitiye sovetskogo voennomorskogo iskusstva" ("Development of Soviet Naval Art of War"), *Morskoy sbornik (Navy Journal)*, No. 2, 1967.

3. "Soviets Bank on 'Third Baku,' " *The Oil and Gas Journal,* April 11, 1966, p. 64.

4. "There is so much oil [near Tyumen] " says Nesterov, "that they are leaving the little deposits and going after the big ones. In the United States a field that contains only 200,000 tons of oil is considered good," he remarks. "Here a deposit of 15 million tons is not deemed profitable."

". . . If you gather the United States' reserves of natural gas in one spot they would total perhaps 8 trillion cubic meters," comments Nesterov, who has visited Texas and California. In the Tyumen region the Urengoi deposit alone has supplies estimated at between 5 trillion and 8 trillion cubic meters. In the north we have already opened up deposits reaching 10 trillion cubic meters, and we have yet to survey another 30 trillion." (C. Saikowski, "Siberan Boom Town," *Christian Science Monitor,* September 17, 1972, p. B-3. Quoted by permission from *The Christian Science Monitor,* ©1972, The Christian Science Publishing Society. All rights reserved.

5. S.V. Goryunov, as quoted in "Soviets Bank on 'Third Baku,' " p. 64.

6. T. Honta, "Some Problems in the Development of the Oil and Gas Industry in Ukraine," *Kommunist ukrainy,* January, 1967, pp. 9-11. Trans. *Digest of Soviet Ukrainian Press,* PROLOG (April, 1967), pp. 10-11.

7. V.A. Bugrov and N.P. Smirnov, *Analiz ekonomicheskoy effektivnosti novoy tekhniki i tekhnologii v gobyche nefti (An Analysis of the Economic Effectiveness of New Technology and Equipment in the Production of Petroleum)* (Moscow: Nedra Press, 1966), p. 1

8. "Russian Energy: Bring the Gift in Barrels," *Economist,* September 23, 1967, p. 1129.

9. Paul Wohl, "Soviet Investment Search Ties Up East European Bloc," *Christian Science Monitor,* February 15, 1967, p. 6. Quoted by permission from *The Christian Science Monitor,* ©1967, The Christian Science Publishing Society. All rights reserved.

10. Yu. Belyayev, "The Economy of the CEMA Member-Countries in the New Five-Year Plan," *Kommunist,* No. 8, May, 1967, pp. 98-107. Trans. by Joint Publications Research Services, Department of Commerce, Washington, D.C., No. 41, 638 (June 29, 1967), pp. 81-82.

11. R. Andreasyan, "The Arab East: Clash with Oil Imperialism," *World Economics and International Relations,* No. 3, p. 113.

12. "Oilfields in Siberia Lost Many Workers," New York *Times,* June 9, 1967, p. 17.

13. C. Saikowski, "Siberian Boom Town," *Christian Science Monitor,* September 17, 1972, p. B-3.

14. "Our successes in the development of chemistry could have been considerable. In a number of Krays and oblasts of the RSFSR, the plan for capital investments and building and assembly work in the development of the chemical and oil-refining industries over the first six months of this year was not fulfilled." *"Udarny front semiletki"* ("The Shock Front of the Seven-Year Plan"), *Pravda,* July 11, 1964, p. 1.

15. "For the Needs of Daily Life," *Robitnycha hazeta (Workers' Daily),* October 5, 1966, p. 2. Trans. *Digest of the Soviet Ukrainian Press,* PROLOG, October, 1966, p. 7.

16. Henry Kamm, "Soviet Refinery 'Fulfills' Its Plan: Grozny Processed Same Oil Over and Over to Meet Goal," New York *Times,* November 18, 1967, p. 5.

17. "Progress in Science is Progress in Production," *Pravda,* November 30, 1966, p. 1. Trans. by Joint Publications Research Service, U.S. Department of Commerce, Washington, D.C., No. 38,972, p. 12.

18. "Waste," *Pravda,* April 28, 1964, p. 3. Trans. by Joint Publications Research Service, U.S. Department of Commerce, Washington, D.C., No. 24,453 (May 1, 1964), pp. 5-6.

19. T. Honta, "How Long Will the Volcanoes Be Active?" *Robitnycha hazeta,* July 10, 1966, p. 3. Trans. *Digest of the Soviet Ukrainian Press,* PROLOG, X, No. 8 (August, 1966), pp. 12-13.

20. "Red Oil: Eastern Europe Fuel Problem Turns Attention to Siberia," *Christian Science Monitor,* February 13, 1967, p. 13. Quoted by permission from *The Christian Science Monitor,* ©1967, The Christian Science Publishing Society. All rights reserved.

21. Frank J. Gardner, "Watching the World," *Oil and Gas Journal,* July 17, 1967, p. 59.

22. "Russian Energy: Bring the Gift in Barrels," *Economist,* September 23, 1967, p. 1130.

23. "Red Oil: Eastern Europe," p. 13. Quoted by permission from *The Christian Science Monitor,* © 1967, The Christian Science Publishing Society. All rights reserved.

24. Tomashpol'skiy, "Mirovoy energeticheskiy balans: problemy posledney treti veka" ("The World Energy Balance: Problems of the Last Third of the Century"), *Mirovaya ekonomika i mezhunarodnye otnosheniya (The World Economy and International Relations),* February, 1967, p. 28.

25. *Ibid.*

26. *Ibid.,* pp. 24-25.

27. "Political gains are just a by-product. Simple economics and a clear need for more oil are the real reasons why the Russians drill deep in the Middle East . . . in the end, it may have no more serious significance than any other competitor's house flag." Edward Hughes, "The Russians Drill Deep in the Middle East," *Fortune* (July, 1968), pp. 102-105. Courtesy of *Fortune* Magazine.

28. Soviet Oil Minister Valentin Shashin, reportedly predicted the U.S.S.R. would surpass the United States in oil production by 1975. ("Soviets Predict Oil Leadership within 4 Years," Reuters from Moscow. *Christian Science Monitor,* January 21, 1971, p. 3.

29. Marshall I. Goldman, "Economic Revolution in the Soviet Union," *Foreign Affairs,* XLV (January, 1967), p. 319.

30. "The nature of the commodities most frequently sought in exchange—steel pipe, tankers, chemical plants, electronic instruments—suggests that the Soviets opened their trade in the West in 1958-59 primarily to secure goods essential to the fulfillment of the goals of the seven-year plan . . . . Crude oil and petroleum products offered Moscow its best opportunity to break into a well-established market by bartering those commodities at attractive prices. The bloc could best acquire the goods to meet its economic needs by adopting that tactic." Michael P. Gehlen, "The Politics of Soviet Foreign Trade," *The Western Political Quarterly,* Vol. XVIII, No. 1 (March, 1965), p. 114.

31. Harvey O'Connor, *World Crisis in Oil* (New York: Monthly Review Press, 1962), p. 391.

32. Discussion of the extension of the trans-Czechoslovakian gas pipeline to service the energy needs of capitalist countries for the long term is presented, for example, in the following: "Soviet Natural Gas for France," *New Times* (Moscow), August, 1971, p. 5 ; and "Russia Pushes Gas Sales in West to Pay for Building 100-Inch Lines from Siberia," *Wall Street Journal,* November 20, 1969, p. 40.

33. "Russia's surplus, after home requirements are met, will not entirely go to its allies. It already has hard-currency customers in Western Europe—France, Italy, Austria, etc.—with whom it might conceivably be doing more business by 1980, especially if the East Europeans should fail meantime to fall in with Russia's investment proposals." "Red Oil: Eastern Europe." p. 13. Quoted by permission from *The Christian Science Monitor,* © 1967, The Christian Science Publishing Society. All rights reserved.

34. Karl-Heinz Domdey, "Economic Contacts between the Socialist and Capitalist, Countries of Europe," *World Marxist Review,* Vol. VIII, No. 9 (September, 1965), pp. 10-13.

35. Ibid.

36. Girey Anisimov, "The Five-Year Plan of the U.S.S.R. and Problems of Science and Technology," *World Marxist Review,* April, 1966, p. 42.

37. "The Soviets have . . . played a part in the charade. They have offered oil at a price to British and other boycotted markets. Soviet traders take a very pragmatic view when the acquisition of foreign exchange is concerned." Erwin D. Canham, "Oil and Politics." *Christian Science Monitor,* July 8, 1967, p. 16. Quoted by permission from *The Christian Science Monitor,* © 1967, The Christian Science Publishing Society. All rights reserved.

"Russia . . . has made an unconfirmed attempt to win oil markets for itself that formerly belonged to the Arabs. The state-controlled refinery, Repesa, has diverted a 60,000-ton tanker to an undisclosed Black Sea port to pick up oil. It had been headed for a port in the Middle East.

From another report it was learned that a 40,000-ton Italian flag tanker was already at the Black Sea port of Tuapse slated to deliver its cargo in Spain. It was asserted that the Russians worked through diplomatic channels to sell its own oil after the Arabs had imposed an embargo." Robert Kearns, "Arab States Fear Loss of Markets," *Journal of Commerce,* June 15, 1967, p. 1.

"The Soviet Union is running an oil sales drive in Western Europe in an effort to take advantage of the embargoes imposed by the Arab countries and the closure of the Suez Canal.

"Importers in several countries have been approached, including the U.K., despite the long-standing British ban on the importation of Russian oil. In the last few days several license applications have been made to the Board of Trade in an effort to get the restriction removed." Christopher Tugendhat, "Russia Pushing Oil Sales in West—U.K. Reviewing Ban," *Financial Times,* June 16, 1967, p. 1.

38. "Behind the Algerian government's abrupt decision to break off talks on the sale of 4.5 billion cubic metres of gas per year to Austria, Italy, Germany, Yugoslavia, and Czechoslovakia lies a major crisis in Algeria's relations with Russia. The Algerians are furious with what they see as a conscious Russian policy of undercutting them in their potential markets so as to force Russian natural gas into central and western Europe. This, the Algerians feel, is hardly appropriate behavior for a country that claims to be a friend of the underdeveloped—and particularly of Algeria." "Algerian Gas: Behind the Row, the Russians," *Economist,* February 4, 1967, p. 433.

39. "The Soviet-Japanese Economic Conference," *New Times,* November 27, 1967, p. 22; and C. Saikowski, "Siberian Boom Town," *Christian Science Monitor,* September 17, 1972, p. B-3.

40. C. Saikowski, "Siberia—Warmer for Japan?" *Christian Science Monitor,* January 20, 1971, p. 1.

A Soviet Future for
Middle East Petroleum?

Resolution of the petroleum paradox would seem to depend
upon rectification of the deficiencies in petroleum production
in order to meet both short- and long-range requirements. As
we have seen, the deficiencies of the economic system, and the
petroleum industry as case in point, were of two categories.
The operational problem, in day-by-day waste and inequities,
results from faulty planning, production, processing, and distribution functions. This type of deficiency is evident in its
effect upon the Soviet capacity to meet short-range requirements: yet, unless corrected, it will work against the ability
to meet long-range needs as well. The other inadequacy is in
the long-range planning, or petroleum developmental function,
of the Soviet economy. This deficiency exacerbates the
problem of meeting long-range petroleum requirements.

Since these operational deficiencies of the U.S.S.R.
petroleum industry apparently cannot be dealt with in order
to permit Soviet petroleum reserves to be translated into short-
range demand satisfaction, Middle East petroleum has been
called upon by the Soviet bloc for oil and natural gas deliv-
ies during the 1970s, permitting the U.S.S.R. to satisfy domestic demands and to retain its present status of marketing

competitor by providing supplies to help meet foreign requirements. Thus, Middle East petroleum resolves the short-range
deficiency of the petroleum paradox by its compensating
function.

While a portion of short-range Soviet exports are serving
to accumulate foreign capital, hard currency, and Western
technology to be applied toward rationalizing the long-range
development of the Soviet petroleum industry, they do not
solve the developmental deficiency of the Soviet economy.
Moscow's petroleum industry is of great importance to the
cause of overall U.S.S.R. and Soviet bloc industrialization and
must, therefore, be developed through sound, long-range planning. Importation of Middle East petroleum on a long-range
basis appears designed to liquidate this deficiency by permitting
the U.S.S.R. to expand its petroleum exports (despite its own
inadequate native production) as a marketing competitor of
the Middle East. In this manner, the Soviet Union can obtain
the wherewithal to develop its broad economy through acquisition of foreign loans, hard currency, and advanced technology. In overcoming this deficiency of the petroleum
paradox, Middle East petroleum is called upon to serve a
corrective function.

Thus, the short- and long-range deficiencies contributing
to the Soviet petroleum paradox are resolved by Soviet bloc
foreign economic planning, using Middle East petroleum as,
respectively, a compensating and a corrective agent. The compensating technique of resolving the short-range deficiencies
through short-range importation of Middle East oil and natural
gas does not call for further elaboration. However, in order to
examine the long-range approach to help liquidate the developmental deficiency of the entire Soviet economy, it is necessary
to deal with strategic economic planning. Here, we have viewed
Soviet interest in Middle East petroleum as a means of gaining
strategic economic dominance over the Middle East. From
the evidence of Soviet policy toward the Middle East, coupled
with the state of the Soviet petroleum industry, it appears that
the U.S.S.R. seeks progressively to move into greater

involvement with the Middle East petroleum industry, ultimately achieving a function as strategic middleman.

An Ideological Formula

A tie has already been established, according to various Soviet writings, between Middle East petroleum and Marxist-Lenninist ideology: ". . . northern Iranian oil . . . [is related to] the world struggle between the forces of democracy and the forces of reaction[1] . . . oil concessions represent . . . the foundation of the entire edifice of Western political influence in the world"[2] . . . and the Middle East region with "the richest oil deposits in the capitalist world . . . is also an extensive zone of the Arab national liberation movement."[3] In the future as well, Soviet strategy can be expected, it seems, to remain attentive to the relevance of Middle East petroleum to a Communist orthodoxy.

While there may be various theories concerning the future of the Communist movement and the forms which political relations between superpowers with conflicting ideologies may assume, this study accepts an authoritative American view that rival global strategies are "ultimately a struggle about how this small planet shall be organized."[4] Furthermore, Soviet strategy, as an amalgam of aims derived from both national interests and ideology, seems to be suitably characterized in one Western appraisal as seeking "to put the West on the final defensive primarily by sheer growth of the Communist system — an international system to include ultimately all states in the world built upon a uniform ideology and led by the Soviet Union."[5] Furthermore, currently espoused Marxist-Leninist ideology appears appropriately to wed recent Soviet policy toward Middle East petroleum with Soviet long-range national aspirations.

World Socialist Planned Economy

> The optimal utilization of the various energy supplies on a world scale will be provided only under conditions of a world socialist planned

economy, and until its establishment, the dissipation of the most powerful energy riches of the planet will not be halted.

— L. Tomashpol'skiy, Moscow, 1967.[6]

In this projection of Soviet ideology the world's richest petroleum region, the Middle East, seems clearly intended for a major role in that future epoch, which envisages a "world socialist planned economy" presumably under the leadership of the pioneer socialist state, the Union of Soviet Socialist Republics. Presumably, intermediate steps would be required to develop the Soviet Union's increasing economic and political activity with the Middle East in a direction toward "socialist relations," within the framework of a world socialist planned economy. Bridging the gap between present reality and such Marxist-Leninist theory would seem to be an international order patterned somewhat after relations existing now within the Soviet bloc. With the latter considered to be a kind of theocratic microcosm, under the predominant rule of the Soviet Union's Party leadership elite, ideologists may perceive the economic relationships encompassed by the Council for Mutual Economic Assistance to be a preliminary model for the world socialist planned economy. A similar parallel may exist between the present concept of pipeline and tanker fuel energy distribution within COMECON member states and the "world energy delivery system" envisaged in Marxist-Leninist doctrine.

World Energy Delivery System

... the insufficiency of energy in certain countries and regions of the world will in large measure be provided by other countries and regions. The world energy delivery system will play an important role in this regard.

— L. Tomashpol'skiy, Moscow, 1967.[7]

The Soviet concept of a world energy delivery system, which would serve the world socialist planned economy, can be perceived, it would seem, to evolve from present commercial relationships providing crude oil and natural gas resources of petroleum-exporting countries to consumer states. In this regard, theorists such as Tomashpol'skiy would seem to anticipate the eventual incorporation of the petroleum riches of the

103

Middle East into such a Soviet-dominated world energy delivery system.

Steps toward achievement of such a system could be expected to be built upon present and planned Soviet-Middle East relationships; the U.S.S.R. is now participating in exploration and production of crude oil, and, along with other members of the Soviet bloc, has contracted to import oil or natural gas on long-term barter arrangements. Future Soviet-Middle East relations could result in the U.S.S.R. undertaking preliminary roles in the region's petroleum industry, and, ultimately, that of strategic middleman, leading in the general direction of a world energy delivery system.

The "Paradox" Resolved? Soviet Roles in Middle East Petroleum

The Communist Party of the Soviet Union will continue, as acknowledged by one of its leading officials, to exercise its leadership role in Party and governmental affairs, determining suitable means for advancing the cause of Communism while accommodating the aspirations expressed in ideology to realities bearing upon the Soviet Union's national interests.[8]

Preliminary Phase

In efforts to realize the ideological projections of economist Tomashpol'skiy concerning a world socialist planned economy and world energy delivery system, Soviet economic policy makers can be expected to adopt interim measures in matters involving the U.S.S.R. with the Middle East petroleum industry. Progressive roles, which would tend to move toward greater Soviet influence with the petroleum-exporting countries, seem to include the following: producer, importer, broker, and strategic middleman.

The U.S.S.R. is already participating as producer of Middle East oil, although not in the traditional capitalist sense. Moscow became involved in exploration and production through its export of technicians and oil-drilling equipment, beginning with

Algeria, Egypt, and Syria in the late 1950s, in accordance with the new policy of aid and trade with countries of the Middle East. We have noted the subsequent expansion of Soviet initiatives in the realm of petroleum relations. Negotiations with major oil-exporting countries were undertaken in earnest by 1966, when arrangements were worked out between Moscow and Teheran for joint exploration efforts in the promising Caspian area of northern Iran, outside the area of the Western-owned consortium. Subsequently, toward the end of 1967, the U.S.S.R. reached an accord with Iraq, which provided for Soviet exploration and production operations in fields outside the area being worked by the Western major companies of Iraq Petroleum Company and, in 1972, contributed to its nationalization by a friendship treaty and a major investment in Iraqi oil production. It can be anticipated that, if trade relations with other major oil-exporting countries of the Middle East tend to expand, the U.S.S.R. will reach additional agreements with those governments for development operations. Whether or not Soviet negotiations with the Middle East lead to conventional concession arrangements, the very participation in oil development and production operations creates the beginnings of an economic interdependency between the oil-producing nations and the U.S.S.R. The extent to which the Soviet Union becomes involved in further petroleum development in the region would seem to stem in large measure from her capacity to offer satisfactory barter terms to Middle East producers, who determine the course they will follow toward national development and industrialization.

The U.S.S.R. and other members of the Soviet bloc have, as already noted, contracted to become importers of Middle East petroleum. In 1966, the U.S.S.R. became the first member of the bloc to contract for the purchase of Middle East petroleum — natural gas, which Iran had been flaring, unable to realize any economic gain. The long-term nature of the Soviet-Iranian gas pipeline contract, which promises to aid development of steel, zinc, and lead industries of Iran, and to provide arms, suggests that economic relations between

Moscow and Teheran will require increasing co-ordination of high-level economic planning throughout the 1970s and beyond. The large capital investments in such a pipeline project suggests extension of gas deliveries toward the end of the century and opens the opportunity, as already suggested, for installation of a parallel crude oil line. Soviet arrangements for joint oil exploration in the Caspian region have indicated the possibility that the U.S.S.R. will purchase oil that is discovered there. Furthermore, Russia's agreement with Iraq late in 1967 and again in 1972, which indicated Moscow as a future purchaser of Iraqi crude, established the perspective for a probable further expansion of Soviet Middle East petroleum imports in the future.

Negotiations by other members of the Soviet bloc for the import of Middle East crude oil give credence to estimates already noted that COMECON is losing its self-sufficiency in oil and must look increasingly to Middle East supplies. Long-term barter contracts that have been concluded, as in the Soviet-Iranian natural gas pipeline agreement, between East European Communist countries and Iraq National Oil Company (INOC), National Iranian Oil Company (NIOC), Kuwait National Petroleum Company (KNPC), Saudi Arabia's Petromin, and governments of other Gulf producers, as well as Libya, Algeria, Egypt, and Syria, indicate a comprehensive new dimension in Middle East petroleum-marketing operations. Thus, the Soviet Union, both directly and indirectly as predominant power in the Soviet bloc and COMECON, is becoming increasingly involved in Middle East petroleum exports through the next decades. To the extent that the producing states become committed in their national economic planning to the exchange of petroleum for industrial and military equipment under the terms of these long-term barter contracts, Middle East states are becoming, at least in part, economically dependent upon the U.S.S.R. and other members of the Soviet bloc. Whether the Soviet Union can succeed in developing such a partial dependency into a one-sided commercial relationship to the ultimate disadvantage of the Middle East states will result from the determination by producing states of the course they wish to follow.

The Soviet Union has already hinted that it might take the opportunity to become a broker for Middle East petroleum. In her negotiations with Iraq concerning exploration and production of certain oilfields both inside and outside the region exploited by Iraq Petroleum Company, Moscow indicated, as already noted, its willingness to find markets for oil produced.

The growing Soviet tanker fleet may well be able to facilitate such a role as marketer of Arab and Iranian oil, in a further encroachment upon the West's formerly secure preserve of Middle East petroleum operations. Such a prospect provides an opportunity, particularly in recent years, for exploiting differences between foreign oil companies and host governments, eager to obtain a greater share of oil revenues.

The national companies and ministries of Middle East oil-exporting countries welcome opportunities for expanding their operations and diversifying their role, gaining increased profits, and exploiting a growing proportion of oil fields vis-à-vis the Western operating companies. Therefore, the Soviet Union can continue to expect enthusiastic response to reasonable overtures for Soviet proposals to act as broker for crude oil, perhaps ready to provide investment in new port facilities in support of such operations. Soviet tankers have been under contract with national Middle East companies for crude oil purchases to deliver to the Soviet Union's own East-of-Suez clients, which include India, Ceylon, North Vietnam, and Japan. The Soviet agreement already noted with British Petroleum (BP) permitting Soviet tankers to load Abu Dhabi crude for delivery to Japan in exchange for providing BP clients in Europe with Soviet crude, suggests that Moscow could, through such a broker role, perhaps even withstand the indefinite closure of the Suez Canal without serious hindrance in service to its customers. Thus, while offering the Middle East's national companies the opportunity of producing oil for Soviet clients, the U.S.S.R. may ultimately acquire a position to bargain with these companies for low-priced oil which Moscow might substitute for its own costlier deliveries to industrialized or developing countries.

Such a broker role could become important to national petroleum interests in the Middle East and tend to institutionalize a measure of economic dependency upon the U.S.S.R.

Ultimate Phase

In the long term of several decades, the U.S.S.R. may move toward a theoretical strategic economic dominance over the Middle East, dispelling the seeming contradictions of the petroleum paradox, through a function of strategic middleman. At the same time, Moscow would appear to be proceeding in a logical development of commercial activities already indicated in the producer, importer, and broker roles. While the previous examples would, in the Marxist-Lenist conceptual systems for world socialist planning and world energy delivery, be considered primitive stages, the U.S.S.R. as strategic middleman could become an operational embodiment of both systems.

Recent developments already point to Moscow's potential for such a middleman role, based upon new petroleum trade patterns emerging between the Middle East and its new Soviet bloc customers, superimposed over Moscow's recent planning for its own petroleum export operations westward and eastward. These plans seem to complement the economic rationale outlined in the last chapter, which explained Soviet interest in Middle East petroleum in terms of a growing Soviet bloc demand for petroleum along with uncertain prospects for development of its Soviet "raw material appendage," coupled with the Soviet Union's rival position vis-à-vis Middle East petroleum-exporting states.

The barter basis, upon which the new Middle East long-term petroleum export agreements with the U.S.S.R. and states of Eastern Europe are being established, would appear to be a viable element[9] in any larger scheme to create a Soviet strategic middleman role. The 1966 U.S.S.R.-Iran natural gas agreement and 1972 oil agreement between Moscow and Baghdad suggest a model for the advocacy of yet closer economic ties in the future between the Soviet Union and other Middle East petroleum capitals.[10]

There is an apparent irony in earlier Soviet plans for the nearly 1,000-mile Soviet-Iranian natural gas pipeline to the border of the U.S.S.R. to be extended northward to the Caucasus, "one of the largest natural gas regions of the U.S.S.R."[11] Evolution of a pipeline system of strategic proportions is also suggested in the agreement with Afghanistan for a natural gas pipeline to deliver fuel to Central Asia, where the U.S.S.R. found its richest resources . . . fields estimated to contain about half the Soviet Union's potential natural gas reserves, while the U.S.S.R. boasted "about one-third of the world's known gas reserves."[12] By 1964, this Bukhara wealth was flowing into a pipeline to the Ural region, reputed to become "the largest gas pipeline in the world."[13] At present, this Central Asian gas, termed "the most economical of all types of fuel in the nation,"[14] is already available to the Moscow-Leningrad region by pipeline, a distance of over 1,700 miles.[15] In addition, the promising new fields of western Kazakhstan, just being developed, are programmed to contribute to the gas pipeline system to the north.[16]

The recent series of oil barter agreements between Eastern Europe and the major producing countries of the Middle East, viewed together with indications of developing Soviet imports from Iraq, Iran, and other Middle East states, seem to correlate with growing signs of an approaching oil deficit condition within the Soviet bloc.

Having considered the outlook for crude oil and natural gas development within the U.S.S.R., and observed an expanding pattern of crude oil imports from the Middle East to the Soviet bloc, we turn to the export side of a "potential strategic middleman."

Soviet oil export policy, which, since exploitation of the Volga-Ural "second Baku" in the late 1950s, has led to expanding crude deliveries for barter to Eastern Europe through "Druzhba," the Friendship Pipeline, and for hard currency and advanced technology to Western Europe by tanker, apparently continues despite prospects of inadequate production in the Soviet bloc. Meanwhile, Soviet natural gas has been flowing through "Bratsvo," the Brotherhood Pipeline, into Eastern Europe. Continuation of Moscow's oil-export policy, which seemed to be borne out by reported efforts of the U.S.S.R. during the 1967 Arab oil boycott to penetrate further into the Middle East's markets of Western Europe, would appear to comprise the export side of a potential "middleman system" to be administered by GOSPLAN (State Economic Planning Committee) in Moscow.

Negotiations carried out by the U.S.S.R. indicate a clear intention to expand her exports of crude oil and natural gas further, which, significantly, it seems were conducted during the precise period when she and her COMECON fellow members were carrying on other negotiations with the Middle East for the import of oil and gas. Thus, Moscow's agreement with Czechoslovakia in 1966 for the latter to build an additional crude oil pipeline from Russia, originating in the recently discovered Siberian Ob' River fields, and her negotiations with Japan for construction of another crude pipeline from the same region to the eastern Siberian coast suggest a planned oil-middleman role. Similarly, successful Soviet negotiations with West European countries, including Austria, Italy, West Germany, and France, as well as continuing discussions with Japan, to arrange for construction of Soviet natural gas pipelines in exchange for deferred payment by fuel deliveries, tend to round out a strategic conception approximating the Marxist-Leninist blueprint for a future world energy delivery system.[17]

The evolution of such a strategic middleman role in the petroleum trade could perhaps be realized over a period of decades, during which Middle East exports from the national sector of the countries' petroleum industries would steadily be expanded toward the Soviet bloc and the U.S.S.R. The operations of Western producing interests in the Middle East would not necessarily appear to be immediately affected, although, in the long run, an expansion in Soviet sales of oil and natural gas, partly of Middle East origin, might destabilize prices on the world market. However, the rising petroleum demand that is predicted for "Free World" and Communist states would presumably tend to counter such instability in that market. Such a Soviet strategic middleman for petroleum would, of course, limit the prospects Western companies may entertain for developing the national sector of the Middle East's petroleum-exporting countries.

Whether there would be an evolution toward such a "world energy delivery system" within the framework of a "world socialist planned economy" will depend, it would seem, upon at least two factors: will evolving trade patterns in Middle East petroleum be restrained by "unfavorable developments" in relations between the Soviet Union and the United States? And, seemingly of primary importance, will the states of the Middle East, Japan, and the countries of Western Europe perceive the development of such trade patterns to be in their own best interests?

Lessons from the Soviet Bloc Experience[18]

If the U.S.S.R. does seek a dominant economic position in the Middle East, as concluded above, and, in turn, a role as predominant superpower in the region, she could be expected to turn attention to the problem of political stability. She would be faced with consolidating her economic dominance over states that have shown they have a limited capacity to cooperate with one another and do not relish hegemony by outside powers.

The Middle East provides a range of problems that Moscow has not experienced in establishing and preserving its political and economic predominance over the Soviet bloc and COMECON. In order to establish and preserve her economic dominance in the Middle East, the U.S.S.R. would have to offer, it would seem, an economic relationship which that region would perceive both to be advantageous and to respect the sovereignty and political independence of Middle East states. The task would be the greater, when compared with the conditions prevailing in the Soviet bloc, because Moscow would not, in the foreseeable future, be able to install reliable Communist or Socialist parties in the Middle East countries, as she has generally been able to do in Eastern Europe.

It would be doubtful as well that the U.S.S.R. could expect to impose, without opposition, a major military presence as a means of giving support to any Moscow-oriented regimes in the region. The degree of success the U.S.S.R. might expect to achieve in becoming predominant superpower in the area would probably depend upon the resolve of the United States to stand in the way of a Soviet southward expansion, whether economic, political, or military. Equally, or perhaps more significant to Soviet future plans in the Middle East, are attitudes of the states themselves and how they perceive their own relations with the U.S.S.R. and the Soviet bloc.

Soviet progress toward a greater position of economic influence in the region will depend, it would seem, upon the image of friendship and co-operation the Soviet Union will be able to maintain. As in the past, she will attempt to appear as "protector against imperialism" Thus, a number of months before the 1967 Arab-Israeli crisis, when the U.S.S.R. gave the Arabs only vocal and diplomatic support, a Soviet political writer, speaking of the tenth anniversary of the Anglo-French-Israeli intervention in Suez, boasted of Soviet resolve in behalf of the Arabs:

> At a time of dire need, Egypt had the solid backing of the U.S.S.R. The socialist world acts as a shield for the oppressed nations, as the guarantor of the independence of developing nations. In the past ten years imperialist dictation has nowhere been manifested with the same force as at Suez. The events of ten years ago demonstrated to all the small and weak nations that they would never be left in the lurch, that there is in the world a force which will never abandon them to the tender mercies of the imperialists.[19]

Despite such reassurances, the apparent lack of substantive Soviet assistance during the 1967 Arab-Israeli War brought Arab criticism.[20] One Arab Minister for External Affairs, and Chairman of the Federal Supreme Council, reportedly expressed bitter views:

> Sheikh Farid, in a recorded interview broadcast on Aden Radio, accused
> Russia of having taken part in a worldwide conspiracy against the Arabs.
> The Soviet attitude in the Middle East War had been inactive and weak,
> and had shattered Arab hopes, he added.[21]

The report went on to say:

> Aden Radio alleged that Taiz, the Yemeni twin capital, had been the
> scene of anti-Soviet demonstrations during the last few days.[22]

In addition to a continuing policy of championing the Arab
cause in the face of apparent setbacks as in Egypt in 1972, the
U.S.S.R. will probably continue to offer declarations in support
of the rights of free nations:

> All countries, big and small, have the same right to respect of their
> sovereignty, independence, and territorial integrity. And nobody has
> the liberty to violate this right.[23]

Faithful to Marxist-Leninist dogma, Soviet publicists can be
expected to stress the "inherent advantages" of relations within the socialist fraternity, in contrast with relations between
capitalist states:

> The mutual relations between the People's Democracies and the Soviet
> Union, and also those between the People's Democracies themselves,
> are founded on absolutely different principles — principles of mutual
> aid and co-operation.[24]

The Party may be expected to continue to refute allegations wherein Western critics have suggested implications for
countries entering into agreements with the U.S.S.R. which serve
to tie together their economies on a long-term basis. The Party's
propaganda has acknowledged criticism of such agreements by
foreigners who question "the innocence" of Soviet motives,
but, as in a commentary in Moscow's journal on international
affairs, appears to avoid the inference that smaller partners to
such agreements are vulnerable to economic blackmail by the
U.S.S.R.:

> The great economic importance of [the "Friendship Pipeline"] is
> indisputable, but has not prevented Agaston [a Swiss "bourgeois
> critic"] from questioning the "purely economic advantages" of the
> pipeline, and casting doubt on the political consequences of its con-
> struction for the Socialist countries in Europe. . . . As for the political
> side of it, the pipeline helps to reinforce the economies of a number
> of Socialist countries in Central and Eastern Europe, thereby also
> strengthening their positions on the international arena.[25]

The U.S.S.R. may hope ultimately to superimpose its own economic planning system over the Middle East, whereby the rationale now applied to COMECON (also CEMA) could be a model for urging petroleum-exporting countries to attain economic plan fulfillment. One Communist ideologist, writing in the Soviet Party Central Committee's official journal, expressed political innuendoes in outlining the integration of these national economies. It is germane to reflect upon the Middle East's petroleum-exporting countries in Moscow's ambitions, as one reads his commentary describing the last five year period (1966-1970) as:

> undoubtedly an important step forward in the further economic development of the CEMA countries, in intensifying their economic and scientific and technical co-operation, and in strengthening positions in the economic competition with the developed capitalist countries. The fraternal countries are now entering into that stage when not only the requirements of the domestic market, but also conscious shaping of the basic branches of industry — taking into account the division of labor and requirements of the scientific and technical revolution — will become one of the decisive factors of their economic progress. Given this situation, the elaboration and realization of new effective forms and methods for international economic activity of CEMA countries are becoming more and more important and require the further pooling of collective efforts.[26]

Presumably the role of indoctrination, as carried out by Communist Party propagandists in seeking East European co-operation within COMECON, would be employed to persuade Middle East petroleum-exporting countries to accept the "international socialist division of labor" concept, and the thesis that "political co-operation among the socialist countries is a necessary prerequisite for . . . solving the most important international problems":

> The international socialist division of labor continues to develop and intensify. New problems arise in its progress along with difficulties. At the CEMA conference of July, 1966, the countries' members reasserted their decision to continue with their efforts to intensify and improve forms of co-operation and increase its effectiveness.
>
> It is very important for the propagandists to explain why political co-operation is necessary and important. The students must understand that the political co-operation among the socialist countries is a necessary prerequisite for the elaboration of a common line and joint activities for solving the most important international problems,

for the successful struggle against imperialist reaction and for peace, socialism, and social progress. Such a co-operation may take a variety of forms. Particularly important, however, are the friendship, co-operation, and mutual aid agreements.[27]

By 1972, the most radical of the Arab countries, Iraq, demonstrated the extent to which Soviet penetration had been successful by reportedly expressing an interest in joining COMECON, the first non-Communist state to seek admission to the economic structure of the Soviet bloc.[28]

Political Rationale for Soviet Economic Dominance

While economic penetration could eventually assume a form of political penetration, other consequences having political overtones could emerge from Soviet economic dominance over the Middle East.

In the sense that the U.S.S.R. looks to trade with the West as a source of hard currency and advanced technology to support plans for modern industrialization,[29] Soviet foreign economic policy seeks to enhance the viability of the state. Soviet petroleum exports to Western Europe have served this purpose; a similar aim is embodied in negotiations to add Japan as a major oil customer and arranging to ship gas to both Western Europe and Japan, as we have seen. Deliveries of Middle East crude to Eastern Europe, and natural gas and crude to the U.S.S.R., all on a barter basis, are making available added increments of energy fuel which can contribute toward satisfaction of domestic needs and export for hard currency or advanced technology in the West. Under a condition of Soviet economic dominance of the Middle East, such procedures might be expected to continue and perhaps to expand, making possible greater Soviet oil and gas trade to the West, with significant increases of hard currency.

Furthermore, if the U.S.S.R. should become dominant in economic relations with the Middle East to the point of pressuring oil-exporting countries to redirect their East European exports through Soviet transport facilities, the Soviet Union could again become East Europe's sole oil and gas supplier, with the political connotation that goes with such an arrangement.

Soviet political rationale concerning relations with the Middle East can be expected to be shaped by the marked dependency of the West upon that region. (See Figures 2, 3, and 4.) For example, Britain not only relies heavily on the Middle East for supply of her energy needs; she also has large capitalist investments which assist in her balance of payments; has a sizeable tanker fleet, 15 percent of those engaged in oil trade, providing significant earnings and assisting in the balance of payments; and still retains sovereignty and base rights in the Middle East.[30]

The U.S.S.R. is aware of France's interests in the Middle East: the import of the preponderance of her oil supplies, certain capital holdings in Middle East petroleum production, and her large number of tankers, 4.5 percent of the world fleet, engaged in oil trade.[31]

Soviet Russia knows the interests of other West European countries in the Middle East: West Germany, Italy, the Netherlands, and Belgium import significant quantities of crude oil; West Germany, Italy, the Netherlands, and Spain have capital investments in petroleum production; Norway, with 15 percent of the world's tankers, and several other West European countries, have a stake in petroleum trade.[32] Japan's growing economic involvement with the Middle East, including its major dependence upon Persian Gulf oils, has strong implications of a political and strategic nature.[33]

Finally, the U.S.S.R. is aware of U.S. interests in the region: control of the largest proportion of Middle East oil production; likely growing dependent upon the importation of Middle East oil in the near future;[34] maintenance of the Sixth Fleet in the Mediterranean and the Seventh Fleet in the Indian Ocean; air supply to U.S. installations in Ethiopia and the Persian Gulf; and U.S. interest in Western Europe's continued access to Middle East petroleum,[35] fueling the vast strategic forces stretching from the heart of Europe to the far corners of

Asia,[36] and in the free movement of Western naval and maritime forces in the area.

While Soviet political-economic planners may well be concerned with their own rising demand for petroleum products, Moscow's strategists concerned with the Middle East can be expected to keep a close watch upon the accelerating demand for oil in Western Europe and the United States, despite new finds as in Alaska and the North Sea. For strategic reasons, it could be important to Party aspirations for the U.S.S.R. to be in a position progressively to deny Western Europe and the United States access to Middle East petroleum. Particularly, it would seem to be a matter of interest to the Kremlin that the Middle East's petroleum resources appear to be growing more important to Western Europe and the United States in the period of the 1970s and beyond, just as the region's petroleum becomes more significant to the U.S.S.R. and the Soviet bloc. Estimates suggest that both the United States, whose oil production capacity now is three-quarters of her current requirements, and Western Europe, already heavily dependent upon the Middle East, will be inclined to look to that region with continuing urgency through the coming decades.[37]

Soviet writers have frequently expressed a keen awareness of the strategic significance of the Middle East region over the years, in terms that unfailingly recognized the importance of its petroleum wealth. In the late 1940s, the question of oil in northern Iran had "in our time become one of the vital questions of international politics, and the struggle ensuing with respect to it is a part of the world struggle between the forces of democracy and the forces of reaction."[38] In the mid-1950s, it was noted that "possession of the oil of the Middle East gives the imperialist monopolies what is in effect the opportunity to dominate the economic and political life of the countries in this part of the world."[39] At the beginning of the 1960s, oil concessions were seen to represent "the foundation of the entire edifice of Western political influence in the world, of all military bases and aggressive blocs. If this foundation cracks, the entire edifice may begin to totter and then come tumbling down."[40]

In the wake of the Arab-Israeli War of 1967, a similar appreciation for the importance of Middle East petroleum appeared in the context of recent heightened tensions in the area: ". . . an important junction of world communications, [which] has the richest oil deposits in the capitalist world and is also an extensive zone of the Arab national liberation movement."[41] "Oil is the most effective weapon the Arabs have. Together with Iran they account for nearly 75 percent of the total world exports. With Iran and North Africa, the Middle East possesses three-quarters of the world's oil reserves. Moreover, its oil is of top quality."[42] A writer on foreign economic relations expressed the significance of Middle East petroleum in a geopolitical sense:

> . . . the oil concessions serve as the basis of the political influence of the West in this strategically important region, located on the shortest routes from the North Atlantic to the basins of the Indian and Pacific Oceans, at the southern borders of the Soviet Union. It is not surprising that in the Near East any conflict over oil takes on a significance extending far beyond the limits of the dispute about the share of incomes.[43]

The vulnerability of future U.S. oil supplies as a result of Soviet subversive potential in the Middle East continues as a theme of the U.S.S.R.'s public media at the very time of apparent increasing U.S.–Soviet understanding at the 1972 Moscow summit. Referring to the growing U.S. need to import half of its oil by 1980-85, a Moscow dispatch was noted to have stated that up to a third of such imports

> ". . . will be carried from the Middle East to the United States – but the scale of the national liberation movement of the peoples of Asia and the Middle East is inflicting blows on the predatory plans of the American monopolists."[44]

If the U.S.S.R. attains a position as predominant superpower in the Middle East, she would appear to gain a capability, through developing petroleum relations suggested in this study, to apply economic, political, and perhaps military pressure throughout the region in support of any aggressive campaign she might choose to undertake. Furthermore, noting the increasing dependency Western capitalist countries appear to be

118

developing for external sources of petroleum such as those of the world's richest producing region, the Soviet leadership would seem to have the capability of hampering or halting the flow of Middle East petroleum westward and to Japan. One Arab leader, just prior to the 1967 crisis with Israel, had asserted that precisely such a capability was Moscow's main objective in the Middle East.[45]

Conclusions

This study has reached an evaluation of Soviet interest in Middle East petroleum, describing it in terms of a long-range, strategic motivation based upon development of a comprehensive pattern of petroleum import and export trade.

Typical of long-term planning under the Soviet system is the significant role of Marxist-Leninist ideology, pointing the general direction for Soviet political and economic planning. The Communist Party of the Soviet Union through its leadership elite is being guided by the goal of establishing a world socialist planned economy, embracing a world energy delivery system that could well be supported by the Middle East in conjunction with Soviet resources.

This Soviet strategy contains elements of Czarist expansionism, which aspired to achieve access to the warm waters of the Mediterranean and of the Persian Gulf; it reflects the imperialistic ambitions of world Communism; and it exhibits the economic pragmatism of a superpower determined to organize the necessary resources to support its unhurried world aspirations.[46]

During the course of Soviet relations with the Middle East, petroleum appeared as a factor of varying prominence. It would be difficult to justify a contention that Middle East petroleum has ever comprised the U.S.S.R.'s primary interest in the region, in view of the geopolitical importance of Russia's southern approaches to the Mediterranean, Persian Gulf, and Indian Ocean area. However, petroleum-bearing regions, such as in Iran, have long been a target of Communist political aspirations; and the contemporary Middle East, the world's leading petroleum region for production and reserves, has in recent years attracted a major Soviet bloc campaign of trade and aid.

Middle East petroleum has been used as a symbolic device to encourage anti-Western sentiment, already activated by currents of nationalism and revolution among Arabs and non-Arabs of the region. Crude oil and natural gas as exploitable resources and as industries have merged as objects of U.S.S.R. and Soviet bloc policy in both short- and long-term planning. Moscow's policy makers have been guided both by Marxist-Leninist ideology and by Russian national self-interest as they have attempted to erode Western economic predominance in the region and create an opening for increasing Soviet bloc participation in the Middle East petroleum industry as advisers, operators, and long-term trading partners.

In seeking an underlying strategic rationale to Soviet petroleum policies, the author has noted Moscow's "petroleum paradox," the seeming contradiction posed by appraisals that the Soviet petroleum industry is, at once, deficient and competitive. The former case is suggested by the contrast of abundant reserves with reports of continuing discrepancies in planning, development, and operation of Soviet oil and natural gas industries, such that Soviet production appears inadequate to meet rising petroleum requirements; it is given credence by a recent series of agreements providing for the import of Middle East petroleum by the U.S.S.R. and the majority of the Soviet bloc. At the same time, the Soviet industry appears competitive as a rival marketer of Middle East petroleum—exporting countries, based upon present Soviet exports to Eastern and Western Europe and Japan, coupled with Soviet negotiations for long-term expansion of her deliveries of crude oil and natural gas to Western Europe, Japan, and recently the United States.

Thus, it seems feasible to dispel the petroleum paradox by turning to the Marxist-Leninist formula for a world socialist planned economy and a world energy delivery system. Such ideology suggests that the U.S.S.R. may assume preliminary roles of producer and major importer of Middle East petroleum and a broker for the region's industry.

Ultimately the U.S.S.R. could, within the world energy delivery system concept, acquire a strategic middleman role by simultaneously importing major quantities of petroleum from the national sector of Middle East countries on a barter basis, and after satisfying domestic needs, exporting crude oil and natural gas from its reservoir of Middle East and indigenous production to traditional Middle East customers of the capatalist world.

Development of such a trade pattern would seem to be in the distinct interest of the Soviet Union as a means of gaining increased hard currency for Western technology judged by prominent Soviet scientists to be inherently superior to that which the U.S.S.R. can produce.[47] Middle East countries, eager to develop the national sector of their petroleum industries in return for machinery and assistance to broaden their industrialization and for arms, would appear to welcome such a development, at least until a delayed reaction undermining Western price structures might ultimately be felt by the producing states. Western companies would, perhaps find themselves on the sidelines, watching the U.S.S.R. and Soviet bloc acquire a pre-eminent position in the further development of the Middle East's national petroleum industry.

The concept of strategic middleman would presumably entail increasing integration of petroleum imports from the Middle East and exports to western countries under the predominant influence of the Moscow center. In ideological terms, the U.S.S.R. would be working toward a world energy delivery system within a world socialist planned economy; in practical terms, Moscow would expect eventually to achieve a position of strategic economic dominance over the Middle East. Such a development would promise acquisition of political leverage commensurate with the level of economic integration achieved. In the meantime, the U.S.S.R. may aspire through economic penetration to achieve a level of political authority as predominant superpower in the Middle East. Then she would be able, according to her own choosing, to continue in the use of politics and oil to exert pressures upon capitalist states by threatening their strategic interests, which include the unhampered flow of petroleum from the Middle East.

Notes

1. E. L. Shteinberg, *Sovetsko-iranskiye otnoshenii i prioski v anglo-amerikanskom imperializme v Irane 1947 (Soviet-Iranian Relations and the Intrigues of Anglo-American Imperialism in Iran, 1947)* (Moscow: *Pravda* Press, 1947), p. 23.

2. R. Andreasyan, "Middle Eastern Oil: Present and Future," *International Affairs*, July, 1960, p. 26.

3. L. Sedin, "The Arab People's Just Cause," *International Affairs*, August, 1967, p. 23.

4. Walter W. Rostow, "Perspective of the Tasks of the 1960's," *Patterns of Competitive Coexistence*, ed. Young Hum Kim (New York: G. P. Putnam's Sons, 1966), p. 60.

5. Jan F. Triska and David D. Finley, *Soviet Foreign Policy*, (New York: Macmillan, 1968), p. 438.

6. L. Tomashpol'skiy, "Mirovoy energeticheskiy balans: problemy posledney treti veka" ("The World Energy Balance: Problems of the Last Third of the Century"), *Mirovaya ekonomika i mezhdunarodniye otnosheniya* (The World Economy and International Relations), February, 1967, p. 29.

7. *Ibid*, p. 29.

8. Communist Party Secretary B. Ponomaryov discusses the Party's role in the formulation of Soviet foreign policy: "At present, on the basis of a study of the objective development of socialist society and scientific assessment of its needs and possibilities, the CPSU is working out and implementing political solutions which offer the maximum scope for the country's advance toward Communism." B. Ponomaryov, "The Historic Significance of the Seventh Congress of the Comintern and Our Time," *World Marxist Review*, December, 1965, Vol. VIII, No. 12, p. 8.

9. ". . . the expansion of trade with countries which can use the simple capital goods the Soviet Union has the ability to export and can provide raw materials which can be absorbed usefully by the Soviet economy may not impose any economic burden upon the Soviet Union. Rather, it may well result in a small net economic gain. The Middle East is such an area." Robert Loring Allen, *Middle Eastern Economic Relations with the Soviet Union, Eastern Europe, and Mainland China* (Charlottesville, Va.: University of Virginia Press, 1958), p. 60.

10. "Co-operation with the U.S.S.R. contributes to economic development and a balanced pattern of foreign trade. Soviet-Iranian economic contacts are developing, helping to raise prosperity standards in both countries and making for closer relations between them." V. Spandaryan, "Soviet Trade With Iran," *New Times*, March 29, 1967, p. 11.

11. "Neft i gaz v stroitel'stve kommunizma," ("Petroleum and Natural Gas in the Construction of Communism,") *Kommunist vooruzhennykh sil (Communist of the Armed Forces)*, No. 14, July, 1965, p. 79.

12. "Soviet Spurs Use of Gas with Pipeline to Moscow," New York *Times*, September, 23, 1967, p. 37. © 1968/67 by the New York Times Company. Reprinted by permission.

13. "The tasks set forth by the Party and the government in connection with providing the industrial Ural area with natural gas from the extremely rich Bukhara reserves have been implemented. The building of the first section of the largest gas

pipeline in the world has been completed." "Samiy moshchniy v mire gazoprovod Bukhara-ural—postroyen!" ("Largest gas pipeline in the world, Bukhara-Ural—complete!") *Pravda*, January 17, 1964, p. 15.

14. *Ibid.*

15. A. Kortunov, "Central Asian Gas Flows into the Capital," *Moscow News*, No. 41 (1967), p. 3.

16. "Petroleum and Natural Gas in Construction of Communism," p. 80.

17. The most recent efforts in this direction were illustrated in 1970 agreements Moscow concluded with West Germany and Italy, the former providing for shipments to at least the year 1992. J. M. van Dijck, "East and West Linked by Pipes," *Common Market*, No. 4, April, 1970, pp. 96-98, pp. 96-97.

18. "In the sphere of international policy our Party takes a realistic view of the world situation and the concrete conditions and possibilities of each of the revolutionary detachments, and upholds flexibly, in true Leninist fashion, the interests of the socialist community, the national liberation movement and the working class movement." B. Ponomaryov, "The Historic Significance of the Seventh Congress of the Comintern and Our Time," *World Marxist Review*, Vol. VIII, No. 12, (December, 1965), p. 8.

19. Georgy Mirskiy, "Suez in Retrospect," *New Times*, October 26, 1966, p. 11.

20. "Arabs Dismayed by Soviet's Stand," *New York Times*, June 8, 1967, p. 21.

21. "Warning Against Faith in Russia by S. Arabian Minister," *Financial Times*, June 15, 1967, p. 7.

22. *Ibid.*

23. A. Yermonskiy and O. Nakropin, "General Line of Soviet Foreign Policy," *International Affairs*, September, 1966, p. 83.

24. G. Andreyev, "United States Imperialist Expansion in Guise of 'AID' to Underdeveloped Countries," *International Affairs*, No. 2, February, 1955, p. 45.

25. L. Lukin and S. Zavolzhskiy, "Bourgeois Criticism of Socialist Economic Cooperation," *International Affairs*, January, 1967, p. 13.

26. Yu. Belyayev, "The Economy of the CEMA Member-Countries in the New Five-Year Plan," *Kommunist*, No. 8, May, 1967, pp. 98-107. Trans. by Joint Publications Research Service, U.S. Department of Commerce, Washington, D. C., No 41,638 (June 29, 1967), p. 85.

27. "The international socialist division of labor continues to develop and intensify. New problems arise in its progress along with difficulties. At the CEMA conference of July, 1966, the countries' members reasserted their decision to continue with their efforts to intensify and improve forms of co-operation and increase its effectiveness."

"It is very important for the propagandists to explain why political co-operation is necessary and important. The students must understand that the political co-operation among the socialist countries is a necessary prerequisite for the elaboration of a common line and joint activities for solving the most important international problems, for the successful struggle against imperialist reaction and for peace, socialism and social progress. Such a co-operation may take a variety of forms. Particularly important, however, are the friendship, co-operation, and mutual aid agreements." St. Goranov, "The World Socialist System: Materials for Propagandists in Primary Political Education Schools," *Politicheska Prosveta* ("Political Education"), No. 3, March, 1967, pp. 61-68. Trans. by Joint Publications Research Service, U.S. Department of Commerce, Washington, D. C., No. 40,921 (May 8, 1967), p. 4.

28. Henry Shapiro, "COMECON Membership Eyed," Washington *Post*, September 26, 1972, p. A-20.

29. "Progress nauki-progress proizvodstva" ("Progress in Science is Progress in Production"), *Pravda*, November 30, 1966, p. 1.

30. "Sources of Conflict in the Middle East," *Adelphi Papers*, No. 26, March, 1966, (London: The Institute for Strategic Studies), pp. 3-4.

31. *Ibid.*, p. 4.

32. *Ibid.*, p. 5.

33. Sevinc Carlson, "Japan's Inroads into the Middle East and North Africa," *The New Middle East* (London) July, 1970, p. 17.

34. Of singular importance in purely economic terms is the contribution made by U.S. private investment in the Middle East to U.S. balance of payments, estimated in 1971 to be near $1 billion. *United States Foreign Policy — 1971: A report of the Secretary of State*, (Department of State Publication 8634, March, 1972), p. 104.

35. *Ibid.*, pp. 5-6.

36. Rouhollah K. Ramazani, *The Persian Gulf: Iran's Role*, (Charlottesville, Va: University Press of Virginia, 1972), p. vii.

37. By 1972, the U.S. Secretary of the Interior was quoted as saying "that the United States is facing 'a fuel and power crisis' and a prospect that by 1985 it will have to import half of its oil requirements." Meanwhile, the Under Secretary of State declared that "about one-third of the total would have to come from the Middle East if current patterns continue." M. Berger, "Fuel Crisis, Big Oil Imports Face U.S. by '80s," Washington *Post*, April 11, 1972, p. A-3.

President Nixon's action to increase U.S. oil imports in 1972 tended to confirm the reported trend toward growing dependency on foreign petroleum. C. Kilpatrick, "Limits on Oil Imports Increased [*sic*] by Nixon," Washington *Post*, September 19, 1972, p. A-13.

38. Shteinberg, *Soviet-Iranian Relations*, p. 23.

39. Belinkov, "Battle for Oil," p. 121.

40. R. Andreasyan, "Middle Eastern Oil," p. 26.

41. Sedin, "Arab People's Just Cause," p. 23.

42. "Baghdad Agreement," *New Times*, August 30, 1967, p. 1.

43. Andreasyan, "The Arab East: Clash With Oil Imperialism," *World Economics and International Relations*, No. 3, p. 112.

44. Moscow Radio dispatch, as quoted in Victor Zorza, "Soviet Oil Moves Threaten West," Washington *Post*, June 7, 1972, p. A-19.

45. "What the Russians Are Up to in the Middle East: Interview With King Hussein of Jordan," *U.S. News and World Report*, December 26, 1966, p. 39.

46. The deliberate pace of pursuing Soviet long-term objectives, however, often conflicts with short-term policy; for example, Soviet patience with the development of a permanent presence in the Middle East argues against supporting Egyptian bellicosity against Israel which could result in a Soviet confrontation with the United States; this apparently led to Sadat's decision in 1972 to call for the humiliating withdrawal of Soviet forces.

47. In the past decade the national economy of our country has begun to show threatening signs of dislocation and stagnation. . . . The growth rate in national income has been going inexorably down. A rift has opened up between what is necessary for normal development and the real introduction of new production capacities. . . . Defects

in the system of planning, accounting and incentives often lead to a contradiction between local or bureaucratic and state or national interest. The result is that reserves are not available and used for production research as they should be, and technological progress is severely retarded. . . . In our country labor productivity continues, as before, to be many times lower than in capitalist countries, and its growth rate is sharply declining. . . .

When we compare our economy with that of the United States, we see that ours is lagging behind, not only quantitatively, but — and this is the saddest part — also qualitatively. The more novel and revolutionary the aspect of the economy, the wider becomes the gap. . . . We are ahead of the U.S. in the production of coal but behind in the production of oil, gas, and electric power, ten times behind in chemistry, and immeasurably behind in computer technology. The latter is especially essential, for the introduction of electronic computers into the national economy is of decisive importance and could radically change the face of the system of production and culture in general. This phenomenon has rightly been called the "second industrial revolution." Meanwhile, the total capacity of our pool of computers is hundreds of times less than in the U.S.A., and as for the use of electronic computers in the national economy, here the difference is so enormous that it is impossible to measure. We are simply living in a different era. . . .

In the late 1950s, our country was the first to launch a sputnik and to send a man into space. By the end of the 1960s, we have lost the lead in this field (as in many others). The first men to set foot on the moon were Americans. This is one of the outward signs of an essential and ever-growing gap between our country and the West extending through the whole spectrum of scientific technological activity. From the appeal of scientists A. D. Sakharov, V. F. Turchin and R. A. Medvedev to Soviet party and government leaders, March 19, 1970. Translated in *Survey* (London), Summer 1970, pp. 160-70.

Appendix 1

Communiqué on Visit of Foreign Commissar Molotov to Berlin*

Pravda, November 15, 1940

During his stay in Berlin from 12 to 13 November of this year the Chairman of the Council of People's Commissars of the U.S.S.R. and People's Commissar for Foreign Affairs, Comrade V. M. Molotov, had an interview with Reichschancellor Herr A. Hitler and the German Foreign Minister Herr von Ribbentrop. The exchange of views proceeded in an atmosphere of mutual confidence and established mutual understanding on all important questions of interest to the U.S.S.R. and Germany.

Comrade V. M. Molotov also had an interview with Reichsmarshal Goering and Herr Hitler's deputy in the National Socialist Party, Herr Hess.

Comrade V. M. Molotov left for Moscow on the morning of 14 November.

*From *Soviet Documents on Foreign Policy*, Vol. III, ed. Jane Degras (Oxford University Press under the auspices of the Royal Institute of International Affairs).

Appendix 2

Statement by Molotov to the German Ambassador on the
Proposed Four-Power Pact, November 25, 1940*

The Soviet Government has studied the contents of the statements of the Reich Foreign Minister at the concluding conversation on 13 November and its attitude toward them is as follows:

The Soviet Union is prepared to accept the draft of the Four-Power Pact which the Reich Foreign Minister outlined in the conversation of 13 November, regarding political collaboration and reciprocal economic support, subject to the following conditions:

1. Provided that the German troops are immediately withdrawn from Finland, which, under the agreements of 1939, belongs to the Soviet Union's sphere of influence. Here the Soviet Union undertakes to ensure peaceful relations with Finland and safeguard German economic interests in Finland (export of lumber and nickel).

*Document: Germany: *Die Beziehungen zwischen Deutschland und der Sowjetunion 1939-1941. Dokumente des Auswärtigen Amtes,* Tübingen, Germany: Laupp' sche Buchhandlung, 1949. (*Relations between Germany and the Soviet Union, 1939-1941. Documents of the Foreign Office*), p. 296, from *Soviet Documents on Foreign Policy.*

2. Provided that within the next few months the security of the Soviet Union in the Straits is assured by the conclusion of a mutual assistance pact between the Soviet Union and Bulgaria, which geographically is situated inside the security zone of the Black Sea boundaries of the Soviet Union, and by the establishment of a base for land and naval forces of the U.S.S.R. within range of the Bosphorus and the Dardanelles on a long-term lease.

3. Provided that the area south of Batum and Baku in the general direction of the Persian Gulf is recognized as the focal point of the aspirations of the Soviet Union.

4. Provided that Japan renounces her rights to concessions for coal and oil in Northern Sakhalin.

In accordance with the foregoing, the draft of the protocol concerning the delimitation of the spheres of interest as outlined by the Reich Foreign Minister would have to be amended to the effect that the focal point of the aspirations of the Soviet Union is stipulated to be south of Batum and Baku in the general direction of the Persian Gulf.

Likewise, the draft of the protocol or agreement between Germany, Italy, and the Soviet Union with respect to Turkey would have to be amended so as to ensure a base for land and naval forces of the U.S.S.R. on the Bosphorus and the Dardanelles on a long-term lease, and also — in case Turkey declares herself willing to join the Four-Power Pact — to have the independence and territory of Turkey guaranteed by the three States named.

This protocol could have to provide that, in case Turkey refuses to join the four Powers, Germany, Italy, and the Soviet Union agree to work out and to carry through the requisite military and diplomatic measures, on which a special agreement would have to be concluded.

Furthermore, there would have to be agreed:

(a) a third secret protocol between Germany and the Soviet Union concerning Finland (see Point 1 above);

(b) a fourth secret protocol between Japan and the Soviet Union concerning the renunciation by Japan of the oil and coal concessions in Northern Sakhalin (in return for an adequate compensation);

(c) a fifth secret protocol between Germany, the Soviet Union, and Italy recognizing that Bulgaria, in view of her geographical position, is located inside the security zone of the Black Sea boundaries of the Soviet Union and that it is therefore held to be a political necessity that a mutual assistance pact be concluded between the Soviet Union and Bulgaria, her sovereignty and independence.

Illustrations

Figure 1

Soviet Crude Oil and Natural Gas Production, 1971

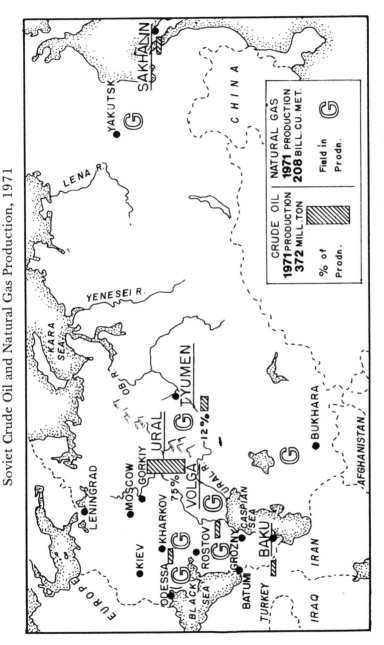

Sources: *B.P. Statistical Review of the World Oil Industry — 1971,*
London: The Baynard Press, 1972; "Russian Bloc Hikes Oil Output,"
World Oil, August 15, 1972, p. 91.

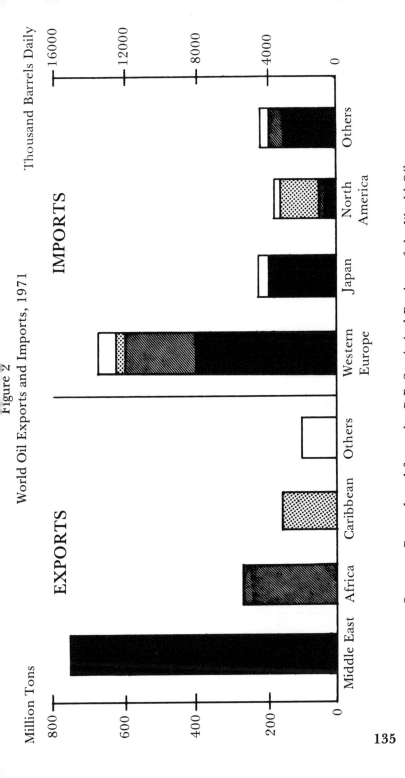

Figure 2
World Oil Exports and Imports, 1971

Source: Reproduced from the *B.P. Statistical Review of the World Oil Industry—1971*, by courtesy of the British Petroleum Company, Limited.

135

World Oil Supply and Demand, 1971

Canada

U.S.A.

Caribbean

Mexico

South America

West Africa

North Africa

Western Europe

Middle East

U.S.S.R. etc.

South Asia

Japan

South East Asia

E. & S. Africa

Australasia

CONSUMPTION

PRODUCTION

Source: Reproduced from the *B.P. Statistical Review of the World Oil Industry—1971,* by courtesy of the British Petroleum Company, Limited.

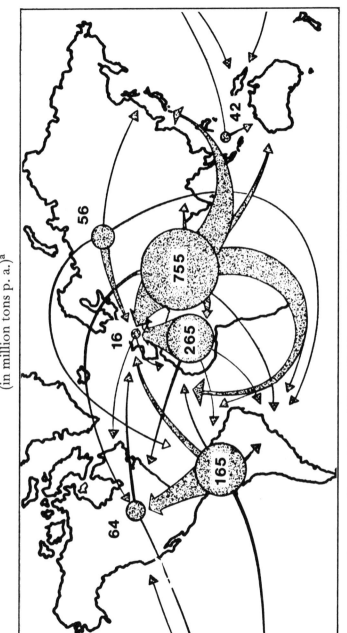

How Oil Moved Round the World, 1971
(in million tons p. a.)[a]

Sources: Format from "How Oil Moves Round the World," London *Times*, July 31, 1968, p. 17; data from *B.P. Statistical Review of the World Oil Industry—1971*, London: The Baynard Press, 1972.

[a]Excluding movements within North America and the Communist areas.

Relationship between World Oil Production and Reserves, 1971

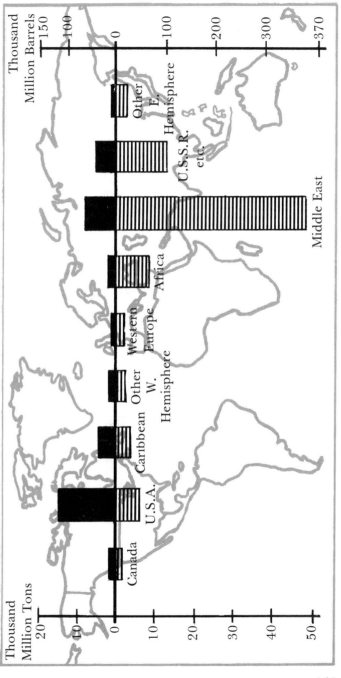

Source: Reproduced from the *B.P. Statistical Review of the World Oil Industry—1971*, by courtesy of the British Petroleum Company, Limited.

Bibliography

Primary Source Books

Aleksandrov, V. V. *Sovremennoye mezhdunaradnoye kommunisti-cheskoye, rabocheye, i natsional'noye dvizheniye ("Contem-porary International Communist, Workers, and National Liberation Movement")*, Vols. I and II. Moscow: State Publishing House for Party Senior School, 1963.

Alekseyev, L. *Sovetskiy soyuz i iran ("The Soviet Union and Iran")*. Moscow: Institute of International Relations Publishing House, 1963.

Brenner, M. *Tekhpromfinplan neftedobyvayushchevo tresta.* Moscow: State Scientific-Technical Publishing House for Petroleum and Fuel Extracting Literature, 1951.

_____. *Neftyanaya i gazovaya promyshlennosti, sssr (Economy of the Petroleum Industry, U.S.S.R.).* Moscow: State Scientific-Technical Publishing House for Petroleum and Fuel Extracting Literature, 1962.

_____. *Neft': Voprocy ekonomiki ("Oil: Economic Questions")*. Moscow: State Publishing House for Political Literature, 1957.

Bugrov, V. A., and Smirnov, N. P. *Analiz ekonomicheskoy effectivnosti novoy tekhniki tekhnologii y dobyche nefti ("An Analysis of the Economic Effectiveness of New Technology and Equipment in the Production of Petroleum")*. Moscow: *Nedra* Press, 1966.

The Century of Rumania's Oil Industry. Bucharest: Foreign Languages Publishing House, 1959.

Chernikh, A. V. *Neftyanaya i gazovaya promyshlennosti, sssr ("Petroleum Industry, U.S.S.R.")*. Moscow: *Vyshaya Shkola*, 1964.

Ivanova, M. N. *Oktyabrskaya revolyutsiya i iran ("The October Revolution and Iran")*. Moscow: State Publishing House for Political Literature, 1953.

Malyshev, Yu. Tushchenko, V. Shampov, and O. Koposova, *Ekonomika neftyanoy i gazovoy promyshlennosti ("Economics of the Petroleum and Natural Gas Industry")*. Moscow: *Nedra* Press, 1966.

145

Milovanov, I. V., et al. *Rabochiy klass i rabochiye dvizheniya v stranakh azii i afriki ("The Working Class and Workers' Movements in the Countries of Asia and Africa")*. Moscow: *Nauka* Press, 1965.

Pyat'desiat' let sovetskoy vneshney torgovli ("Fifty Years of Soviet Foreign Trade"). Moscow: State Publishing House for International Relations, 1967.

Popov, I., and L. M. Tomashpol'skiy. *Toplivno-energetiches-kaya baza mirovoy sotsialisticheskoy sistemi ("Energy Fuel Basis of the World Socialist System")*. Moscow: State Publishing House: Ekonomika, 1964.

Potemkin, V. P., ed. *Istoriya diplomatii 1919-1939 ("History of Diplomacy, 1919-1939")*. Vol. III. Moscow: Government Printing Office for Political Literature, 1945.

Radek, K. *Vneshnyaya politika sovetskoy rossii, 1923*, p. 74, quoted in I. Spector, *The Soviet Union and the Muslim World, 1917-1956*. Seattle: University of Washington Press, 1956.

Shteinberg, E. L. *Sovetsko-iranskiye otnoshenii i proiski v anglo-amerikanskom imperializme v irane 1947 ("Soviet-Iranian Relations and the Intrigues of Anglo-American Imperialism in Iran in 1947")*. Moscow: *Pravda* Press, 1947.

Trukhanovskiy, V. G., ed. *Istoriya mezhdunarodnykh otnoshenii 1917-1939 ("History of International Relations 1917-1939"*. Moscow: State Publishing House for International Relations, 1964.

Vishinskiy, A. Y. *The Law of the Soviet State*. New York: The Macmillan Co., 1948.

Vneshnyaya torgovlya SSSR — statisticheskiy obzor ("U.S.S.R. Foreign Trade — Statistical Survey). Moscow: State Publishing House, 1966.

Zinner, P. E. *National Communism and Popular Revolt in Eastern Europe*. New York: Columbia University Press, 1956.

Primary Source Articles

"Aggression Against the Arab World," *New Times* (Moscow), June 14, 1967, pp. 1-3.

Andreasyan, R. "Arabskiy vostok: novoye stolknoveniye s neftyanym imperializmom" ("The Arab East: New Clash with Oil Imperialism"), *Mirovaya ekonomika i mezhdunarodniye otnosheniya ("World Economics and International Relations")* (Moscow), No. 3, pp. 111-113.

_____. "Middle Eastern Oil: Present and Future," *International Affairs* (Moscow), July, 1960, pp. 23-30.

_____. "New Aspects of Middle East Countries' Oil Policy," *International Affairs* (Moscow), September, 1968, pp. 28-36.

Andreyev, G. "United States Imperialist Expansion in the Guise of 'AID' to Underdeveloped Countries," *International Affairs* (Moscow), February, 1955, pp. 29-46.

Anisimov, Girey. "The Five Year Plan of the U.S.S.R. and Problems of Science and Technology," *World Marxist Review* (Prague), IX, No. 4 (April, 1966), pp 38-42.

"The Arab World and the U.S.S.R.," *New Times* (Moscow), December 7, 1966, p. 5.

"Architect of Soviet Foreign Policy," *New Times* (Moscow), April 26, 1967, pp. 1-2.

Ardekani, A. "Toward a National Democratic Front in Iran," *World Marxist Review* (Prague), VIII, No. 9 (September, 1955), pp. 29-34.

Astakhov, S. "More about the Secret Springs of the Israeli Aggression," *International Affairs* (Moscow), October, 1967, pp. 33-40.

"Baghdad Agreement," *New Times* (Moscow), August 30, 1967.

Belinkov, S. "Battle for Oil," *International Affairs* (Moscow), January, 1955, pp. 120-122.

Belyayev, Igor, and Yevgeniy, Primakov. "Lessons of the 1967 Middle East Crisis," *International Affairs* (Moscow), March, 1968, pp. 40-46.

_____. "The Situation in the Arab World," *New Times* (Moscow), September 27, 1967, pp. 8-11.

"C.E.M.A.—Iraq Cooperation Aids in Social, Economic Gains," Radio Moscow in Arabic to Arab World, September 4, 1972, *Foreign Broadcast Information Service — Soviet Union*, September 6, 1972, Volume III, No. 174, p. B-2.

Charakcheyev, Asen. "Internationalism — An Effective Force," *World Marxist Review* (Prague), IX, No. 3, (March, 1966), pp. 17-20.

"Chronicle of Grand Achievements — Fifty Years of Soviet Foreign Policy," *International Affairs* (Moscow), August, 1967, pp. 95-97.

Combo, Juan. "Venezuelan Oil," *New Times* (Moscow), July 26, 1967, pp. 20-21.

"Communique' on the Visit of Foreign Commissar Molotov to Berlin," *Pravda* (Moscow), November 15, 1940, as quoted in *Soviet Documents on Foreign Policy*, III (1933-1941). Issued under auspices of the Royal Institute of International Affairs London: Oxford University Press, 1953, pp. 476-477.

"Concerning the Frontier Incident in the Gaza Area," *International Affairs* (Moscow), April, 1955, pp. 112-113.

"To Consolidate Further the Forces of Socialism on the Basis of Marxist-Leninist Principles," *Pravda* (Moscow), November 23, 1956; *National Communism and Popular Revolt in Eastern Europe*, Part IV. New York: Columbia University Press, 1956.

"Czechoslovak-Egyptian Economic Relations Grow Stronger," *International Affairs* (Moscow), May, 1956, p. 135.

"Declaration by the Government of the U.S.S.R. on the Principles of Development and Further Strengthening of Friendship and Co-operation between the Soviet Union and Other Socialist States, October 30, 1956," *National Communism and Popular Revolt in Eastern Europe*, Part IV. New York: Columbia University Press, 1956.

Dmitriyev, Y. "Arab Oil Resources," *International Affairs* (Moscow), August, 1967, pp. 101-102.

Domdey, Karl-Heinz. "Economic Contacts between the Socialist and Capitalist Countries of Europe," *World Marxist Review* (Prague), VIII, No. 9 (September, 1965), pp. 15-21.

Domrachev, M., and V. Galakhov. "Soviet Trade Unions — School of Communism," *Kommunist* (Moscow), No. 3 (February, 1958), pp. 23-29.

Doudera, Karel. "Eliminate the Consequences of the Aggression," *World Marxist Review*, X, No. 8 (August, 1967), pp. 3-6.

Drambyants, G. "The King and the Arabs," *New Times* (Moscow), March 22, 1967, pp. 20-22.

_____. "The Oil Embargo," *New Times* (Moscow), June 21, 1967, pp. 4-5.

Dymshits, V. "Ekonomika sssr za 50 let," ("The Soviet Economy During 50 Years"), *Kommunist*, No. 15 (October, 1967), pp. 32-43.

"For the Needs of Daily Life," *Robitnyoha Hazeta (Workers' Daily)* (Kiev, Ukraine), October 5, 1966, p. 2. Trans. *Digest of the Soviet Ukrainian Press*, PROLOG (October, 1966).

"The Fraternity Pipeline," *Soviet Union* (Moscow), No. 202 (1966), pp. 24-27.

"Friendship between the Great Powers," *International Affairs* (Moscow), May, 1956, pp. 5-11.

Gerasimov, G. "Anti-Communism and the Foreign Policy of Imperialism," *International Affairs* (Moscow), September, 1966, pp. 85-92.

Gevorkyan, P. "Aden: The Struggle Continues," *International Affairs* (Moscow), August, 1967, pp. 81-82.

_____. "Syria: Political Aspects of the Oil Conflict," *International Affairs* (Moscow), February, 1967, pp. 86-87.

Gorshkov, Admiral S. G. "Razvitiye sovetskogo voennomorskogo iskusstva" ("Development of Soviet Naval Art of War"), *Morskoy sbornik* ("Naval Journal") (Moscow), No. 2 (1967), pp. 9-21.

Grigoryev, Kh. "An Action Contrary to the Interests of Iran and International Security," *International Affairs* (Moscow), December, 1955, pp. 54-64.

Guseinov, K. A. "O mezhdunarodnom znachenii bratskikh svyazey sovetskikh profsoyuzov s profsoyuzami stran azii i afriki" (" The International Significance of Relations between Soviet Trade Unions and Trade Unions of the Countries of Asia and Africa"), in *Rabochiy klass i rabocheye dvizheniye v stranakh azii i afriki ("The Working Class and Workers' Movements in Countries of Asia and Africa")*. Ed. I. V. Milovanov *et al.* Moscow: *Nauka* Press, 1965, pp. 5-38.

Honta, T. "Hekotoriye problemy razvitiya neftyanoy i gazovoy promyslennosti ukrainy" ("Some Problems in the Development of the Oil and Gas Industry in Ukraine"), *Kommunist ukrainy* ("Communist Ukraine"), No. 1 (January, 1967), pp. 79-83. Trans. *Digest of Soviet Ukrainian Press*, PROLOG (April, 1967), pp. 10-11.

_____. "How Long Will The Volcanoes Be Active?" *Robitnycha Hazeta* (Kiev), July 10, 1966, p. 3. Trans. *Digest of the Soviet Ukrainian Press*, PROLOG, X, No. 8 (August, 1966), pp. 12-13.

Husseini, A. "Another Wave of Terror in Iran," *World Marxist Review* (Prague), VIII, No. 6 (June, 1965), pp. 64-65.

Ikonnikov, I. "The CMEA Countries in 1966-1970," *International Affairs* (Moscow), October, 1967, pp. 27-32.

"An Important Contribution to Peaceful Coexistence," *International Affairs* (Moscow), June, 1956, pp. 12-16.

"Infringement on Iranian National Interests," *International Affairs* (Moscow), October, 1955, pp. 135-136.

"The Iranian Oil Problem," *International Affairs* (Moscow), July, 1955, pp. 147-149.

Ivanov, K. "Soviet Foreign Policy and the Present International Situation," *International Affairs* (Moscow), November, 1955, pp. 16-31.

Ivanov, Valentin. "Refinery on the Red Sea," *New Times* (Moscow), October 12, 1966, pp. 29-31.

Kafman, A. "U.S. Big Stick in the Mediterranean," *International Affairs* (Moscow), August, 1967, pp. 71-75.

Kaftanov, Sergey. "Ten Years of Soviet-Arab Friendship," *Culture and Life* (Moscow), No. 7 (1968), pp. 14-15.

Karpov, S. "The Closed Canal," *New Times* (Moscow), June 19, 1968, pp. 24-25.

Kasatkin, D. "Middle East: Assault on the Oil Monopolies," *International Affairs* (Moscow), January, 1967, pp. 93-94.

Khrushchev, Nikita S. "On Peaceful Coexistence," in *Patterns of Competitive Coexistence/USA vs USSR*. Edited by Young Hum Kim. New York: G. P. Putnam's Sons, 1966, pp. 428-444.

Kortunov, Alexey. "Nature's Generous Gift," *Culture and Life* (Moscow), No. 7 (1968), pp. 12-15.

_____. "Central Asian Gas Flows into the Capital," *Moscow News*, No. 41 (1967), p. 3.

Kremnev, M. "Arab East: Provocation Continues," *New Times* (Moscow), November 30, 1966, p. 17.

_____. "Tension Centre in the Arab East," *New Times* (Moscow), December 21, 1966, pp. 6-7.

Kruglov, M. "Arab East: Complex Problems," *New Times* (Moscow), September 13, 1967, p. 14.

Kudryavtsev, V. "Concerning Events in Arab East," *Izvestiya,* April 14, 1963, p. 5, in *Current Digest of the Soviet Press*, XV, No. 15 (May 8, 1963), p. 28.

_____. "Unity is the Course," *Izvestiya*, January 26, 1964, p. 4, in *Current Digest of the Soviet Press*, XVI, No. 4 (February 19, 1964), pp. 25-26.

"Kul'tura sovetskogo cheloveka" ("The Culture of Soviet Man"). *Pravda* (Moscow), December 2, 1966, p. 1.

Lebedev, I. "Australia's Role in Western Military Plans," *International Affairs* (Moscow), November, 1967, pp. 52-57.

Lenin, V. I. "The Proletarian Revolution and the Renegade Kautsky," in *Selected Works*, Vol. III. Moscow: Foreign Languages Publishing House, 1961.

Levchenko, L. "Oil Monopolies Attacking," *International Affairs* (Moscow), August, 1967, pp. 78-79.

Lukin, L., and S. Zavolshskiy. "Bourgeois Criticism of Socialist Economic Co-operation," *International Affairs* (Moscow), January, 1967, pp. 9-13.

Makhynya, M. "Known on All Continents, Ukraine and the World" *Radyanska Ukraina*, February 28, 1967, *Digest of Soviet Ukrainian Press*, XI, No. 4 (April, 1967), pp 27-28.

Marx, Karl. "Manifesto of the Communist Party," in *Selected Works of Marx and Engels*, Vol. I. Moscow: Foreign Languages Publishing House, 1962.

Medvedko, L. "Arabskuyu neft'— arabam!" ("Arab Oil for the Arabs!"), *Pravda* (Moscow), March 6, 1967.

"The Mighty Banner of Internationalism," *Pravda* (Moscow), May 21, 1964, p. 1. Trans. Joint Publications Research Service, U.S. Department of Commerce, Washington, D.C., No. 24,781, May 26, 1964, pp. 1-4.

Mirskiy, Georgiy. "Arab East: Moment of Truth," *New Times* (Moscow), November 12-20, 1967, pp. 27-29.

_____. "Israeli Aggression and Arab Unity," *New Times* (Moscow), July 12, 1967, pp. 4-7.

_____. "Suez in Retrospect," *New Times* (Moscow), October 26, 1966, pp. 9-11.

Mstislavskiy, P. "Strategy of the New Five-Year Plan," *New Times* (Moscow), July 13, 1966, pp. 7-10.

Nakaryakov, V. "Iranian Oil Production Dispute," *Izvestiya* (Moscow), November 11, 1966, p. 6. Trans. the Joint Publications Research Service, U.S. Department of Commerce, Washington, D. C., No. 39,174, December 19, 1966.

"Neft' i gaz v stroitel'stve kommunisma" ("Petroleum and Natural Gas in the Construction of Communism"), *Kommunist vooruzhennykh sil ("Communist of the Armed Forces")*, No. 14, (July, 1965), pp. 78-89.

"New U.S. Plans for 'AID' to Underdeveloped Countries," *International Affairs* (Moscow), February, 1956, pp. 21-27.

"On the Policy of the Soviet Union in Connection with the Israeli Aggression in the Middle East," *Information Bulletin*, No. 12 (1967), pp. 4-6.

Osipov, A. "Neft' nigerii" ("Oil of Nigeria"), *Mirovaya ekonomika i mezhdunarodniye otnosheniya ("World Economics and International Relations")* (Moscow), No. 5 (1967), pp. 123-125.

Osokin, S. "East of Suez," *Soviet Military Review* (Moscow), No. 9 (September 21, 1966), pp. 51-53.

Palynkatis, I. I. *Ekonomicheskoye razvitiye irana ("The Economic Development of Iran")*. Moscow: State Publishing House; *Ekonomika,* 1966, as quoted in "The Present Soviet View of Persia," *Mizan* (London), VIII, No. 5 (September/October, 1966), pp. 214-217.

"The 1961 Party Programme," *The USSR and the Future* (Appendix pp. 255-312). New York: Frederick A. Praeger, 1963.

"The 1919 Party Programme," *The USSR and the Future* (Appendix B, pp. 313-324). New York: Frederick A. Praeger, 1963.

Patolichev, Nikolay. "Trade with 100 Countries," Moscow *News*, No. 32 (August 19-26, 1967), p. 8.

Perlo, Victor. "American Oil Companies and the Middle East," *International Affairs* (Moscow), December, 1967, pp. 39-44.

"Political Economy in the Soviet Union," *Pod znamenem marksizma ("Under the Banner of Marxism")*, Nos. 7-8 (July/August, 1943). Trans. New York: International Publishers, 1944.

Potapova, S. M. "The System of Organs Directing Union-Republic Industry in the Current Period," *Pravovedeniye ("Jurisprudence")* (Leningrad: University Press), No. 3, 1960, pp. 3-14.

Proshik, N. I. "Polozheniye rabochikh-neftyanikov v saudovskoy arabii" ("The Situation Concerning Oil Workers in Saudi Arabia"), in *Rabochiy klass i rabocheye dvizheniye v stranakh azii i afriki ("The Working Class and Workers' Movements in Countries of Asia and Africa")*. Ed. I. V. Milovanov et al. Moscow: *Nauka* Press, 1965, pp 210-230.

Suchkov, N., and I. Garshin. "Zhizn' i bor'ba molodezhi arabskogo vostoka" ("The Life and Struggle of the Youth of Arab East"), *Molodoy Kommunist ("Young Communist")* (Moscow), No. 4 (April, 1955), pp. 104-109.

Ponomaryov, B. "The Historic Significance of the Seventh Congress of the Comintern and Our Time," *World Marxist Review* (Prague), VIII, No. 12 (December, 1965), pp. 5-12.

Prazsky, Jan. "Imperialist Intrigues in the Middle East," *World Marxist Review* (Prague), X, No. 7 (July, 1967).

Primakov, Y. "Behind the Scenes of the Israeli Gamble," *International Affairs* (Moscow), No. 7, pp. 58-61.

"Progress nauki — progress proizvodstva" ("Progress in Science is Progress in Production"), *Pravda* (Moscow), November 30, 1966, p. 1.

"Provocative Imperialist Bustle in the Persian Gulf," *International Affairs* (Moscow), March, 1968, pp. 75-76.

Rachkov, B. "Neft' bez mifov" ("Oil Without Myths"), *Izvestiya* (Moscow), May 24, 1966, p. 2.

_____. "The Russian Stake in the Middle East," *The New Middle East,* (London), May, 1969.

_____. "Za kulisami — neft'" ("Oil — Behind The Scenes"), *Izvestiya* (Moscow), July 11, 1967, p. 5.

_____. "The Imperialist Stake in the Middle East Oil," *New Times* (Moscow), June 14, 1967, pp 2-3.

_____. "The Petroleum Monopolies and the Israeli Aggression," *Kommunist* (Moscow), No. 12 (August, 1967), pp. 109-117. Trans. Joint Publications Research Service, U. S. Department of Commerce, Washington, D. C., No. 42,903, October 10, 1967, p. 90.

Rubenstein, G. "Nekotoriye voprosy razvitiya vneshney torgovli" ("Several Questions Concerning the Development of Foreign Trade"), *Voprosy ekonomiki* (Moscow), September, 1966, pp. 111-117.

"Rumanian Trade with the East," *International Affairs* (Moscow), April, 1956, pp. 133-134.

Salen, Amin, and Tigani, Babiker. "Consolidation of Anti-Imperialist Forces Is the Path to Progress of Arab Peoples," *World Marxist Review* (Prague), X, No. 10 (October, 1967), pp. 4-7.

"Samiy moshchniy v mire gazoprovod Bukhara-Ural — postroyen" ("Largest Gas Pipeline in the World, Bukhara-Ural — Completed"), *Pravda* (Moscow), January 17, 1964, p. 1.

Sedin, L. "The Arab Peoples' Just Cause," *International Affairs* (Moscow), August, 1967, pp. 23-29.

Seiful-Mulyukov, Farid. "Iraq Today," *New Times* (Moscow), July 26, 1967, pp. 12-13.

"Session of Baghdad Pact Council," *International Affairs* (Moscow), May, 1956, pp. 132-133.

Shimmel, N. "Damascus Journalist Tells of His Visit to Syria," *New Times* (Moscow), February 23, 1966, pp. 29-32.

Skuratov, L. "Oil Consortium against Iran," *New Times* (Moscow), November 23, 1966, pp. 14-16.

"The Soviet-Japanese Economic Conference," *New Times* (Moscow), November 27, 1967, p. 22.

"Soviet Natural Gas for France," *New Times* (Moscow), No. 34, August, 1971.

"The Soviet Press Tradition," *New Times* (Moscow), May 10, 1967, pp. 9-10.

"Soviet Union Expands Its Foreign Trade," *International Affairs*(Moscow), April, 1956, pp. 134-135.

Spandaryan, V. "Soviet Trade With Iran," *New Times* (Moscow), March 29, 1967, pp. 10-11.

Stepakov, V. "Aktivno formirovat' marksistkoleninskoye mirovozzreniye i kommunisticheskuyu moral' sovetskikh lyudey" ("Actively Forming the Marxist-Leninist World Outlook and the Communist Morality of Soviet People"), *Kommunist* (Moscow), No. 17 (November, 1966), pp. 14-28.

"Successful Negotiations," *International Affairs* (Moscow), January, 1955, pp. 94-95.

Sultan-Galiev, M. "K obyavlenii azerbaidzhanskoy sovetskoy respublik" ("Declaration of the Azerbaijanian Soviet Republic") *Zhisn' natsional'nosti* (*"Life of Nationalism"*) (Moscow), No. 13, May 5, 1920, p. 1; as quoted in Xenia J. Eudin, and Robert C. North, *Soviet Russia and the East 1920-1927.* Stanford, California: Stanford University Press, 1957, p. 96.

Svetlov, R. "USSR—USA: Possibilities and Reality," *International Affairs* (Moscow), February, 1972.

"Svet oktyabrya" ("The Light of October"), *Kommunist* (Moscow), No. 15 (October, 1966), pp. 3-13.

"Syria, Lebanon and Oil Companies," *International Affairs* (Moscow), June, 1956, pp. 118-120.

"Teoreticheskiy seminar — aktual'niye problemy politicheskoy ekonomii sotsializma" ("A Theoretical Seminar — Actual Problems in the Political Economy of Socialism"), *Kommunist* (Moscow), No. 14 (September, 1966), pp. 47-56.

"Theses of the Central Committee of the CPSU," *Information Bulletin* (Prague), No. 13, 1967, pp. 50-52.

Tomashpol'skiy, L. "Mirovoy energeticheskiy balans: problemy posledney treti veka" ("The World Energy Balance: Problems of the Last Third of the Century"), *Mirovaya ekonomika i mezhdunarodniye otnosheniya* (*"The World Economy and International Relations"*) (Moscow), February, 1967, pp. 15-29.

"Tomsk Oil," *Moscow News,* No. 27 (July 13-20, 1968), p. 2.

"Triumph of Friendship and Brotherhood of People of Labor," *Pravda* (Moscow), May 18, 1964, p. 3. Trans. *Current Digest of the Soviet Press*, XVI, No. 20 (June 10, 1964), pp. 7-9.

Tunkin, G. I. "New Principles of International Law," *New Times* (Moscow), August 30, 1967, p. 305.

"The Turko-Iraqi Treaty," *International Affairs* (Moscow), April, 1955, pp. 111-112.

"Udarny front semiletki" ("The Shock Front of the Seven-Year Plan") *Pravda* (Moscow), July 11, 1964, p. 1.

"U.S. and British Armed Forces and the Middle East Crisis,"
  International Affairs (Moscow), August, 1967, pp. 104-106.
"U.S. Big Stick in the Mediterranean," *International Affairs*
  (Moscow), August, 1967, pp. 71-75.
"U.S.S.R., Iraq Sign Cooperation, Trade Agreements," TASS
  International Service (Moscow), September 5, 1972,
  reported in *Foreign Broadcast Information Service — Soviet
  Union*, September 6, 1972, Volume III, No. 174, p. B-1.
Varchuk, V. V., and V. R. Razin. "Studies in the Area of the
  Political Organization of Socialist Society," *Voprosy
  filosofii* ("Philosophical Questions") (Moscow), No. 4,
  1967, pp. 134-143. Trans. Joint Publications Research
  Service, U.S. Department of Commerce, Washington, D.C.,
  No. 41,995, July 28, 1967.
Varkony, Endre. "Terminal of the Oil Pipeline," *Hungarian
  Review* (Budapest), XII, 1966, pp. 5-8.
Vilba, M. "'Islam Pact' Seen as Tool for Promoting Western
  Oil Interests," *Pravda ukrainy* (Kiev), May 17, 1966.
  Trans. Joint Publications Research Service, U.S.
  Department of Commerce, Washington, D.C., No.
  36,009, June 15, 1966, p. 8.
Vinogradisky, D. "Pervoye sobraniye aktiva rabotnikov
  neftedobyvayushchey promyshlennosti" ("First Meeting
  of the Organization of the Oil-Production Industry"),
  Neftyanoye khosyaystvo ("Petroleum Industry")
  (Moscow), June, 1966, p. 72.
Volskiy, Dmitry. "Arab East: Time of Great Change," *New
  Times* (Moscow), April 19, 1967, pp. 10-12.
_____. "Into The Twentieth Century," *New Times*
  (Moscow), May 17, 1967, pp. 15-17.
_____. "On the Persian Gulf," *New Times*
  (Moscow), February 7, 1968, pp. 14-16.
_____. "Troubled Spring," *New Times* (Moscow),
  May 31, 1967, pp. 14-16.
Yermonskiy, A., and O. Nakropin. "General Line of Soviet
  Foreign Policy," *International Affairs* (Moscow),
  September, 1966, pp. 76-84.

Secondary Source Books

Allen, Robert Loring. *Middle Eastern Economic Relations with the Soviet Union, Eastern Europe, and Mainland China.* Charlottesville, Virginia: University of Virginia Press, 1958.

_____. *Soviet Economic Warfare.* Washington, D.C.: Public Affairs Press, 1960.

Avtorkhanov, A. *Tekhnologiya vlasti (The Technology of Power: Formation of the CPSU).* Munich, Germany: Central Union of Political Emigrants, 1959.

Badeau, John S. *The American Approach to the Arab World.* New York: Harper and Row, 1968.

Barghoorn, Frederick C. *Soviet Russian Nationalism.* New York: Oxford University Press, 1956.

Baykov, A. *The Development of the Soviet Economic System.* New York: The Macmillan Co., 1948.

Beloff, Max. *The Foreign Policy of Soviet Rusia, 1936-1941.* Vol. III. London: Oxford University Press, 1949.

Berdyayev, Nicolas. *The Russian Idea.* New York: The Macmillan Company, 1948.

Bergson, Abram. *Economic Trends in the Soviet Union.* Cambridge, Massachusetts: Harvard University Press, 1963.

Bibliography of Recent Soviet Source Material on Soviet Central Asia and Its Borderlands (including the Middle East). No. 1. London: Central Asian Research Centre, 1961.

Bolton, A. R. C. *Soviet Middle Eastern Studies: An Analysis and Bibliography.* Part II, Arabs and the Arab World; Part III, The Arab Peninsula; Part IV, Egypt; Part V, Iraq; Part VI, Palestine (Israel) and Jordan; Part VIII, Syria and Lebanon. London: Royal Institute of International Affairs, 1959.

BP Statistical Review of the World Oil Industry — 1971. The British Petroleum Company, Ltd. London: The Baynard Press, 1972.

Bullard, Sir Reader. *Britain and the Middle East from the Earliest Times to 1950*, pp. 165-166, as quoted in Heinrich Hassmann, *Oil in the Soviet Union*. Trans. Alfred M. Leeson. Princeton, N.J.: Princeton University Press, 1953.

_____, ed. *The Middle East (A Political and Economic Survey)*. London: Oxford University Press, 1958.

Campbell, R. W. *Soviet Economic Power*. Cambridge, Mass.: The Riverside Press, 1960.

Carman, E. D. *Soviet Imperialism: Russia's Drive Toward World Domination*. Washington, D.C.: Public Affairs Press, 1950.

Cattan, Henry. *The Evolution of Oil Concessions in the Middle East and North Africa*. Dobbs Ferry, N.Y.: Oceana For the Parker School of Foreign and Comparative Law, 1967.

Churchill, Winston. *The World Crisis*. New York: Charles Scribner's Sons, 1963.

Cottam, R. W. *Nationalism in Iran*. Pittsburgh: University of Pittsburgh Press, 1964.

Dallin, David J. *The New Soviet Empire*. New Haven, Conn.: Yale University Press, 1951.

_____. *Soviet Foreign Policy After Stalin*. Philadelphia: J. B. Lippincott Company, 1961.

Degras, Jane, ed. *Soviet Documents of Foreign Policy*, Vol. II (1925-1932) and Vol. III (1933-1941). London: Oxford University Press, 1952.

Ebel, Robert E. *The Petroleum Industry of the Soviet Union*. Washington, D.C.: American Petroleum Institute, 1961.

Ellis, Harry B. *Challenge in the Middle East: Communist Influence and American Policy*. New York: The Ronald Press, 1960.

Elwell-Sutton, L. P. *Persian Oil: A Study in Power Politics*. London: Lawrence & Wishart, 1955.

Eudin, Xenia J., and Robert C. North. *Soviet Russia and the East 1920-1927*. Stanford, Calif.: Stanford University Press, 1957.

Fatemi, N. *Oil Diplomacy: Powderkeg in Iran*. New York: Whittier Books, Inc., 1954.

Feller, Albert. *Erdöl und Erdgas in der sowjetischen Machtpolitik: Ein Diskussionsbeitrag über die Bedeutung und Folgen Westlicher Lieferungen für das östliche Pipelinesystem ("Crude Oil and Natural Gas in Soviet Power Politics: Discussion Paper on the Significance and Consequences of Western Deliveries for the Eastern Pipeline System")*. Bonn: Büro Bonner Berichte, 1965.

Fischer, Louis. *The Soviets in World Affairs*. Vols. I and II. London: Jonathan Cape, 1930.

Florinsky, Michael T. *Russia*. Vols. I and II. New York: The Macmillan Company, 1955.

Frankel, Paul H. *Mattei, Oil and Power Politics*. New York: Frederick A. Praeger, 1966.

Goodman, E. R. *The Soviet Design for a World State*. New York: Columbia University Press, 1960.

The Gulf: Implications of the British Withdrawal. Special Report Series No. 8, The Center for Strategic and International Studies, Georgetown University, February, 1969.

Hartshorn, J. E. *Oil Companies and Governments*. London: Faber & Faber, Ltd., 1967.

Hassmann, Heinrich. *Oil in the Soviet Union*. Trans. Alfred M. Leeston. Princeton, N.J.: Princeton University Press, 1953.

Hodgkins, Jordan. *Soviet Power: Energy Resources, Production and Potentials*. Englewood Cliffs, N.J.: Prentice-Hall, 1961.

Hoskins, Halford L. *Middle East Oil in U.S. Foreign Policy*. Washington, D. C.: Library of Congress, 1950.

_____. *The Middle East: Problem Area in World Politics*. New York: The Macmillan Co., 1954.

Hurewitz, J. C., ed. *Soviet-American Rivalry in the Middle East*. Proceedings of the Academy of Political Science, Columbia University, March, 1969.

Ingram, D. *The Communist Economic Challenge*. New York: Frederick A. Praeger, 1965.

Issawi, Charles, and Mohammed Yeganeh. *The Economics of Middle Eastern Oil.* New York: Frederick A. Praeger, 1963.

_____. *Oil, The Middle East and the World. The Washington Papers,* No. 4. The Center for Strategic and International Studies, Georgetown University. New York: The Library Press, 1972

Jelavich, Charles. *Tsarist Russia and Balkan Nationalism.* Berkeley: University of California Press, 1958.

Kaser, Michael. *Comecon.* London: Oxford University Press, 1965.

Kazemzadeh, Firuz. *The Struggle for Transcaucasia (1917-1921).* Birmingham, England: Templar Press, 1951.

Kennan, George F. *Russia and the West under Lenin and Stalin.* Boston: Little, Brown and Co., 1960.

_____. *Soviet Foreign Policy, 1917-1941.* Princeton, N.J.: D. Van Nostrand Co., 1960.

Khadduri, Majid. *Independent Iraq.* London: Oxford University Press, 1960.

_____. *The Islamic Law of Nations.* Baltimore: The Johns Hopkins University Press, 1966.

_____. *Major Middle Eastern Problems in International Law.* Published by the American Enterprise Institute for Public Policy Research. Washington, D. C., June, 1972.

_____. *Republican Iraq.* London: Oxford University Press, 1969.

_____. *Political Trends in the Arab World.* Baltimore: The Johns Hopkins University Press, 1970.

Kim, Young Hum, ed. *Patterns of Competitive Coexistence: USA vs USSR.* New York: Putnam, 1966.

Kulski, W. W. *The Soviet Regime: Communism in Practice.* Syracuse, N.Y.: Syracuse University Press, 1963.

Laqueur, W. *Communism and Nationalism in the Middle East.* London: Routledge and Kegan Paul, 1956.

Lee, Dwight E. "The Liberation of the Balkan Slavs." *A Handbook of Slavic Studies.* Ed. L. Strakhovsky. Cambridge, Mass.: Harvard University Press, 1949.

161

Lenczowski, George. *The Middle East in World Affairs.* Ithaca, N.Y.: Cornell University Press, 1962.

_____. *Oil and State in the Middle East.* Ithaca, N.Y.: Cornell University Press, 1949.

Lobanov-Rostovsky, A. *Russia and Asia.* Ann Arbor: George Wahr Publishing Co., 1951.

London, Kurt L., ed. *The Soviet Union: Half a Century of Communism.* Baltimore: The Johns Hopkins Press, 1968.

Longrigg, S. H. *Oil in the Middle East: Its Discovery and Development.* London: Oxford University Press, 1961.

Lubell, H. *Middle East Oil Crises and Western Europe's Energy Supplies.* Santa Monica, Calif.: Rand Corporation, 1963.

Marder, Arthur J. *The Anatomy of British Sea Power.* Hamden, Conn.: Archon Books, 1964.

_____. *From the Dreadnought to Scapa Flow.* London: Oxford University Press, 1961.

Marshall, Charles Burton. *The Cold War.* New York: Franklin Watts, Inc., 1965.

Marx, Karl, and Friedrich Engels. *The Russian Menace to Europe.* Glencoe, Ill.: The Free Press, 1952.

McClellan, G. S. *The Middle East in the Cold War.* New York: Wilson Co., 1956.

Mikesell, Raymond F., and Hollis B. Chenery. *Arabian Oil: America's Stake in the Middle East.* Chapel Hill: University of North Carolina Press, 1949.

Mosely, Philip E. *The Kremlin and World Politics.* New York: Alfred A. Knopf, 1960.

Nollau, Günther, and Hans Jürgen Wiehe. *Russia's South Flank: Soviet Operations in Iran, Turkey, and Afghanistan.* New York: Frederick A. Praeger, 1963.

Nove, A. *Economic Rationality and Soviet Politics.* New York: Frederick A. Praeger, 1964.

O'Connor, Harvey. *World Crisis in Oil.* New York: Monthly Review Press, 1962.

Park, Alexander G. *Bolshevism in Turkestan 1917-1927.* New York: Columbia University Press, 1957.

Penrose, Edith. *The International Oil Industry in the Middle East.* Cairo: National Bank of Egypt, 1968.

Polk, William R. *The United States and the Arab World.* Cambridge, Mass.: Harvard University Press, 1965.

Ramazani, Rouhollah K. *The Persian Gulf: Iran's Role.* Charlottesville: University Press of Virginia, 1972.

Schapiro, Leonard. *The Communist Party of the Soviet Union.* New York: Random House, 1960.

_____. ed. *The USSR and the Future: An Analysis of the CPSU.* New York: Frederick A. Praeger, 1963.

Schurr, Sam H., and Homan, Paul T. *Middle Eastern Oil and the Western World.* New York: Elsevier Publishing Company, Incorporated, 1971.

Schwartz, Harry. *Russia's Soviet Economy.* Englewood Cliffs, N.J.: Prentice Hall, 1958.

_____. *The Soviet Economy Since Stalin.* New York: J. B. Lippincott Company, 1965.

Shamma, Samir. *The Oil of Kuwait: Present and Future; an Arab Point of View.* Beirut: The Middle East Research and Publishing Center, 1959.

Sharabi, Hisham B. *Governments and Politics of the Middle East in the Twentieth Century.* Princeton, N.J.: D. Van Nostrand Company, 1962.

_____. *Nationalism and Revolution in the Arab World.* Princeton, N.J.: D. Van Nostrand Company, 1966.

Shimkin, Dmitri B. *Minerals – A Key to Soviet Power.* Cambridge, Mass.: Harvard University Press, 1953.

Shwadran, Benjamin. *The Middle East, Oil and the Great Powers.* New York: Council for Middle Eastern Affairs, 1959.

Siksek, Simon G. *The Legal Framework for Oil Concessions in the Arab World.* Beirut: Middle East Research and Publishing Center, 1960.

Smal-Stocki, Roman.. *The Captive Nations.* New York: Bookman Associates, 1960.

Spector, I. *The Soviet Union and the Muslim World 1917-1956.* Seattle: University of Washington Press, 1959.

Sumner, Benedict H. *Russia and the Balkans (1870-1880).*
Hamden, Conn.: Archon Books, 1962.

Tatu, Michel. *Power in the Kremlin from Khrushchev to
Kosygin.* New York: The Viking Press, 1969.

Triska, Jan F., and David D. Finley. *Soviet Foreign Policy.*
New York: The Macmillan Company, 1968.

Tugendhat, Christopher. *Oil — The Biggest Business.* London:
Eyre and Spottiswoode, 1968.

Ulam, Adam B. *Expansion and Coexistence: The History of
Soviet Foreign Policy 1917-1967.* New York, Frederick
A. Praeger, 1968.

*United States Foreign Policy — 1971: A Report of the
Secretary of State.* Department of State Publication
8634, Washington, D. C., March, 1972.

Wellisz, Stanislaw. *The Economies of the Soviet Bloc.*
New York: McGraw-Hill Co., 1964.

Wiles, P. J. D. *The Political Economy of Communism.*
Cambridge, Mass.: Harvard University Press, 1962.

Zabith, Sepehr. *The Communist Movement in Iran.* Berkeley:
University of California Press, 1966.

Secondary Source Articles

"Abu Dhabi Oil Deal with Japan," *Financial Times* (London),
May 22, 1968, p. 7.

"L'achat de sous-marins soviétiques est confirmé,"
Le Monde (Paris), April 3, 1968, p. 4.

Achminow, Herman F. "Karl Marx Embarrasses the Soviet
Ideologists," Institute for the Study of the U.S.S.R.
(Munich), *Analysis of Current Developments in the
Soviet Union,* No. 27, 1966/1967, pp. 1-7.

"Alarms Ring From Mideast to Atlantic," Washington *Post*,
April 9, 1967, p. 1.

"Algerian Gas: Behind the Row, the Russians," *The Economist*
(London), February 4, 1967, p. 433.

"Algeria Takes Control of 13 U.S. Companies," *Financial Times*
(London), June 15, 1967, p. 7.

Allen, Robert Loring. "Soviet Russian Economic Penetration in the Middle East," *Free World Forum,* I, No. 5 (September/ October, 1959), pp. 32-38.

Allen, Robert S., and Paul Scott. "U.S. — Russian Oil Deal is Puzzling," *Northern Virginia Sun,* February 22, 1967.

"All Seas Open to Russia," *London Times,* February 17, 1968, p. 5.

"America and the Middle East," *The Annals of the American Academy of Political and Social Science,* May, 1972.

Amery, Julian. "East of Suez Up For Grabs," *Reporter,* December 1, 1966, pp. 16-21.

Anable, David J. H. "Paris Stakes Claim For Libyan Oil," *Christian Science Monitor,* April 15, 1968, p. 11.

Anderson, Raymond H., "Pravda Cautions Czechs on Trade," New York *Times,* September 3, 1968, p. 7.

Anthony, John Duke. "The Lower Gulf States: New Roles in Regional Affairs," *Middle East Institute Panel Discussion Resume' Series* No. 5 (1972), August, 1972.

"Arab Pledges to Attend Khartoum Summit," *Financial Times* (London), June 15, 1967, p. 7.

"Arabs Dismayed By Soviet's Stand," New York *Times,* June 8, 1967, p. 21.

"Arabs Make a Deal on Oil," *Business Week,* September 30, 1972.

"Arabs Said to Increase Canal Force," Washington *Post,* October 28, 1967, sec. A, p. 10.

Arendt, H. "Totalitarian Imperialism: Reflections on the Hungarian Revolution," *The Journal of Politics,* No. 1 (February, 1958), pp. 71-76.

Babich, Andrey V. "Ministerial Bureaucracy Still Hamstringing the New Soviet Economic Reform," Institute for the Study of the U.S.S.R. (Munich), *Analysis of Current Developments in the Soviet Union,* No. 26 (1966/1967), pp. 1-7.

"Back from the Brink," *Business Week,* June 10, 1967, pp. 35-36.

"A Bad Arab Summer," *The Economist* (London), August 27, 1966, pp. 799-800.

Badeau, J. S. "The Soviet Approach to the Arab World," *Orbis*, III, No. 1 (Spring, 1959), pp. 75-84.

"Bad Russian Advice," *Christian Science Monitor,* August 23, 1967, p. 14.

Bala, Mirza. "Die Aspiration der sowjets auf Aserbaidschan," *Sowjet Studien* (Munich), No. 1 (July, 1956), pp. 75-81.

Ballis, W. B. "Soviet-Iranian Relations during the Decade 1953-1964," *Bulletin* of the Institute for the Study of the U.S.S.R., XII, No. 11 (November, 1965), pp. 9-22.

Barry, John, "Oil and Soviet Policy in the Middle East," The *Middle East Journal,* Volume 26, No. 2, Spring, 1972.

Berger, M. "Fuel Crisis, Big Oil Imports Face U.S. by '80s," Washington *Post*, April 4, 1972, p. A-3.

_____. "Oil, Foreign Policy and Energy Crises," Washington *Post*, April 16, 1972, p. B-5.

Berliner, J. S. "Soviet Economic Policy in the Middle East," *Middle Eastern Affairs* (Council for Middle Eastern Affairs, New York) (August/September, 1959), pp. 286-290.

Berreby, Jean-Jacques. "Does America Need Arab Oil?" *The New Middle East* (London) April, 1970.

"Bombing of Saudi Arabian Oasis by Egyptian Planes Is Reported," New York *Times*, November 7, 1966, p. 8.

Borowiec, Andrew. "Russia May Gain from Oil Crisis in Mideast," Washington *Star*, December 14, 1966, sec. A, p. 31.

"Bourguiba Denounces UAR Soviet Aid," *Teheran Journal,* May 20, 1968, p. 1.

Bowen, Maj. Gen. Frank S., Jr. "Middle East: Strategy and Oil," *Army*, XII, No. 3 (October, 1961), pp. 50-52.

Brady, Thomas F. "Iran Beginning Wide Exchanges With Soviet," New York *Times,* July 14, 1966, p. 6.

_____. "Iran Said to Consider Buying Soviet Missiles," New York *Times,* July 14, 1966, p. 6.

Brewer, William D. "Yesterday and Tomorrow in the Persian Gulf," *Middle East Journal,* Spring, 1969, Volume 23, No. 2.

"Brezhnev's Renegade Features Revealed More Clearly," Peking *Review,* July 21, 1967, pp. 8-11.

"A Business For Giants," *The Economist* (London), March 2, 1968, pp. ix-xiii.

Campbell, John C. "The Communist Powers and the Middle East," *Problems of Communism,* September-October, 1972.

"The Middle East in the Muted Cold War," *Monograph Series in World Affairs,* No. 1 (1964-1965).

Canham, Erwin D. "Oil and Politics," *Christian Science Monitor,* July 8, 1967, p. 16.

Carlson, Sevinc. "Japan's Inroads into the Middle East and North Africa," *The New Middle East* (London), July 1970.

Carlson, Verner R. "The Soviet Maritime Threat," *United States Naval Institute Proceedings,* XCIII, No. 5 (May, 1967), pp. 39-48.

Carmical, J. H. "Soviet Union Seeks Greater Role in Europe's Fuel Market," New York *Times,* December 11, 1966, p. 1.

Cattell, David T. "The USSR and the West," *Current History,* LI, No. 302 (October, 1966), pp. 193-240.

Cazes, B. "Rationality and Doctrine in Economic Thought," *Problems of Communism,* IX, No. 2 (March/April, 1960), pp. 9-15.

Chabagi, V. G. "Forty Years of Soviet Near-Eastern Policy," *The East Turkic Review* (Munich), No. 2, 1959, pp 28-36.

"The Communist Oil Conundrum," *The Economist* (London), January 7, 1967, pp. 46-47.

"Un Consortium de pétroliers européens indépendants anime par Elf-E.R.A.P. negocie l'obtention de permis de recherche en Iran," *Le Monde* (Paris), April 30, 1968, p. 26.

"Cooking Up a Gas Deal," *Business Week,* January 20, 1968, p. 34.

Cooley, John K. "Algerian Nationalization Move Jolts Foreign Oil Interest," *Christian Science Monitor*, December 15, 1966, p. 2.

_____. "Arab Leftists Scent Gain From Oil Crisis," *Christian Science Monitor*, December 15, 1966, p. 2.

_____. "Arabs Act: New U.A.R. — Syrian Agreement Stiffens Arab World Defense," *Christian Science Monitor,* November 7, 1966, p. 11.

_____. "Arab Oil Embargo Squeezes Arabs, Too," *Christian Science Monitor,* June 22, 1967, p. 1.

_____. "Egyptian Oil Outlook Brightens," *Christian Science Monitor,* December 19, 1966, p. 5.

_____. "Flurry Over Oil in Middle East," *Christian Science Monitor,* January 15, 1968, p. 1.

_____. "Iran Development Floats on Oil," *Christian Science Monitor,* March 15, 1968, p. 4.

_____. "Iraq to Develop Vast Oil Field," *Christian Science Monitor,* April 15, 1968, p. 12.

_____. "Moscow Aim Probed in Oil Deal," *Christian Science Monitor,* December 29, 1967, p. 2.

_____. "Oil Crisis Bubbles in Mideast," *Christian Science Monitor,* April 22, 1967, p. 2.

_____. "Politics and Petroleum Mix in Arab Congress," *Christian Science Monitor,* March 8, 1967, p. 4.

_____. "Saudi Bid Seen As Policy Shift," *Christian Science Monitor*, July 6, 1968, p. 2.

_____. "Syria Closes Pipeline — Oil Cutoff Pinches Iraqi Income," *Christian Science Monitor,* December 14, 1966, p. 6.

Cordtz, Dan. "But What Do We Do about the Arabs?" *Fortune,* September 1, 1967, pp. 75-186.

Cottrell, Alvin J., and Burrell, R. M. "No Power Can Hope to Dominate the Indian Ocean," *The New Middle East* (London), September, 1971.

Coxe, D. G. M. "The African Gambit," *Rally,* II, No. 2 (July/August, 1967), p. 9.

Cromley, Ray. "Soviets Seek Deal," Washington *Daily News,* October 2, 1967, p. 17.

"Czechs Conclude $200 m. Oil-Machinery Deal With Iran,"
Financial Times (London), May 7, 1968, p. 5.

Dabernat, Rene. "France's New Oil Line-Up," *Paris Match.*
Reprinted in London *Times*, December 18, 1967, p. 18.

Dallin, A. "Soviet Policy toward Eastern Europe," *Journal of International Affairs,* XI, No. 1 (1957), pp. 48-59.

Davis, David. "Russians Intensify Petrol Battle," London
Times, March 8, 1968, p. 17.

Dietsch, Robert. "Glubb Sees Soviets as Mid-East Victors,"
Washington *Daily News,* October 6, 1967, p. 9.

Douglas-Home, Charles. "Russia's Growing Sea Power," London
Times, February 15, 1968, p. 5.

"Early Soviet Contacts With Arab and African Countries,"
Mizan VIII, No. 2 (March/April, 1966), pp. 87-91.

"Economic Problems in the USSR," *Nashe Obshcheye Delo
(Our Common Cause)* (Munich), No. 10 (May, 1960), p. 2.

"Egypt," *The Atlantic,* April, 1968, pp. 10-20.

"Egyptians Show Off Soviet Air-Ground Missiles in Parade,"
Washington *Post*, July 24, 1966, sec. A, p. 18.

"Egypt Lost 700 Million Pounds of Soviet Equipment,"
Financial Times (London), June 14, 1967, p. 14.

Ellis, Harry B. "The Arab-Israeli Conflict Today," in *The
United States and the Middle East.* Georgianna G. Stevens,
ed. Englewood Cliffs, N.J.: Prentice Hall, Inc., 1964,
pp. 113-147.

"Erdöl ins Feuer" ("Pouring Oil into the Fire"), *Der Klare Blick*
(Berne), June 14, 1967.

Farnsworth, Clyde H. "A Bar to Soviet Oil Is Asked in Belgium,"
New York *Times,* May 31, 1968, p. 41.

_____. "Soviet Pushes Fuel Sales in West," New
York *Times,* December 9, 1967, p. 71.

"Finding Future Oil Reserves Difficult But Not Impossible,"
Oil and Gas Journal, June 10, 1968, pp. 38-39.

Foel, Earl W. "Have Soviets Gained in Mid-East Aftermath?"
Christian Science Monitor, September 19, 1967, p. 1.

"Foreign Trade in Communist Development," *Communist Affairs* (University of Southern California), IV (September/October, 1966), pp. 6-11.

"Foreign Trade of Centrally Planned Economies," *Communist Affairs* (University of Southern California), V (March/April, 1967), pp. 3-12.

Francis, David R. "Soviets Peddle Oil to Nations Cut Off by Arabs," *Christian Science Monitor*, June 20, 1967, p. 12.

Friedman, Milton. "Oil and the Middle East," *Newsweek,* June 26, 1967, p. 63.

Gardner, Frank J. "The Middle East—1 Year after the War," *Oil and Gas Journal,* June 10, 1968, pp. 54-56.

_____. "Russia Claims Steady Gains in Refining," *Oil and Gas Journal*, September 16, 1968, pp. 39-41.

_____. "Russian Oil: Threat or Mirage?" *Oil and Gas Journal*, July 17, 1967, p. 59.

_____. "Watching the World," *Oil and Gas Journal,* July 17, 1967, p. 59.

Gasteyger, Curt. "Moscow and the Mediterranean," *Foreign Affairs* (July, 1968), pp. 676-687.

Gehlen, Michael P. "The Politics of Soviet Foreign Trade," *The Western Political Quarterly,* XVIII, No. 1 (March, 1965), pp. 104-115.

Getler, Michael. "Pentagon to Brief Iran on Latest Arms," Washington *Post*, September 9, 1972, p. A-8.

"Glassboro," Washington *Post,* June 27, 1967, sec. A, p. 16.

Goldman, Marshall I. "Economic Revolution in the Soviet Union," *Foreign Affairs* (January, 1967), pp. 319-331.

Graham, J. D. S. "U.S. Companies Agree on Emergency Oil Plans," *Financial Times* (London), June 16, 1967, p. 1.

Grose, Peter. "Kosygin Goes to Cairo Today in Effort to Bolster Soviet Influence in Mideast," New York *Times,* May 10, 1966, p. 12.

Gross, George. "Rumania: The Fruits of Autonomy," *Problems of Communism,* XV, No. 1 (January/February, 1966), pp. 16-27.

Hajenko, F. "The Mamai System of Socialist Competition," *Bulletin* of the Institute for the Study of the U.S.S.R., V, No. 6 (June, 1958), pp. 29-40.

_____. "The Wage Reform and the Curtailment of the Working Day," *Bulletin* of the Institute for the Study of the U.S.S.R., VI, No. 1 (January, 1959), pp. 16-24.

"Handbook on the Middle East," Foreign Policy Association, *Intercom,* IX, No. 6 (November/December, 1967).

Hasib, Khair al-Din. "Towards a National Oil Policy in Iraq," *Supplement* to *Middle East Economic Survey* (Beirut), XI, No. 28 (May 10, 1968), pp. 1-5.

Hayes, Leslie. "Another 32 Years—And No More Oil," *Kayhan* (Teheran), May 21, 1968, p. 1.

Haykal, Muhammad Hasanayn. "Arab-Soviet Friendship," Institute for Strategic Studies (London), *Survival,* IX, No. 11, 1967, pp. 358-362. Broadcast over Cairo Radio, August 25, 1967, monitored by BBC, Reading, England.

Herbert, Nicholas. "Soviet Bombers Visit Syria and Egypt," London *Times*, April 8, 1968, p. 4.

Herman, Leon M. "The Soviet Oil Offensive," *Reporter,* June 21, 1962, pp. 26-28.

Hittle, James D. "Russians May Dominate Middle East with Navy," San Diego *Union,* September 11, 1966, sec. A, p. 7.

Hoagland, John H., Jr., and John B. Teeple. "Regional Stability and Weapons Transfer: The Middle Eastern Case," *Orbis,* IX, No. 3 (Fall, 1965), pp. 714-728.

Hoffman, David. "Navy Warns of Improved Russian Subs," Washington *Post,* March 14, 1968, p. A-8.

Hollingsworth, Clare. "New Arms 'Vital' for Persia," *Manchester Guardian Weekly,* September 1, 1966, p. 5.

Hoskins, Halford L. "Soviet Economic Penetration in the Middle East," *Orbis,* III, No. 4 (Winter, 1960), pp. 458-468.

_____. "The U.S. in the Middle East: Policy in Transition," Current History, XLVIII, No. 285 (May, 1965), pp. 257-262.

Hottinger, Arnold. *"Die Araber nach dem dritten israelisch-arabishen Krieg"* ("The Arabs Following the Third Arab-Israeli War") *Europa-Archiv* (Bonn), No. 15 (August 10, 1967), pp. 533-540.

Hourani, Cecil. "The Moment of Truth," *Encounter* (November, 1967), pp. 3-14.

"How Oil Moves Round the World," London *Times*, July 31, 1968, p. 17.

"How U.S. Could Meet a New Military Test," *Business Week*, June 10, 1967, pp. 38-40.

Howard, Harry N. "The Regional Pacts and the Eisenhower Doctrine," *The Annals of the American Academy of Political and Social Science,* May, 1972.

_____. "The United States in the Middle East Crisis," *Current History,* December, 1967.

Howard, Michael, and Robert Hunter. "Israel and the Arab World: The Crisis of 1967," The Institute For Strategic Studies (London), *Adelphi Papers,* No. 41 (October, 1967).

Hughes, Edward. "The Russians Drill Deep in the Middle East," *Fortune* (July, 1968), pp. 102-105.

Hunter, Robert E. "The Soviet Dilemma in the Middle East, Part II: Oil and the Persian Gulf," *Adelphi Papers*, No. 60 (October, 1969) London: The Institute for Strategic Studies.

"Iran Expects $300 Million in Soviet Credits," *International Herald Tribune,* April 16, 1968, p. 2.

"Iran Oil Deal with Rumania," London *Times*, July 17, 1968, p. 24.

"Iran Seeks Big Rises in Oil Revenue," London *Times,* October 30, 1967, p.17.

"Iranian Oil—Agreement Reached," *The Economist* (London), December 17, 1966, pp. 1275-1276.

"Iran's Breakthrough," *The Economist* (London), January 14, 1967, pp. 139-140.

"Iran's Economy: Taking Its Chance," *The Economist* (London), August 26, 1967, p. 746.

"Iran's Oil Squeeze," *Christian Science Monitor,* November 4, 1966, p. 18.

"Iraq and U.S.S.R. Exchange Letters on Soviet Assistance for Oil Exploration and Development in Iraq," *Middle East Economic Survey* (Beirut), XI, No. 9 (December 29, 1967), pp. 1-5.

"Iraq Challenge to Oil Consortium — Deal Planned with Russia," London *Times,* December 28, 1967, p. 4.

"Iraq's Oil — Good Politics, Bad Business," *The Economist* (London), February 10, 1968, p. 60.

Issawi, Charles. "Iran's Economic Upsurge," *Middle East Journal,* XXI, No. 4 (Autumn, 1967), pp. 447-461.

"Italy and Russia: The New Alliance," *The Economist* (London), September 23, 1967, p. 1125.

"Italy's Oil Firm to Explore, Jointly Develop with Saudi Arabia Oil in Vast Desert Area," *Wall Street Journal,* December 22, 1967, p. 22.

"Japanese Rekindle Siberian Line Negotiations," *Oil and Gas Journal,* January 8, 1968, p. 49.

Jones, J. D. F. "Kuwait Resumes Oil Sales But Not to Britain, U.S.," *Financial Times* (London), June 15, 1967, p. 1.

Joshua, Wynfred. *Soviet Penetration into the Middle East.* New York: National Strategy Information Center, 1970.

Kaiser, Robert G. "Middle East Cloud Bears Strong Silver Lining for Kremlin," Washington *Post*, July 20, 1972, p. A-14.

Kamm, Henry. "Soviet Refinery 'Fulfills' Its Plan: Grozny Processed Same Oil Over and Over to Meet Goal," New York *Times,* November 18, 1967, p. 5.

Kashin, Aleksander A. "Karlovy Vary — A Non-Conference," Institute for the Study of the U.S.S.R. (Munich), *Analysis of Current Developments in the Soviet Union,* No. 35 (1966/1967), pp. 1-7.

Kearns, Robert. "Arab States Fear Loss of Markets," *Journal of Commerce,* June 15, 1967, p. 1.

Kennedy, John F. "Toward a Strategy of Peace," in *Patterns of Competitive Coexistence/USA vs USSR*. Young Hum Kim, ed. New York: G. P. Putnam's Sons, 1966, pp. 419-427.

"Khrushchev: The Popular Prefect," *Spectator*, May 22, 1964, pp. 680-681.

Khrushchev, Nikita S. "The Task of Surpassing the U.S.," in *Patterns of Competitive Coexistence/USA vs USSR*. Young Hum Kim, ed. New York: G. P. Putnam's Sons, 1966, pp. 151-163.

Kilpatrick, Carroll. "Limit on Oil Imports Increased [sic] by Nixon," Washington *Post*, September 19, 1972, p. A-13.

Kimche, Jon. "Soviet Switch over Israel," *Evening Standard* (London), p. 1.

Klinghoffer, Arthur Jay. "Evaluating the Soviet Role in the Middle East," *Mizan* (London) X, No. 3 (May/June, 1968), pp. 86-93.

Knox, Rawle. "Nasser Still Hopes for UN Action: Doubts on Suez Oil Position," London *Times,* October 30, 1967, p. 5.

"Kosygin To Head Russian Team at UN Assembly," *Financial Times* (London), June 16, 1967, p. 20.

"Kosygin The Resilient Bureaucrat," *Communist Affairs*, II, No. 6 (November/December, 1964), and III, Nos. 1, 3 (January/February, May/June, 1965).

Kühne, Von Stefan. *"Nasser ist der Gefangene der reichen ölscheichs"* ("Nasser Is Prisoner of the Wealthy Oil Sheikhs), *Die Welt* (Hamburg), May 27, 1968, p. 5.

Kutt, Aleksander. "Soviet Exploitation of Eastern Europe Continues," *East-West Digest* (London), III, No. 3 (August, 1967), pp. 250-254.

"Kuwait National Petroleum Branches Out," *Oil and Gas Journal*, September 16, 1968, p. 58.

Landis, Lincoln. "Middle East Crises and the U.S.S.R.," *World Affairs* Volume 130, No. 1, 1967.

_____. "Soviet Interest in Middle East Oil," *The New Middle East* (London), December, 1968.

_____. "Der Suezkanal in der politischen Strategie der Sowjetunion," (The Suez Canal in Soviet Strategy), *Europa Archiv* (Bonn), No. 3, 1969.

Laqueur, Walter. "The Outlook: Neither War nor Peace," *Current,* No. 87 (September, 1967), pp. 60-64.

Lee, Dwight E. "The Liberation of the Balkan Slavs," in *A Handbook of Slavic Studies.* Leonid Strakhovsky, ed. Cambridge, Mass.: Harvard University Press, 1949, pp. 271-292.

Leontief, W. "The Decline and Rise of Soviet Economic Science," *Foreign Affairs* (January, 1960), pp. 261-272.

Levy, Walter. "Oil Power," *Foreign Affairs,* July, 1971.

Lewis, Bernard. "Middle East Reaction to Soviet Pressures," *Middle East Journal,* X (Spring, 1956), pp. 125-137.

"Limited Middle East Flow Little Help," *Oil and Gas Journal,* July 17, 1967, pp. 42-43.

Loewenthal, Rudolf. "A Bibliography of Near and Middle Eastern Studies Published in the Soviet Union from 1937 to 1947," *Oriens* (Leiden, Netherlands), No. 2 (1951), pp. 328-344.

Lombardo, Ivan Matteo. "Maritime Routes, Petrol and Soviet Strategy," *NATO Letter* (October, 1964), pp. 22-25.

London, Kurt L. "The Soveit Union and the West," *Current History,* LVII, No. 338, (October, 1969).

Longrigg, Stephen H. "The Economics and Politics of Oil in the Middle East," *Journal of International Affairs,* XIX, No. 1, 1965, pp. 111-122.

Lucas, Walter. "Oil-Export Questions Remain Unanswered," *Christian Science Monitor,* October 3, 1967, p. 13.

Luce, Sir William. "Aden's Shadow Over the Gulf," London *Daily Telegraph,* April 12, 1967, p. 16.

MacDonald, Scot. "STRIKE's Attention is Drawn to Mid-East, Africa," *Armed Forces Management* (August, 1967), pp. 34-76.

Maffre, John. "Ivan Hugs Shores of Tripoli," Washington *Post,* February 25, 1968, sec. D, p. 2.

Marin, Yuri V. "Marxism-Leninism in Retreat Before the March of Science," Institute for the Study of the U.S.S.R. (Munich), *Analysis of Current Developments in the Soviet Union,* No. 467, August 8, 1967, pp. 1-6.

Marshall, Charles Burton. "Reflections on the Middle East," *ORBIS,* XI, No. 2 (Summer, 1967), pp. 343-359.

Masson, Ph., and Labayle Couhat. *"La Présence Navale Sovietiqu en Mediterran'ee,"* Revue de Defense Nationale (Paris), XXIV (May, 1968), pp. 858-873.

May, John Allan. "Any Arab Boycott Two-edged," *Christian Science Monitor,* June 16, 1967, p. 14.

Mazour, Anatole G. "Russia, The Middle East, and Oil," *World Affairs Interpreter* (Los Angeles) (Winter, 1952), pp. 415-423.

McDonald, James, "Shipping Re-routed on Basis of Lengthy Closure of Suez," *Financial Times* (London), June 15, 1967, p. 1.

"The Mediterranean — One Small Symbol," *The Economist* (London), July 13, 1968, p. 28.

"The Mediterranean, Pivot of Peace and War," *Foreign Affairs* (July, 1953), pp. 619-633.

Melloan, George. "Stymied Soviets? Problems of Pricing, Personnel Face USSR in Reforming Economy," *Wall Street Journal,* December 27, 1967, p. 1.

"Middle East Arms Race," *Atlantic* (September, 1966), sec. A, p. 30.

"The Middle East: Chronology," *Survival* (London), August, 1967, pp. 242-245.

"The Middle East in the Soviet Press," *Mizan* (London), Supplement A, No. 1 (January/February, 1967), [London: Central Asian Research Center in association with St. Antony's College Soviet Affairs Study Group].

"The Middle East in the Soviet Press," *Mizan* (London), Supplement A, No. 2 (March/April, 1967).

"The Middle East in the Soviet Press," *Mizan* (London), Supplement A, No. 3 (May/June, 1967).

"The Middle East in the Soviet Press," *Mizan* (London),
    Supplement A, No. 4 (July/August, 1967).

"Middle East Maneuvers: What Is the Soviet up to?" *Christian
    Science Monitor,* November 13, 1967, sec. B, p. 1.

"Middle East Oil," *The British Survey*, No. 281 (January, 1968),
    pp. 2-15.

"Middle East Oil: Asking for More," *The Economist* (London),
    September 9, 1967, p. 914.

"Middle East Oil: Flashpoint Iraq," *The Economist* (London),
    January 28, 1967, p. 350.

"Middle East Oil: Higher Stakes," *The Economist* (London),
    November 26, 1966, pp. 934-935.

"Middle East Oil: New Deal Versus Oil," *The Economist*
    (London), March 18, 1967, pp. 1056-1057.

"Middle East Oil on New Terms," *The Economist,* June 5, 1965,
    pp. 1151-1168. A Survey including separate articles
    entitled "The Plain of Oil," "Oil on New Terms," "Getting
    and Spending," "Cash on the Barrel," and "Politics Over
    the Oil Scene."

"The Middle East: Soviet Anxieties," *Mizan* (London), IX, No. 4
    (July/August, 1967), pp. 145-153.

Middleton, Drew. "Iran — A Strategic Pawn," New York *Times,*
    April 7, 1968, sec. D, p. 6.

_____. "The Arab World: Soviet Role Widens,"
New York *Times*, July 16, 1968, p. 1.

Millar, T. B. "Soviet Policies South and East of Suez," *Foreign
    Affairs*, October, 1970, Vol. 49, No. 1.

Monroe, Elizabeth. "British Bases in the Middle East — Assets
    or Liabilities?" *International Affairs* (London), XLII, No. 1
    (January, 1966), pp. 24-34.

Morgan, Carlyle. "French Mirage Deal Seen as Jab at Soviets,"
    Christian Science Monitor, April 15, 1968, p. 12.

Morison, David. "Ideology and 'Common Sense,' " *Mizan*
    (London), VIII, No. 6 (November/December, 1966),
    pp. 242-249.

_____. "Russia, Israel, and the Arabs," *Mizan* (London), IX, No. 3 (May/June, 1967), pp. 91-107.

_____. "Soviet Influence: Prospects for 1967," *Mizan* (London), IX, No. 1 (January/February, 1967), pp. 31-37.

_____. "Soviet Interest in Middle East Oil," *Mizan* (London), X, No. 3 (May/June, 1968), pp. 79-85.

Morris, Joe Alex, Jr. "Mideast Oil Crisis Seen as Threat to West's Ownership," Washington *Post*, December 19, 1966, sec. A, p. 19.

_____. "Reds Spotted in Syria Near Border of Israel," Washington *Post*, October 9, 1966, sec. A, p. 20.

_____. "Russia Seeks Entry to Iran's Gulf Oil Fields — Kosygin Eyes Region Dominated by West," *International Herald Tribune*, April 5, 1968, p. 2.

_____. "Soviets Advance in Mideast," Washington *Post*, February 21, 1968, sec. E, p. 1.

"Moscow Pushes Arctic Trade Route," Washington *Evening Star*, June 5, 1968, sec. E, p. 16.

Mosher, Lawrence. "Nasser's Drive for South Arabia," *Reporter*, February 9, 1967, pp. 24-27.

Mostert, Noel. "High Stakes Southeast of Suez," *Reporter*, March 7, 1968, pp. 17-20.

_____. "Russia Bids for Ocean Supremacy," *Reporter*, February 10, 1966, pp. 24-28.

Murarka, Dev. "Soviet Leaders Tighten Control Over Arts, Culture," London observer of Washington *Post*, September 7, 1972, p. E-6.

"The National Liberation Movement: A Lower Soviet Rating?" *Mizan* (London), IX, No. 2 (March/April, 1967), pp 41-49.

"New Oil Discovery in Egypt," *Interplay*, (August/September, 1968), p. 34.

"Newsletter," *Oil and Gas Journal*, September 16, 1968, pp. ii-v.

Nossiter, Bernard. "Kosygin Visits Pakistan Today: Arms and Aid Seen Topics," Washington *Post*, April 17, 1968, sec. A, p. 17.

"Now a New Ocean for U.S. to Defend — Huge Vacuum as
Britain Pulls Back," *U.S. News and World Report,* August
28, 1967, pp. 32-33.

Ofner, Francis. "Israeli Pipeline to Link Oil Ports," *Christian
Science Monitor,* July 13, 1968, p. 11.

"Oil Agreement," Washington *Post,* December 25, 1967, p. C-4.

"Oil Deal Aids Soviet in Mideast," Washington *Post*, December
27, 1967, p. A-14.

"Oilfields in Siberia Lost Many Workers," New York *Times,*
June 9, 1967.

"Oil in Egypt, Through Israel," *The Economist* (London),
June 8, 1968, pp. 71-72.

"Oil — Iraq Settlement," *The Economist* (London), May 6,
1967, p. 597.

"Oilmen Confident on Alternative Supplies if Arab-Israeli War
Bars Suez Shipments," *Wall Street Journal,* May 24, 1967,
p. 4.

"Oil Minister Outlines Syria's Oil Plans," *Middle East Economic
Survey* (Beirut), XI, No. 28 (May 10, 1968), p. 506.

"The Oil Squeeze," *The Economist* (London), March 2, 1968,
pp. 47-48.

"Oil: Syria Wins, Iraq Loses," *The Economist* (London),
March 4, 1967, p. 854.

O'Toole, Thomas. "U.S. Energy Crisis: Light Dims at End of
the Tunnel," Washington *Post,* April 4, 1972, p. 1.

Pace, Eric. "Egypt Rules out Bases for Soviet," New York
Times, November 27, 1967, p. 1.

_____. "Oil Boom Aiding Shah of Iran's Reform
Programs," New York *Times*, September 25, 1967, p. 1.

Parrott, John. "British White Paper Outlines New Alternatives
For Fuel," *Christian Science Monitor,* November 18,
1967, p. 8.

Pennar, Jaan. "The Soviet Road to Damascus," *Mizan*
(London), IX, No. 1 (January/February, 1967), pp. 23-29.

"Pipelines for Russia — Golden Chance in Siberia," *The
Economist* (London), May 6, 1967, pp. 592-594.

"Pointers from the 23rd CPSU Congress," *Mizan* (London), VIII, No. 3 (May/June, 1966), pp. 95-99.

"Polish President Visits Abadan," *Daily Star* (Beirut), May 13, 1968, p. 2.

"Putting a Bear in Britain's Tank," *Business Week,* July 20, 1968, p. 80.

"Radio Address by Imre Nagy Promising New Policies and an Adjustment in Relations with the Soviet Union, October 25, 1956," *National Communism and Popular Revolt in Eastern Europe,* Part III, New York: Columbia University Press, 1956.

Ramazani, Rouhollah K. "Iran's Changing Foreign Policy," *Middle East Journal,* Autumn, 1970.

"Recent Soviet Articles on the UAR," *Mizan* (London), VIII, No. 1 (January/February, 1966), pp. 33-37.

"Red Oil: Eastern Europe Fuel Problem Turns Attention to Siberia," *Christian Science Monitor,* February 13, 1967, p. 13.

"Red Navy Patrols Mediterranean — Soviet Maritime Power Disturbing," *The German Tribune* (Hamburg), June 24, 1967, p. 1. Reprinted from *Süddeutsche Zeitung* (Munich).

Reese, Howard C. "The Arab-Israeli Dispute and the Major Powers," *Military Review* (April, 1966), pp. 53-64.

_____. "The Search for Equilibrium in the Middle East," *Military Review* (April, 1968), pp. 29-40.

Revai, J. "The Character of a 'People's Democracy,'" *Foreign Affairs* (October, 1949), pp. 143-152.

"Rich Sea Gas Source For Italy," London *Times,* September 16, 1968, p. 22.

Rossow, Robert J. "The Battle of Azerbaijan, 1944," *Middle East Journal,* X (Winter, 1956), pp. 17-32.

Rostow, Walter W. "Perspective of the Tasks of the 1960s," in *Patterns of Competitive Coexistence/USA vs USSR.* Young Hum Kim, ed. New York: G. P. Putnam's Sons, 1966, pp. 54-61.

"Russia Increases Her Aid to Iran," Washington *Star,* June 23, 1968, sec. A, p. 14.

"Russia in the Middle East," New York *Times,* January 16, 1968, p. 38.

"Russia, Iran Sign Pact on Military Aid," Washington *Post,* February 8, 1968, p. 10.

"Russia Launching Oil Sales Drive in West Europe," London *Times,* November 24, 1967.

"Russia Moves into Middle East Oil," London *Times,* December 28, 1967, p. 7.

"Russian Bloc Hikes Oil Output," *World Oil,* August 15, 1972, p. 91.

"Russian Energy: Bring the Gift in Barrels," *The Economist* (London), September 23, 1967, p. 1129.

"Russia Pushes Gas Sales in West to Pay for Building 100-Inch Lines from Siberia," *Wall Street Journal,* November 20, 1969, p. 40.

"Russia to Equip UAR Refinery," London *Times,* November 21, 1967, p. 4.

"Russians Say U.S. Promoted Persian Gulf Defense Grouping," Washington *Post,* March 6, 1968, p. A-30.

Saikowski, C. "Resource Gap Nags Soviets," *Christian Science Monitor,* October 27, 1970, p. 1.

_____. "Siberian Boom Town," *Christian Science Monitor,* September 17, 1972, p. B-3.

Salem, Elie A. "Islam in the Cold War," *Free World Forum,* II, No. 4 (1960), pp. 1-10.

Sarkis, Nicolas. "Les pays arabes veulent 'décoloniser' le pétrole," *Le Monde* (Paris), April 16, 1968, p. 1.

Schlesinger, R. "New Forms of Workers' Participation in Management," *Soviet Studies* (Glasgow), X, No. 1 (July, 1958), pp. 101-103.

Schmidt, Dana Adams. "Nasser's Road to Oil Runs through Yemen," New York *Times,* November 13, 1966, sec. E, p. 4.

_____. "Strategy Shifts on Persian Gulf," New York *Times*, January 14, 1968, p. 9.

Schroeder, Gertrude E. "Soviet Technology: System vs. Progress," *Problems of Communism,* September-October, 1970.

"Scorpion's Sting: The Arabs Have the Most to Lose from an Oil Boycott," *Barron's,* July 10, 1967, p. 1.

"Search for Petroleum Sources Intensified," *Financial Times* (London), May 22, 1968, p. 7.

Shabad, Theodore. "Cost-Conscious Soviet Planners Seek More Efficient Use of Natural Resources," New York *Times,* October 31, 1967, sec. C, p. 26.

Shabecoff, Philip. "East-West Trade Hurdles Ideology," New York *Times,* March 9, 1967, sec. C, p. 15.

Shapiro, Henry. "COMECON Membership Eyed," Washington *Post,* September 26, 1972, p. A-20.

"Shoring Up the Arab States," *East Europe,* February, 1968, pp. 24-28.

"Short- Versus Long-Term Considerations in Planning a National Oil Policy," *Letter for Executives: Review of Arab Petroleum and Economics* (Beirut), I, No. 11 (May 7, 1968), pp. 6-8.

"Shrewd Russian Move," *Christian Science Monitor,* December 6, 1966, sec. B, p. 14.

Shub, Anatole, "Soviet Push in Siberia is Costly," Washington *Post,* October 13, 1967, sec. A, p. 10.

_____. "Soviets Mum in Mideast Shifts," Washington *Post,* November 15, 1967.

Shwadran, Benjamin. "Soviet Posture in the Middle East," *Current History,* LIII, No. 316 (December, 1967), pp. 331-336.

Sieniawski, Michael. "World Oil Output," *Christian Science Monitor,* July 5, 1967, p. 12.

Silvestri, Stefano. "Problems and Prospects of the Mediterranean Area," *Lo Spettatore internazionale* (English edition), III, No. 2 (April/June, 1968), Istituto affari internazionale (Rome), pp. 148-156.

Skala, Martin. "West's Oil Firms Face Up to Search for Alternatives," *Christian Science Monitor,* June 19, 1967, p. 10.

Smith, Hedrick. "Egyptians Divide on Kosygin Visit," New York *Times,* May 22, 1966, p. 22.

_____. "Soviet Navy Said to Increase Use of UAR Ports," New York *Times,* April 5, 1966, p. 10.

_____. "Ex-U.S. Envoy to Cario Believes Soviet Aided Nasser's Challenge to Israel," New York *Times,* September 12, 1967.

Smith, Robin. "Visiting Historian Says Revolution, Palestine Resistance Linked," *Daily Star* (Beirut), July 23, 1968, interview with Hisham B. Sharabi; Georgetown University.

Smith, William D. "Mideast Catalyst: The Arabs' Oil and American Money," New York *Times,* April 7, 1968, sec. 3, p. 1.

_____. "Oil Industry Widens Horizons to Meet Demands in the Future," New York *Times,* November 12, 1967, sec. F, p. 1.

_____. "Soviet Union Tastes Middle East's Oil," New York *Times,* December, 1967, sec. F, p. 1.

Smithies, Arthur. "The Primrose Path to Economic Development," *Challenge* (January/February, 1967) pp. 30-42.

Smolansky, O. M. "Moscow and the Persian Gulf: An Analysis of Soviet Ambitions and Potential," *Orbis,* XIV, No. 1 (Spring, 1970), pp. 92-108.

"Some British Firms Seek to Buy Soviet Oil: Russia Seen Gaining from Current Shortage," *Wall Street Journal,* June 19, 1967, p. 4.

"Sources of Conflict in the Middle East," *Adelphi Papers,* No. 26 (March, 1966); London: The Institute For Strategic Studies.

"Sources of OPEC Oil," London *Times,* July 9, 1968, p. 21.

"Soviet Comments," The Institute For Strategic Studies (London), *Survival* (August, 1967), pp. 261-262.

"The Soviet Dilemma," *Mizan* (London), VIII, No. 2 (March/April, 1966), pp. 49-52.

"Soviet Economic Policy since 1953: A Study of Its Structure and Changes," *Soviet Studies* (Glasgow), XVII, No. 1 (July, 1965), pp. 1-43.

"Soviet Export Drive Sputters," *Oil and Gas Journal,* May 30, 1966, pp. 25-27.

"Soviet Flank Attack Threatens Unity of the West," *Business Week,* March 24, 1956, pp. 24-26.

"Soviet Influence in Gulf Rises," *Kayhan* (Teheran), May 18, 1968, p. 1.

"Soviet Interest in Syria," *Mizan* (London), VIII, No. 1 (January/February, 1966), pp. 23-33.

"Soviet Interest in the Middle East," *Mizan* (London), VIII, No. 3 (May/June, 1966), pp. 142-144.

"Soviet Is Called Maritime Threat," New York *Times,* August 28, 1967, sec. M, p. 48.

"Soviet Navy Is Developing as Global Strategic Force," Washington *Post*, August 24, 1967, p. F-1.

"Soviet Navy on NATO's Flanks," *NATO Review,* July/August, 1972.

"Soviet Oil Flow Headed up Fast," *Oil and Gas Journal,* January 8, 1968, pp. 47-48.

"Soviet Opinions on Syria and the Ba'th," *Mizan* (London), VIII, No. 2 (March/April, 1966), pp. 73-78.

"Soviet Warships to Visit Pakistan," *Teheran Journal,* May 20, 1968, p. 1.

"Soviets Bank on 'Third Baku,' " *Oil and Gas Journal*, July 17, 1967, p. 59.

"Soviets Plan World's Biggest Pipeline," *Oil and Gas Journal,* November 7, 1966, p. 70.

"Soviets Plan New Egypt Oil Search," *Oil and Gas Journal,* July 17, 1967, p. 59.

"Soviets Predict Oil Leadership within 4 Years," Reuter, *Christian Science Monitor,* January 21, 1971.

"Soviet Spurs Use of Gas with Pipeline to Moscow," New York *Times,* September 23, 1967, p. 37.

"Soviet Push Work on Huge Gas Line," *Oil and Gas Journal,* June 10, 1968, p. 76.

"Soviets Strengthen Navy," Washington *Post,* October 26, 1967, p. A-25.

"Soviets Tackle Deeper Caspian Waters," *Oil and Gas Journal,* June 10, 1968, pp. 59-69.

Spencer, D. L. "The Role of Oil in Soviet Foreign Economic Policy," *American Journal of Economics and Sociology,* XXV (January, 1966), pp. 91-107.

"Start Near for Iran-to-Soviet Line," *Oil and Gas Journal,* April 17, 1967, pp. 111-113.

Sterling, Claire. "The Soviet Fleet in the Mediterranean," *Reporter,* December 14, 1967, pp. 14-18.

Stolte, S. C. "Soviet Economic Integration Plans for the Communist Bloc," *Bulletin* of the Institute for the Study of the U.S.S.R. (Munich), No. 9 (September, 1958), pp. 31-38.

Strakhovsky, Leonid. "Imperial Russia," in *A Handbook of Slavic Studies.* Edited by L. Strakhovsky. Cambridge, Mass.: Harvard University Press, 1949.

Strausz-Hupe, Robert. "The Real Communist Threat," *International Affairs,* Royal Institute of International Affairs (London), XLI, No. 4 (October, 1965), pp. 611-623.

"Supertanker Threat to the Canal," London *Times,* July 31, 1968, p. 21.

Taborsky, Edward. "The Communist Parties of the 'Third World' in Soviet Strategy," *Orbis,* XI, No. 1 (Spring, 1967), pp. 128-148.

"Taking It Out on the Oil Companies," *The Economist* (London), June 24, 1967, pp. 1368-1369.

Tarokh, Ahman. "Iranian-Soviet Trade Gathers Momentum," *Christian Science Monitor,* July 9, 1968, p. 10.

Tether, C. Gordon. "Making 'Arab Solidarity' A Force For Good," *Financial Times* (London), June 14, 1967, p. 15.

Texaco, Incorporated. "Texaco Chairman Predicts Rising Oil Demand," *Newsletter,* May 9, 1967 (New York: Texaco, Inc. Public Relations Division), p. 1.

Thorpe, Willard L. "American Policy and the Soviet Economic Offensive," in *Patterns of Competitive Coexistence/USA vs USSR.* Young Hum Kim, ed. New York: G. P. Putnam's Sons, 1966, pp. 163-175.

_____. "Soviet Economic Growth and U.S. Policy," in *Comparisons of the United States and Soviet Economies,* a report of the Joint Economic Committee, U.S. Contress (3 parts; Washington: Government Printing Office, 1959), III, pp. 571-588.

Tidmarsh, Kyril. "Russia's Worries with Her Economic Bloc," London *Times,* April 10, 1968, p. 10.

Tugendhat, Christopher. "Rapid Growth for 'High Seas Gas,' " *Financial Times* (London), May 22, 1968, p. 8.

_____. "Russia Pushing Oil Sales in West — U.K. Reviewing Ban," *Financial Times* (London), June 16, 1967, p. 1.

"The UAR and 'Proletarian Dictatorship,' " *Mizan* (London), VIII, No. 2 (March/April, 1966), pp. 67-72.

Urban, George R. "The Concept of Propaganda," *Communist Affairs* (University of Southern California), IV, No. 3 (May/June, 1966), pp. 3-6.

"The USSR and the Persian Gulf," *Mizan* (London), X, No. 2 (March/April, 1968), pp. 51-57.

"USSR — A New Naval Power, Says Sir Alec," *Teheran Journal,* May 18, 1968, p. 9.

van Dijck, J. M. "East and West Linked by Pipes," *Common Market* (The Hague) No. 4 (April, 1970), pp. 96-98.

Verrier, Anthony. "Western Aces in Iraq's Oil Gamble," London *Sunday Times,* April 14, 1968, p. 44.

Vicker, Ray. "Russia Pushes Gas Sales in West to Pay for Building 100-Inch Lines from Siberia," *Wall Street Journal,* November 20, 1969, p. 40.

Volk, Sigmund. "The Long Soviet Shadow on the International Fuel Market," Institute for the Study of the U.S.S.R. (Munich), *Analysis of Current Developments in the Soviet Union*, No. 464, July 18, 1967, pp. 1-5.

"Warning against Faith in Russia by South Arabian Minister," *Financial Times* (London), June 15, 1967, p. 7.

Waskovich, G. "The Ideological Shadow of the U.S.S.R.," *The Annals of the American Academy of Political and Social Science*, CCLXXI (September, 1950), pp. 43-54.

Watt, D. C. "The Persian Gulf — Cradle of Conflict?" *Problems of Communism* May-June, 1972.

Welles, Benjamin, "Soviet Sea Moves Disturbing to U.S.," New York *Times*, April 17, 1968, p. 5.

Wentworth, Eric. "Emergency Oil Moves Authorized by Interior," Washington *Post*, June 11, 1967, p. A-20.

_____. "Oil Troubles the Waters," Washington *Post*, June 11, 1967, p. C-1.

"What a War Anniversary Says to Oil Industry," *Oil and Gas Journal*, June 10, 1968, p. 40.

"What The Russians Are Up to in the Middle East: Interview with King Hussein of Jordan," *U.S. News and World Report*, December 26, 1966, pp. 39-42.

Wheeler, G. "Middle East Studies in the U.S.S.R.," *Middle East Studies* (London), VI, No. 1 (October, 1964), pp. 84-90.

"Where Western Europe Buys Its Oil," *Financial Times* (London), May 23, 1967, p. 16.

Wierzynski, Gregory H. "Tankers Move the Oil that Moves the World," *Fortune*, September 1, 1967, pp. 80-152.

Winder, David. " 'Oil Power' Tamed," *Christian Science Monitor*. August 23, 1967, sec. B, p. 1.

Wohl, Paul. "Moscow Promotes Pan-Europe," *Christian Science Monitor*, May 1, 1968, p. 6.

_____. "Red Capital Soviet Investment Search Ties Up East European Bloc," *Christian Science Monitor,* February 15, 1967, p. 5.

_____. "Soviets Vow Support for Palestinians," *Christian Science Monitor,* September 26, 1972, p. 1.

"Work Starts on Iran-Soviet 660-Mile Gas Line," *Oil and Gas International* (June, 1967), pp. 125-127.

"The World at Work," *Barron's,* July 24, 1967, p. 7.

"World of 2000 to Run on Oil and Atoms," *Oil and Gas Journal,* January 8, 1968, p. 50.

"Worldwide Crude Production," *Oil and Gas Journal,* June 10, 1968, p. 169.

Yellon, R. A. "The Winds of Change," *Mizan* (London), IX, No. 2 (March/April, 1967), pp. 51-57.

Younger, J. Arthur. "United States-Soviet Confrontation in Mideast Feared," *U.S. Congressional Record,* Appendix, April 6, 1967, sec. A, p. 1644.

"Zakharov Leads Russian Military Mission to Iran," *Kayhan International Edition* (Teheran), May 19, 1968, p. 1.

Zorza, Victor. "Soviet Oil Moves Threaten West," Washington *Post,* June 7, 1972, p. A-19.

Official Publications

Belyayev, Yu. "The Economy of the CEMA Member-Countries in the New Five-Year Plan," *Kommunist* (Moscow), No. 8 (May, 1967), pp. 93-107. Trans. Joint Publications Research Service, U.S. Department of Commerce, Washington, D.C., No. 41,638, June 29, 1967.

"Central Committee of Ukrainian CP Reviews General Progress of Ukraine Under Soviet Power," *Pravda ukrainy* (Kiev), January 26, 1967, pp. 1-2. Trans. Joint Publications Research Service, No. 40,257, March 14, 1967.

Colm, G. assisted by J. Darmstadter. "Evaluation of the Soviet Economic Threat," in *Comparisons of the United States and Soviet Economies.* Report of the Joint Economic Committee, U.S. Congress (3 parts; Washington: Government Printing Office, 1959), II, pp. 529-543.

Dillon, C. D. "Realities of Soviet Foreign Economic Policies," address delivered in New Orleans, Louisiana, January 27, 1959. *Department of State Publication No. 6780.*

Didenko, N. "The Historic Role of the CPSU in Creating the Military and Economic Might of the U.S.S.R.," *Voyennoistoricheskiy zhurnal,* (Moscow) ("Military History Journal"), August, 1967, pp. 3-16. Trans. Joint Publications Research Service, No. 42,811, October 2, 1967.

Dulles, A. W. "The Challenge of Soviet Power," address delivered in New Orleans, Louisiana, April 8, 1959. *Department of State Publication No. 6823.*

Goranov, St. "The World Socialist System: Materials for Propagandists in Primary Political Eduction Schools," *Politicheska Prosveta (Political Education) (Sofia),* No. 3 (March, 1967), pp. 61-68. Trans. Joint Publications Research Service, No. 40,921, May 8, 1967, p. 4.

"An Important Factor In Strengthening Peace," *Pravda* (Moscow), March 23, 1964, p. 1. Trans. Joint Publications Research Service, No. 23,867, March 25, 1964, pp. 5-7.

"In the Name of Peace, for the Good of the Fatherland," *Pravda* (Moscow), December 21, 1966, p. 1. Trans. Joint Publications Research Service, No. 39,316, December 28, 1966, pp. 1-3.

"Large-Scale Chemical Production — In High Gear!" *Pravda* (Moscow), November, 1966. Trans. Joint Publications Research Service, No. 38,729, November 21, 1966, pp. 5-6.

"The Leninist Course of Our Party," *Pravda* (Moscow), December 15, 1966, p. 1. Trans. Joint Publications Research Service, No. 39,192, December 20, 1966, pp. 1-7.

Lovestone, J. "Basic Distinctions between the Soviet Economy and American Economy," in *Comparisons of the United States and Soviet Economies.* Report of the Joint Economic Committee, III, pp. 547-568.

"Nazi-Soviet Relations, 1939-1941," Documents from the
    Archives of the German Foreign Office, U.S. Department
    of State Publication 3023, 1948, p. 257, as quoted in G.
    Lenczowski, *Russia and the West in Iran, 1918-1948,*
    Ithaca, N.Y.: Cornell University Press, 1949, p. 193.
Nutter, G. W. "The Structure and Growth of Soviet Industry: A
    Comparison with the United States," in *Comparisons of the
    United States and Soviet Economies.* Report of the Joint
    Economic Committee, I, pp. 95-120.
N'yersh, Rezhe. "The Reform of the Economic Mechanism and
    the Party," *Kommunist,* No. 16 (November, 1966), pp.
    92-102. Trans. Joint Publications Research Service,
    No. 39,401, January 4, 1967, pp. 8-21.
Peterson, H. C. "Soviet Economic Growth and U.S. Policy," in
    Comparisons of the United States and Soviet Economies.
    Report of the Joint Economic Committee, II, pp. 517-527.
"The Power of the Soviets Is the Power of the People," *Pravda*
    (Moscow), December 5, 1966, p. 1. Trans. Joint
    Publications Research Service, No. 39,009, December 7,
    1966, pp. 4-6.
"The Property of the People," *Pravda* (Moscow), March 13,
    1964. Trans. Joint Publications Research Service,
    No. 23,731, March 18, 1964, pp. 1-4.
Prozhogin, N. "Oil and Gas in Sahara Produced Independently
    by Algeria," *Pravda* (Moscow), November 14, 1966, p. 4.
    Trans. Joint Publications Research Service, No. 39,174.
Prucha, Milan. "Marxism and Trends in Philosophy," *Kulturny
    zivot (Cultural Life)* (Bratislava, Czechoslovakia), No. 5
    (February 3, 1967), p. 10. Trans. Joint Publications
    Research Service, No. 40,190, March 8, 1967, pp. 7-13.
Schwartz, H. "Reflections on the Economic Race," in
    Comparisons of the United States and Soviet Economies.
    Report of the Joint Economic Committee, III, pp. 609-616.
Stefanov, V. "The Party and Communism," *Kommunist*
    (Moscow), No. 8, (May, 1967), pp. 8-23. Trans. Joint
    Publications Research Service, No. 41,638, June 29,
    1967.

"Waste," *Pravda* (Moscow), April 28, 1964, p. 3. Trans. Joint
    Publications Research Service, No. 24,453, May 1, 1964,
    pp. 5-6.
Yemelyanov, D., and K. Morozov. "The Mirror of the Rayon,"
    Pravda (Moscow), February 29, 1968, p. 3. Trans. Joint
    Publications Research Service, No. 44,969, pp. 1-2.

Pamphlets

Binder, Leonard. *The Middle East Crisis: Background and Issues,*
    Center for Policy Study, University of Chicago, June, 1967.
Loewenthal, Rudolf. *Russian Material on Arabs and Arab
    Countries.* Selective Bibliography. Washington, D.C.:
    Department of State, 1958.
Michael, F. *Common Purpose and Double Strategy.* Washington,
    D.C.: Institute for Sino-Soviet Studies, George Washington
    University, November, 1966.
Middle East: Tricontinental Hub (A Strategic Survey). Pamphlet
    #550-2. Washington, D.C.: Department of the Army,
    January 19, 1965.
*The Sino-Soviet Economic Offensive in the Less Developed
    Countries.* Publication No. 6632. Washington, D.C.: U.S.
    Department of State, 1958.

Public Documents

U.S. Senate, Committee on Foreign Relations. *Arms Sales to
    Near East and South Asian Countries: Hearings Before the
    Sub-Committee on Near Eastern and South Asian Affairs.*
    90th Congress, 1st Session, 1967.
_____. Committee Print, *A Select Chronology and
    .Background Documents Relating to the Middle East.* 90th
    Congress, 1st Session, June 6, 1967.
Germany: "Statement by Molotov to the German Ambassador
    on the Proposed Four-Power Pact, 25 November 1940,"

Die Besiehungen zwischen Deutschland und der
Sowjetunion 1939-1941. Dokumente des Auswärtigen
Amtes, Tübingen, Germany" Laupp'sche Buchhandlung,
1949. ("Relations between Germany and the Soviet Union
1939-1941. Documents of the Foreign Office"), p. 296, as
quoted in Soviet Documents on Foreign Policy III
(1933-1941). (Issued under auspices of the Royal Institute
of International Affairs.) London: Oxford University
Press, 1953, pp. 477-478.

Reports

The Communist Economic Threat. Department of Defense
Pamphlet, Washington, D.C.: Government Printing Office,
1960.

Herman, Leon, and Halford L. Hoskins. *Soviet Oil in the Cold
War.* Library of Congress Committee Print. Washington,
D.C.: U.S. Government Printing Office, 1961.

Hoskins, Halford L. *Problems Raised by the Soviet Oil
Offensive.* Library of Congress Committee Print.
Washington, D.C.: U.S. Government Printing Office, 1962.

National Petroleum Council. *Impact of Oil Exports from the
Soviet Bloc.* Vols. I and II, 1962, Supplement, 1964.

*The Soviet Military Aid Program as a Reflection of Soviet
Objectives.* "Georgetown Research Project," # AF49
(638)-1412. Washington, D. C.: Atlantic Research
Corporation, 1965, pp. 158-167; 201-230.

Unpublished Material

Ghoreichi, Ahmad. "Soviet Policies in Iran." Unpublished
Ph.D. dissertation, University of Colorado, 1965.

Martin, Neil A. "Khrushchev and the Non-Russians; A Study of
Soviet Nationality Policy Since the Death of Stalin."
Unpublished Ph.D. dissertation, Georgetown University,
Washington, D.C., 1968.

Smolansky, Oles M. "The Soviet Union and the Arab East, 1947-1957." Unpublished Ph.D. dissertation, Columbia University, New York.

Weaver, Paul E. "Soviet Strategy in Iran, 1941-1957." Unpublished Ph.D. dissertation, University of Michigan, 1958. (Microfilm No. 58-2811.)

Other Sources

Political Affairs (Theoretical Journal of the Communist Party, U.S.A.), XLVI, No. 7 (July, 1967).

WTTG Telecast "Panorama" (Washington, D.C.). Inverview with Dr. Paul S. Ello. "Czechoslovakia." August 6, 1968.

INDEX